WILLIAM S. FAIRHURST, III

Weedsport, N. Y. 13166

THE PENINSULA

DRAWINGS BY GRATTAN CONDON

THE PENINSULA

BY LOUISE DICKINSON RICH

THE CHATHAM PRESS, INC.

RIVERSIDE, CONNECTICUT

DISTRIBUTED BY THE VIKING PRESS, INC.

CONTENTS

To the Memory of Lisle Albright
and to his wife Marjorie
through whose kindness and generosity
I first came to The Peninsula

THE PENINSULA

GUZZL

SILVER MIN

WEST
GOULDSBORO

1

SORRENTO

FIRST   X
SETTLERS

JONES
POND

G O U L D S B

F
R
E
N
C
H

STAVE
I.

186   195

SOUTH
GOULDSBORO

PORCUPINE ISLANDS

JORDAN
I.

W I N T E R   H A R B O R

I
S
M
A
N

WINTER HARBOR

BAR
HARBOR

IRONBOUND I.

G
R
I
N
D
S
T
O
N
E

N
E
C
K

B
A
Y

HERON I.

SPECTACLE I.

NED I.

MARK
I.

ACADIA
NAT.
PARK

NAV
RAD
STA

ACADIA
NAT.
PARK

TURTLE I.

EGG ROCK
L.H.

RAVEN'S
NEST

SCHOODIC
HEAD

THE
ANVI

BIG
MOOSE I.

SCHOODIC
PT.

LITT
MOO

MT. DESERT I.

CHICKEN MILL POND

GOULDSBORO

WEST BAY

GOULDSBORO BAY

186

Dyke Marsh

FORBES POND

HEATH

SAND COVE

195

PROSPECT HARBOR

L.H.

HEATH

COREA

BIRCH HARBOR

CABIN X

CRANBERRY PT.

WINKER'S HARBOR

ONSQUEAK HARBOR

SPRUCE PT.

SCHOODIC I.

STEUBEN

DYER NECK

DYER BAY

PETIT MANAN PT.

BOIS BUBERT I.

CROWLEY I.

EASTERN I.

SALLY I.

SNEEP I.

BAR I.

OUTER BAR I.

WESTERN I.

GREEN I.

PETIT MANAN I.
L.H.

N

W   E

S

ATLANTIC OCEAN

0   1   2   3   4   5 MILES

G.C.

Introduction

MOST OF US, I SUPPOSE, AT ONE TIME OR AN-other experience a longing for another way of life. Suddenly our days and our energies seem to be expended on trivia. We are over-come by a sense of being alien, of not belonging in the world in which we find ourselves, of being out of step with the times and out of sympathy with the attitudes that we encounter. We are hungry for the fundamentals—for the satisfaction of wresting food from the stubborn earth, of raising our own rooftrees with our own hands, of combating successfully man's implacable, hereditary foes, the wind and the weather. We suffer a great nostalgia, which means a sick-ness to return home.

Where is this home? We don't know. We try to find it by spending summers at the beach, by moving to old farmhouses within the commuting zone, by taking do-it-yourself courses, by hunting moose at enormous expense in Nova Scotia, by cultivating herbaceous borders or making our own bread. We try hard to go home, but we can't find the way. In their artificiality, the means we employ are doomed to failure. None of the things we do is of necessity. There is always a safe retreat from our self-imposed hardships.

We can't go home because the home we are seeking never actually existed for any of us. It lies, rather, deep in racial memory of our beginnings on this continent. What we really wish is that time would turn back so that we might live the simple, self-sufficient lives of our ancestors. That's impossible, of course. Even if it were possible, we would almost certainly be disappointed and dismayed by the result; but very few ever have an opportunity to put the matter to the test.

By chance, I have had that opportunity, and I'd like to tell you about it. I'd like to tell what it is like to live in a village that is, in its essentials, the same now as it was a hundred years ago. There is, unavoidably, a thin—a very thin—veneer of modernism; but underneath it lies the unchanged structure of our lost, remembered home.

1. Return to Yesterday

STARTING AT THE KENNEBEC RIVER, THE coast of Maine begins its great sweep to the east and becomes increasingly broken and rugged. Nowhere in the world is there a more irregular coastline; long bays and sheltered estuaries reach far inland, and rocky capes and headlands jut boldly out to sea. About two-thirds of the way along this tremendous eastward curve is the Gouldsboro Peninsula: thirty thousand acres of granite, heath and shallow topsoil, boasting two small fresh-water bodies—Jones and Forbes Ponds, one six-hundred-foot eminence, Mt. Cromer, and a few small streams. The Peninsula is bounded on the west by Frenchman Bay, on the east by Gouldsboro Bay, and on the south by the open Atlantic, stretching away in emptiness to the Caribbean. A string of islands, reefs and ledges encircles it, bearing what are to me fascinating names: The Old Man and Old Woman and Roaring Bull reefs; Stone Horse and Bonny Chess and Abijah Ledges; Ironbound and Outer Bar and Stave Islands; and many, many others. They are the summits of what were once mountains before the weight of the great ice-age glacier bore down upon and drowned this coast beneath the sea.

Half the land of the peninsula is completely unsuited to agriculture. Much of it is solid pink granite, penetrated by veins of galena, zinc and copper, but never in commercially profitable quantities. Some of the rest is given over to heath (pronounced locally "hayth")—flat barrens supporting only moss, coarse salt grasses, low blueberry bushes and a wide variety of tiny subarctic plants. They are pocked with quicksands, very dangerous in fact and bottomless in fancy, although, to return to cold fact, a Navy survey found bottom in the worst of them at sixteen feet. I suppose, however, that if you wander into one, sixteen feet is as bad as sixteen miles, as far as your personal wellbeing and future usefulness are concerned.

Although there are some patches of fairly good soil, most of it is clay or gravelly loam, so that farming above the kitchen-garden level is a far from rewarding occupation. There are no great stands of towering pines such as exist in some other parts of Maine. The thinness of the soil and the constant battering of the off-Atlantic gales keep growth on a dwarf scale, with the result that lumbering is small-scale, too—just an affair of going out into the huddled, wind-tortured thickets of fir to cut a few fence posts, bows for lobster traps, or poles to brace the woodshed roof. It's a bare, open, sparse country, exposed to the sky and to the sea.

Most of the older, more mellowed communities of the Maine coast —the lovely towns between Kittery and Ellsworth—are distinguished by the beauty of their ancient houses. On the Peninsula there are almost no buildings of any architectural interest whatsoever. The houses are plain and small, with little, low-ceilinged rooms and steeply pitched roofs. They are not show pieces but shelters constructed to keep out the elements and to conserve heat. In the winter the foundations are banked with earth and seaweed and boughs against the searching fingers of the icy wind. They look pretty bleak in winter. But in summer the little lawns, hard-won from an uncooperative earth, are bordered with the brightest, most riotous flowerbeds I ever saw. Perhaps it is the iodine in the soil, perhaps it is the warmth of the sun held and reflected by the omnipresent rock, perhaps it is the humidity supplied by the frequent fogs that so encourages growth and bloom. Whatever the reason, in their brief flowering the Peninsula gardens are a joy to behold. The land seems to be trying in a few short weeks to compensate for its long season of austerity.

There are three ways of getting onto the Peninsula from US Route 1. Route 186 diverges at West Gouldsboro and roughly follows the shoreline in a big loop until it rejoins US 1 at Gouldsboro, where it may be considered either an exit or an entrance, depending on your direction. Strung like beads along this loop are the little towns of the Peninsula: West Gouldsboro, South Gouldsboro, Winter Harbor, Wonsqueak, Bunker and Birch and Prospect Harbors, and finally Gouldsboro. All, with the addition of Corea, are parts of the town of Gouldsboro except Winter Harbor, which seceded many years ago. It is just as well that it did. It is the maverick of the lot, having little in common with the others, since it alone has given itself over to the summer people. In Winter Harbor there are luxury hotels, art galleries and a store that carries S. S. Pierce products and Pepperidge Farm bread.

The third route onto the Peninsula, the Pond Road, lies between the other two, splitting the Peninsula in halves and terminating at Prospect Harbor. To reach Corea, which dangles like a pendant from this necklace of villages, you take a side road at Prospect Harbor and go as far as you can on it. It's a dead-end road, beyond which lies only the sea.

It really doesn't make much difference which road you choose. The same phenomenon occurs on any one of them. Within a few yards of US 1 you are aware of having moved from one world into another. Behind you is the busy main artery of traffic, rushing heedlessly to and from Canada over a beautifully surfaced, expertly engineered modern highway. Now you are traveling on a narrow, winding country road, blacktopped as a concession to the motor age, but otherwise unaltered from the era of the horse and the ox-team. The long, steep hills still retain the thank-you-ma'ams of an older day—short stretches where the pitch is leveled so that draft animals may rest; and the original abrupt curves are deadly for any speed over fifteen miles an hour, which was, of course, an unimagined pace at the time of the road's construction. The result is that you are necessarily slowed down to the tempo of Peninsula progress.

But the change is more than a matter of speed or the lack of it. It's a matter of intangibles, of the appearance of the country, of the untroubled faces of the people you see. The first time I visited the Peninsula I wondered how it happened not to be an island. By any of the three roads onto it, you take a sharp dip down and up again from the main highway. It would have been an island if the glacier had been a few million tons heavier, and the sea would have flowed free through Jones Pond and out into the arm of Gouldsboro Bay that is called West Bay. It's only by accident that it isn't an island. I have been on real islands that are far less insular.

Perhaps this is because, as on true islands, the pervading and inescapable element is the sea. It is always there, usually within sight and always within hearing. It is from the sea that most Peninsulans derive their living, some of them—the lobstermen and sardiners—directly; and the others—the packers in the sardine factory, the owners of the little stores, the pound-keepers and bait-sellers—almost as directly.

Nothing—not the fall of governments or the birth of kings or the discovery of new galaxies—is of so much importance and interest as the question of whether the boats will be able to go out today, and whether the lobsters will be crawling and the herring shoaling. When the three-day southeasterlies come whooping in off the Atlantic, so that a triple wall of thundering breakers and driven spume piles up solidly from the Sally Islands to Schoodic Point and no boats can leave any of the little harbors; or when one of the epic fogs, caused by the confluence of the warm Gulf Stream and the cold Labrador Current, marches down from the Bay of Fundy, then the Peninsula seems scarcely to breathe. There is no businesslike puttering of lobsterboats in the early morning, no cheerful shouting along the longlegged wharfs in the afternoon. There are only the crash of the surf and the thin mewing of wind-blown gulls The men sit around the stores in their hipboots and slickers, waiting out the weather and swapping old tales; or they peer from dim windows at the fog and pace down to the harbors to see how the moorings are holding. With the sea barred to them, they are men without occupation and at loose ends.

But the sea is more than a means of livelihood. It is a Presence, impossible to forget or ignore. It fills the eye and the ear and the mind, stretching blue and boisterous or sullen and gray to the horizon, racing through the island passages and breaking in great geysers of spray over the reefs. It is never still. On the rare calm days it is still unresting. Obedient to the moon, it rises to cover the nearshore, kelp-clothed ledges, lifting the seaweed gently and stirring to activity the myriad life beneath it; or it withdraws to lowest ebb, emptying all the little pools and exposing their inhabitants to the sun and the predatory beaks of the gulls.

Its voice is always in the ear, sometimes subdued and wooing, sometimes as murmurous as the slow breathing of a sleeping beast, sometimes as wild and clamorous as a battle cry. All other sounds—the calling of birds, the wind over the heath, the speech of men—are flute notes against the deep orchestration of the sea. At first you watch the tides and are aware of the blowing up of an easterly with its crosschop, or of the brimming moment of silence that marks high tide at noon of a hot day; but very soon the surface of your mind ceases to monitor. You go about your business, whatever it may be, with no thought to the sea. But always at the back of your consciousness you know what it is doing. In the middle of a conversation or waking in the dead of night you know without looking "The tide has just turned" or "The wind has shifted and she's started to pile up on Western Island." The sea has become a part of you, just as the beating of your heart and the rhythm of your breathing are parts of you.

It has been my observation that the gears of life mesh with amazing precision. Usually I have my activities mapped out far enough in advance so that I am not open to suggestions from complete strangers for the spending of the coming summer. For years the routine remained the same: winters in Bridgewater, the Massachusetts town of my green years, so that my two children might attend adequate schools; June to September at Forest Lodge, the isolated house in the Maine woods where I lived my married life, where Rufus was born, where my husband died, and where we were happiest when my children were small. That schedule left no room for experiments in vacations.

That spring of four years ago was different: disorganized, disturbed and disturbing. Rufus, then sixteen and big for his age, informed me that he had a job for the summer, driving a tractor on a farm. I have no patience with clinging widowed mothers, so I bestowed my blessing on this show of initiative; but that left me and Dinah, who was twelve, on our own. Opening Forest Lodge—a rambling ranch of a place—and getting it into running order was a tedious and expensive business, and I saw very little object in undertaking it for one little girl and one middle-aged woman. My reluctance was increased when I discovered that Dinah was not enthusiastic, either. It had been fine, she told me, when she was in the tree-hut-and-Indian-scout stage; but now she was a young lady, and the exclusive society of bunnies, deer and her mother left something to be desired. I saw exactly what she meant.

In addition to this, I had just finished a book and was in that exhausted and depressed state that all writers know—a condition that lasts until you get an idea for another book and have it under way. As far as another book was concerned, my mind was a blank and I was convinced—as most writers are between books—that I had come to the end of the line and would never write another word. I was tired of writing, anyhow. I was tired of myself and of my life. I wished the West had not been opened up. I would have been a big success as a pioneer woman in a covered wagon, I was sure. I wished— I didn't know what I wished. Oh, I was in a bad way, ripe for revolution.

At that precise moment the letter came. It was from a Chicagoan who signed himself L. M. Albright, and who had read some of my books. He and his wife owned a log cabin on Cranberry Point in Corea on the coast of Maine, which they were not going to be using that summer. Judging from my books, he was of the opinion that I wouldn't mind rather primitive living conditions, by which he meant lack of plumbing and electricity. This part of the coast, he told me, was wild and beautiful and unspoiled, and he believed that I would like it. So why didn't I accept the cabin for the summer, with his and Mrs. Albright's compliments?

I thought, "Well, for Heaven's sake! What a remarkably kind

gesture! But of course I can't accept— Why, I don't know the man and he doesn't know me—" Then I wondered, "Where is Corea, anyhow? I never heard of it." I got out a map, and after considerable searching I found it, very obscure and labeled in very small letters. It was about thirty miles east of Bar Harbor on one of the long tongues of land that thrust out into the open Atlantic, way off the beaten track of US Route 1 to Canada. I sat back and looked at the map, at the ragged line of the coast, at the sprinkling of offshore islands, and at the meager scattering of small dots that marked the few villages of the locality. It looked wonderful to me.

So then I thought, "After all, why not?"

And that is how I happened to find myself on the Gouldsboro Peninsula.

I shall never forget my first coming to Corea, late on a June afternoon. I arrived under almost ideally propitious circumstances. Although I had driven with my young daughter Dinah and the black collie, Caro, over three hundred and seventy miles since dawn, it was almost as though I had been transported in my sleep from my familiar bed in the house on an elm-shaded street in Massachusetts to this land of granite, sea and sky. You can't drive that far in that time and pay heed to anything except the ribbon of the road unrolling before you. You have no edge of attention to spare for the changing of the country through which you are passing. Boston dropped behind us, and Portland, and all the charming villages of the western and middle coasts of Maine—Wiscasset, Damariscotta, Camden and Searsport—with no recognition from me, except the due recognition automatically paid to road signs and traffic lights. We were wearing blinders as far as the scenery was concerned.

Since the Pond Road onto the Peninsula seemed shortest on the map we chose it, followed it to Prospect Harbor, and took the abrupt right turn near the post office to Corea, across three miles of the barren level of what I was later to know as The Hayth. There was nothing—nothing at all—to prepare us.

Near the close of the day we came to the edge of the heath, where it breaks and dips sharply. The sun was still up, but definitely westering; and for the first time since sunrise I looked with seeing eyes at the world around me.

There was nothing familiar. The blue of the sea, stretching to the limit of the earth, smote the senses like a blow. A deep ground swell—what I was to learn to call an "old" sea, the fringe of some distant storm—was running, so that as far as the eye could reach great fountains played: far out where the submerged reefs lay,

nearer at hand against the ledges of the islands, and close below us along the rim of the land itself. Far, far out rose the tower of Petit Manan (or 'Titm'nan) Light, unreal and enchanted on its bleak rock, golden and remote as a tower in a fairy tale. And at our feet lay the hamlet and the harbor.

It was just a little harbor, a scooped-out basin in the pink granite, surrounded by high-posted wharfs, each with its shack for gear, and by the unpretentious houses of the region. A narrow passage beyond which the surf pounded on the bars connected it with the sea. There were perhaps thirty boats there, a full harbor, all washed a soft rose against the sea's shouting blue by the declining sun, all faced into the rising tide, bows to the entrance like a herd grazing into the wind. Every single one of them was a workboat, a little lobsterman designed and built for a hard, specific use. There wasn't a pleasure craft in the lot, not one slim yacht or elegant mahogany cruiser. I had never seen a harbor like it, nor one I liked so well. It made all other harbors of my experience seem a little effete and silly.

Perhaps as we grow older we tend to simplify our lives and to prune them of the nonessentials. It's not entirely a matter of choice. Life strips us of most of our youthful illusions and bright dreams; and death takes away, one by one, those whom we loved and upon whom we depended. If we are to survive, we must reconcile ourselves to this plundering, we must learn to distinguish between those things which were ornamental and the true necessities; and we must learn too the possibly more difficult lesson of letting go gracefully the superficial and of treasuring and nurturing the few basic realities which must be our support and comfort for as long as we walk about under the light of the heavens. Perhaps that is why, in that moment on the edge of the heath, something within me responded to the place.

It was beautiful with the only kind of beauty that I was now beginning to recognize as authentic: the great, unadorned beauty and strength of the functional. There was nothing anywhere that was unnecessary; nothing, whether the work of man or of nature, that existed without a purpose. I was a stranger; but in spite of my strangeness the country spoke to some inner need of which I had not until then been fully aware, to a need to know who I was and what I was worth. Here, away from the pleasant, unintentional, fatal seductions and unplanned blackmail of friends and acquaintances, away from the façade I had built over the years to impress a world with the self I wished I were—a false front that I was obliged continually to reinforce—perhaps I could find my real self, whether it be good or bad.

Stranger though I was, I was not completely uninformed about

Corea. Early in our correspondence L. M. Albright had given me a rough idea of the geography of the place. I knew that halfway down the hill, at the combined general store and post office, a road branched to the left, skirted the head of the harbor, and passed over a causeway onto Crowley Island on the east side of the harbor. The main thoroughfare continued straight down the hill on the west harborside, and somewhere near its end was the obscure little side road that led to Cranberry Point. I also knew three names: those of Marcia Spurling and George Crowley, who acted as caretakers for the Albrights during their absences, and that of Herbert Young, the keeper of the store. Acting upon suggestion, I had written to Miss Spurling to inform her of the time of our arrival, and she had assured me that she and Mr. Crowley would have the cabin open and in running order: shutters off, oil range lighted, pump connected, and bottled-gas refrigerator operating. If I would stop at her house, on the right at the top of the hill, first beyond the schoolhouse, she would give me the key and direct me to the Point. So I stopped at her house, but there was nobody at home except a mean-looking white cat who gave me a baleful glare through the screen door.

According to Mr. Albright, the man to see in case I found myself in any predicament was Herbert Young. I rolled down the hill and found the store exactly where I expected to find it, at the fork of the road on a slight elevation overlooking the harbor. I parked the car and went into the big, dim cave of a room. It was like every country store I ever saw, with the post office at the rear, behind its grated wicket and rampart of glass-fronted mail boxes. The walls were lined to the ceiling with canned and packaged goods, boxes of work gloves, slickers, sweat shirts and rubber boots. A great stove, cold now in June, occupied the center of the floor, and along one side ran the universal Liars' Bench, common to all rural stores in New England, where men with time on their hands sit and discuss the affairs of the nation, the weather outlook, and the latest local rumor. It was occupied now by three men in hipboots and long-billed cloth caps, who fell into a watchful silence at my entry. Behind the counter on the opposite side leaned a grizzle-haired man with alert eyes, whom I correctly assumed to be the storekeeper.

"My name is Rich, Mr. Young," I began, "and I—"

That's as far as I got. "Thought prob'ly 'twas you," he informed me. "Minute you drove up, I said 'Bet that's them.'" The three heads on the bench nodded in confirmation. "Got here a little ahead of yourself, didn't you?" I was back in every small town I've ever inhabited, where one's activities are everyone's concern. It was a social climate to which I was accustomed, and I immediately felt at home.

I said yes, I had got ahead of myself, and did he know where Miss Spurling was.

"Marcie? I surmise she and George are down to the Point, gettin' the place ready for you. Jest you rest easy a spell and they'll be back."

Couldn't I follow her down to the Point, I wanted to know. If he would direct me—

"By dear," he said gently, and I thought then and for a long time afterward that he was using a term of affection, until weeks later I realized that *By dear* was his most violent oath, used for emphasis as some others use *By God!* "By dear, I wouldn't advise it. That Point road's terrible. 'Twould be best if you waited for Marcie." I wish I could convey the way he said *road*, but I can't even pronounce it the way he did: somewhere between *rode* and *rud*, but not quite either. "But if you're bound an' determined—"

I was bound and determined, so he and the other three stepped with me out into the road, where by the aid of maps drawn with a stick on the ground, and to an accompaniment of warnings about the blind turn near Wasgatts' house, deep ruts, dangerous outcroppings of ledge and other assorted perils, they sent me on my way. "You'll think you're headed into nowhere," was their final word. "But keep on goin'—if you can—an' you'll get there."

The road wasn't all that bad, but it was no boulevard, and it very shortly did seem to be leading nowhere at all. It deteriorated into what was little more than a rough cart track across an open moor studded with twisted and tangled copses of stunted fir. There wasn't a building in sight—only the wide expanse of coarse-turfed, granite-ribbed land, and beyond it on three sides the glittering, surf-fringed sea. Gulls circled over us, screaming at the intrusion, and the tall grasses and low bushes tossed and flattened in the stiff salt breeze. The whole feeling of the place was primeval.

Then, topping a rocky, fir-crowned knoll, we saw the cabin crouching at the very limit of the land. It was a real cabin, constructed of logs with a huge fieldstone chimney forming most of one side, long and low, hugging the earth and facing bravely the wide expanse of open sea. It looked as though it belonged there, as though it had grown out of the moor and ledges and was as timeless and enduring as they. We loved it on first sight, and grew to love it more throughout the long days of that summer.

It seems very odd to me now that the road across the moor to the end of the Point was ever strange to me, so that I had to proceed over it on the first day with every precaution. Now I can drive over it in the densest fog, when the bushes along its edges are invisible, and never miss a turn or fail to shift on any of the abrupt, unseen pitches; or I can walk over it on the darkest night without stumbling. It seems even odder that the people whom I found working on the stove in the kitchen—they, and the storekeeper, and the Albrights, Lisle and Marjorie—were ever strangers to me. Now we know all that needs to be known about each other; we're as comfortable in each others' company as worn-out old shoes. We are friends now, safe and easy in a confident, undemanding relationship.

Now I know that beneath the courtesy shown me by Herb at the store on that first day, and the formal welcome extended to me by George and Marcia in the kitchen of the cabin, lay a great skepticism and a deep distrust, but I didn't find that out until a year ago, when I stopped at Marcia's one day to have a little chat with her. George Crowley, who is a widower without family, boards at her house; and while we were talking he came in, said "Hi, Louise," patted his white cat, Fuzzy, and started to take off the hipboots which every lobsterman wears from dawn until he gets through the day's work. Marcia started laughing, and I asked her what was so funny.

"I guess it's all right to tell you now, Louise," she said. "You remember that first year you came here? You remember you wrote me a letter about when you and Dinah would arrive? Well, all Lisle had told me was that a friend of theirs and her little girl were going

to use the cabin that summer. I didn't know you from Adam's off
ox; so when your letter came, signed by your name, I guess I was
some old taken aback. I'd read some of your books, you see."

"I said to George, 'You know who that woman *is?* She's that
writer.' And you want to know what George said?" She started
laughing again. "He just looked at me like he'd been poleaxed, and
he said, '*Now* what kind of a damned hellish mess have we got ourselves into?' That's exactly what he said."

George started to laugh, too. "Yup," he admitted, and shook his
head. "Seems like a long time ago now."

It does indeed.

That long-ago summer I spent in beginning to know tne land
and the people. It would seem to be an easy enough assignment to
learn all there was to learn about a handful of men and women and
a country that was reduced to the simplest terms of clean-swept
land, the sea, the sky and the weather. But when was the human
heart ever easy to read, or human conduct subject to immutable laws
of behavior? Where is there a land that never changes, that remains
forever static, frozen in one mood?

This country never looked the same for two days in succession. Sometimes the air sparkled like diamond dust and all the colors were brilliant and the outlines of the islands were sharp against sea and sky, clear as pasted cutouts. Sometimes the atmosphere was slightly pearly and as bland as milk; and with the change the whole world changed. The islands receded into a soft distance and became vague and dreamlike, their colors muted, and the grass-grown track across the moor to the village was a strange road leading to an unknown destination. Sometimes when the day was bright and burnished near at hand, so that every blade of grass and sea-worn pebble was as distinct as a detail of an etching, a wall of fog stood out to sea, blotting out the horizon and concealing 'Titm'nan Light. Boats disappeared into that fog, to emerge suddenly in unexpected places. In the late afternoon rainbows appeared on the face of the fog wall, mile-high columns of dazzling color, like great stained-glass windows.

Often the fog did not stay out at sea, but moved in silently and swallowed up the land. The islands became shadows, and then they were gone. Next the big rugosa bushes among the nearby ledges grew shadowy, until they too melted away. The sunlight changed to a luminous whiteness, and then to a damp, chill gray. The eaves dripped, the invisible surf sounded loud, and every twig was beaded with tiny drops of moisture. All sounds became distorted, so that the barking of the dog at the door seemed muffled and remote, while the clanging of the gong buoy southwest of the Old Woman rang loud and immediate in the ear.

Oh, the lovely sounds of Cranberry Point that I learned to know that summer! Never have I been in a place so seldom silent. The wind blew over the moor constantly, now with a wistful sighing, now with a harplike singing in the grasses, now with the deep tone of an organ. The gulls screamed and mewed overhead, soaring, consulting, turning and coasting together down invisible slopes of air. Flocks of tiny shore birds skimmed along the water's edge, their high, sweet constant calling like a rain of chimes. Under the eaves the cliff swallows chattered continually, filling the rooms with their light and happy voices. Early in the morning the lobster boats puttered cheerfully out to sea; and at night foxes barked on the moor.

The toll of the bell buoys and the hollow hooting of the whistle buoys drifted in from the sea, now loud and demanding, now ghostly and diminished, depending on the direction of the wind. And always, above and below and around all the other sounds, was the sound of the sea.

I thought that summer I had seen every face the country could present, but now I know that I shall never see them all, that I shall never learn its countless aspects in all seasons. in autumn when the blueberry bushes carpet the land with scarlet, so that the firs look black and the sea a deep indigo; in winter when it is blanketed in snow, withdrawn, cold and dormant; in spring when new life flashes like green-gold wildfire over the heath. One lifetime is not enough to memorize all that.

We were very busy that summer. We dug clams, gathered goose-grass greens, picked blueberries, collected shells and ringed pebbles, and, when the tide was out, hunted for sand dollars on the exposed bar off Crowley Island and for sea anemones in the little tidal pools of the Point. We explored the shore, swam, fished with handlines for pollock in the harbor, went out at dawn with the lobster fleet, and in the afternoon lay on the springy turf, improving our suntans. We attended baked bean suppers and ice cream festivals and fancy work sales and picnics, and went to church. We became habituées of the store at mail time, sitting around talking and listening to the talk. We had a wonderful vacation.

But as I grew to know the Peninsula better I saw that it was something more than just another vacation spot on the Maine coast. It wasn't a vacation spot at all. Nobody there cared whether the few stray summer people like me ever returned or not. They put up with us and helped us when they could; they seemed to like us; but we were not necessary to them. They had preserved their old, simple, self-sufficient way of life, independent of summer dollars and summer foibles, so that if every one of us went away and never came back they would still be able to survive through the knowledge handed down to them through the generations.

How unusual this is you will not understand until you have lived in other sea towns along this coast where the whole economy has been altered to meet the demands of the summer influx. There is a beautiful little village not far from the Peninsula which was, twenty-five years ago, self-supporting. Now the harbor is empty of all workboats. Their moorings are occupied by the graceful toys of the invaders, and the fish pier is a yacht club. The lobstermen mow the lawns of the summer estates and teach teen-agers to sail. If summer employment and summer-place taxes were withdrawn, the roads of the town would become grass-grown and the population would starve. The old skills have been lost and forgotten.

I spent another summer in another coastal village where my vegetable man kept me supplied gratis with cut flowers in the expressed hope that one day I would mention him in a book. No one there ever set out traps any more. They were all too busy washing the windows, clipping the hedges, and raking the driveways of the wealthy. I don't blame them for choosing this easier means of making a better living, but I cannot help feeling that they have sold their birthright for a mess of pottage. No longer can they look a man in the eye and say, "Nope, I ain't got the time for any such foolishness." They have thrown away their independence.

People are not like that on the Peninsula. I had the fact brought home to me on° day about a year ago. I had had, that spring, a short article about Corea published in *The Readers' Digest* which caused a certain amount of local excitement, and I was thinking about writing this book concerning the Peninsula. With this idea in mind, I developed a habit of asking questions and writing the answers down in a notebook which I carried always in the hip pocket of my jeans.

I was sitting on the Liars' Bench one noon, asking these questions while I waited for the mail stage to arrive. It finally drew up to the door, and the stage-driver, Horace Myrick, came lugging in the mail sacks. Holly Myrick is one of the two men in town who does not earn his living directly from the sea. The other is Herb Young Holly, in addition to carrying the mail, is also one of the three selectmen of the town of Gouldsboro and therefore more or less *in loco parentis* to the Peninsula. He heard me talking to old Dan Young, who is eighty-three, about his earliest recollections.

Holly dumped the mail sacks in the post office and came back to where I was sitting. "Your name wouldn't be Rich, would it?" he asked. "You wouldn't be the one that's caused all this confusion around here?"

I admitted that I probably was, and added that I was considering writing a book about the Peninsula. Would he, as selectman, be willing to help me find some information that I lacked?

He squared his shoulders, his thin, dark face stern. "Now look here, Miz Rich," he said. "We don't want no book written about us. We're ignorant and we know it, but we got feelings like anybody else. We don't like to be twitted about our ignorance by summer people, in print or out of print. You treat us decent and you won't find anybody, anywhere, kinder or more helpful than we are. But start making fun of us, and we don't like it. It hurts. We're no better than anybody else, but neither are we any worse. We're just hard-working people, trying to get along the best we can. Damn it, we ain't *quaint!* I've read books about some of the towns along here and I don't like them. I ain't going to have that happen to us."

I looked at him, standing there, young, defensive and deadly serious; and I felt a deep respect for him. He meant exactly what he said. It took me a long time to convince him of my good will, but, once convinced, he threw himself wholeheartedly into my project.

No, the Peninsula is not like the despoiled towns to the west; but it cannot retain its immunity from change forever. The straws are already in the wind. Most houses now have electricity and most families own cars. While the majority either pump water or carry it in buckets from wells, a few now have indoor plumbing and bathrooms. It is not, however, the mechanical aspects of the modern age that will alter the place out of recognition. They alone could not affect a way of life and a philosophy of living that have endured for two hundred years. When the change comes, it will come through the capture of the region by the summer people, with their different viewpoints and standards and their comparatively easy money. Already the infiltration has begun. Each year a few more vacationists find their way to this remote country. It is inevitable that they should. All the older vacation areas—Cape Cod, Cape Ann and the western coast of Maine—are overcrowded now. The search for space and quiet and simplicity perforce extends further and further to the east, a search expedited and increased in numbers by the rapid improvement of road and air travel.

I cannot, for the sake of the people, regret this. Their hard lives will be made easier and richer by association with more worldly and experienced individuals. In spite of things I may have seemed to imply, there is nothing wrong with summer people or with the gifts they bring.

Nevertheless, I shall regret the passing of what amounts to a last frontier, an anachronism in the world of today. When the last lobsterman hauls his last trap and turns his boat over to fishing parties from the city, when his son turns from the sea to a full-time caretaker's job, when his wife stops knitting bait bags and opens a gifte shoppe, and when Herb streamlines his store into a gaudy supermarket, something that was American will die.

That is why I think it important to make a record of this last outpost of individualism, from its beginnings to the present day, before it is too late.

2. The Early Settlers

THE FIRST EUROPEANS TO VIEW THE SURF-washed ledges of the Gouldsboro Peninsula were the Vikings under Leif Ericson in the year 1,000 A.D. In all probability they stood well out to sea beyond the vicious reefs. There was no object in an attempt to land on a dangerous coast so obviously barren of what they were seeking: the tall pines which they needed for masts and ship timbers, their supply at home having been depleted. They sailed on past the bleak ledges to the more hospitable shores of the southwest, to the area below the Penobscot, where the forests marched down to the high-tide mark. Even there they never established any permanent settlements. They set up temporary camps, bases for use during their lumbering operations, and when they had completed their errand they abandoned them. After a time, they stopped coming altogether.

The next white men to view the Peninsula from the safety of the horizon were the crew of Estaban Gomês, a Spaniard seeking gold and fabulous treasure such as had been found in Peru and Mexico. In 1525 he coasted all the way from Cuba to Nova Scotia, leaving a record of his progress on the map of today. He it was who named Casco Bay, Saco Bay, the Bay of Fundy and Campobello Island, calling them respectively Bahia de Casco (Bay of the Helmet), Bahia de Saco (Bay of the Sack), Bahia Profundo (Deep Bay), and Campo Bello (Beautiful Country). It is significant that no feature of the long stretch of coast of which Gouldsboro is the central point bears any name of Spanish derivation. Its forbidding aspect daunted even the most avid and reckless. Very soon the Spanish and the Portuguese and all the other fortune seekers accepted the fact that this was no land of inexhaustible emerald mines and gold-paved streets. They too went away, and again the coast was left in peace for almost a century.

Meanwhile the firearm came into common use, giving the European an incontrovertible advantage over the Indian; and the idea that wealth was necessarily a matter of gold and jewels became slightly old-fashioned. Other more prosaic materials in which America abounded—such as fish, fur and timber—were being recognized as the true treasure. In addition to these factors, which alone would have made the conquest of the New World inevitable, there were political and religious changes all over Europe, so that men everywhere were restless, dissatisfied, and ready to embark on new ventures. The West provided the opportunity.

In 1598 a ship outfitted by Sir Humphrey Gilbert and captained by John Walker came to anchor in Penobscot Bay, where Walker went ashore and claimed all the land everywhere in the name of Elizabeth and of England. He did not, however, establish any colony. Only six short years later, in 1604, a French company under the leadership of Pierre du Gast, Sieur de Monts, landed on Dochet's Island in the St. Croix River—now the International Boundary between the United States and Canada—and built a sturdy little settlement. He in turn claimed all the territory in the name of King Henry of France and Navarre. The Peninsula was perfectly bracketed by the two claims, although no representative of either power had set foot on it.

Among du Gast's group was Samuel de Champlain, probably the most important and competent explorer in the history of North America. Using Dochet's as a base, he ranged far down the coast in his ships, mapping the territory carefully and accurately and making the first reliable reports on the nature of the country. The Gouldsboro Peninsula he dismissed as impossible, warning all mariners in no uncertain terms that it was the worst piece of coast he had ever had the misfortune to encounter, continually pounded by thundering surf, shrouded frequently in dense fog, rimmed by lethal reefs, and beset by treacherous crosscurrents. Consequently all shipping gave it a wide margin of safety for a long time, passing well out beyond Petit Manan, which Champlain so named because it reminded him of Grand Manan, back near Dochet's Island. Geography was against early colonization of the Peninsula.

Although the land itself remained unexploited, this was not true of the coastal waters. Starting in about 1614, the sea was alive with fishing boats from southern colonies like Virginia and from Europe. The Catholic countries of the continent furnished a very profitable market for sea food, and the banks off the Isles of Shoals to the west and the Grand Banks to the east provided a wonderful source of supply for this market. Therefore a huge fish business sprang up, with hundreds of vessels making three round trips a year to fill their holds with what was called New England Silver. It was not unusual in stormy weather for forty or more fishermen to lie at anchor in some of the many sheltered coves and harbors along the coast from Massachusetts to Nova Scotia, but not in the little-known coves of the Peninsula. Concurrently a fur-trading business developed, more or less accidentally, when Sir Richard Hawkins visited Maine and happened to pick up a load of pelts from the Indians. He sold them in Europe at a profit which amazed him and everybody else. After that, naturally, trade in furs was energetic, if rather haphazard. The captains of the ships simply accepted any bundles that the Indians felt like bringing down to their moorings to sell. This was a happy arrangement that satisfied all concerned and hurt nobody.

In 1628, however, a new phase of fur trading was evolved. The Pilgrims, who had settled at Plymouth in 1620, found themselves in arrears with their payments on the *Mayflower*, which they had rented on the installment plan. In order to raise the necessary money they decided to go into the fur business. Although the Pilgrims are remembered and revered chiefly for their brave and idealistic attitude toward religious freedom, on weekdays they were far from dreamy-eyed idealists. In business matters their heads were extremely clear and their dealings outstandingly shrewd. With characteristic acumen they concluded that the former method of merely collecting furs according to Indian whim was pretty amateurish. So they established trading posts on the Kennebec and Penobscot Rivers in Maine, which was the best fur country, put the Indians more or less on contract to deliver only to them, and in addition supported their own teams of professional white trappers.

These posts were so successful financially that the Pilgrims were impelled to expand further to the east. Like all before them, they bypassed the Peninsula as being too tough and built their establishment on the Machias River, fifty miles further along. This was a mistake. The French considered Machias too near their own colonies in Acadia for comfort and destroyed the post almost as soon as it was completed. Then, having no use for it themselves, they abandoned it to the wilderness, and again this long stretch of coastline was tenantless.

It remained so for over a century and a quarter. During all this time the French and the English were struggling for supremacy in the New World, inciting the Indians to attack each others' settlements, besieging each others' cities to the east and west of the Peninsula, conducting war at sea, plundering, burning, killing, kidnapping, and wreaking general havoc. Treaties were signed and territory changed hands time and again; and, after short intervals of uneasy truce, war broke out again, more treaties were signed, and new boundaries were drawn. It was a time of change and disturbance in which only the Peninsula remained unchanged and undisturbed.

There the tides rose and fell over the granite ledges as they had since the beginning of time, and great storms swept in from the sea to twist and toughen the little firs. Gulls inscribed their shining geometry over the barren moors, seals rolled and played in the waters of the bay, the wide-eyed herring shoaled in the inlets, and lobsters crawled slowly along the bottoms of the coves. Far out on the horizon sails glinted in the sun—the sails of fishing smacks, of traders beating up the wind to Boston from Halifax, of the French fleet on its way to reduce Castine, of the Massachusetts armada bound for the siege of Louisbourg. But they never drew near. It was almost as though the Peninsula were a quarantine area, insulated from the history being made all around it. Its only history was the immemorial history of nature, of the seasons, the winds and the weather, recorded on the face of the land.

You must remember that at this time all travel was by sea, there being no roads at all through the wilderness; and the sea off the Peninsula was—and is—something to treat with great respect. Perhaps a pattern of behavior that has carried over into the present was established then, when the words Down East had real meaning. You sailed your ship to the east down the prevailing westerly winds; so the place at which you arrived was naturally Down East. Now Down East seems to be practically anywhere north of Boston, and the term has lost its old significance.

But a habit prevails. In the olden days ships put in to the safe ports of western Maine, did whatever provisioning and repair work was necessary, and then proceeded well out from the Peninsula to their more easterly destinations. Now, when wind and high seas can have no possible effect on land travelers' rate and safety of progress, a modern equivalent of the same procedure is commonly observed. The motorist puts in at a service station in the more civilized area, provisions with gasoline and hot dogs, and has his oil and water checked. Thus fortified for the perils ahead, he makes all speed along US 1 to the east, not even glancing down the roads onto the Peninsula.

In 1759 the English captured the stronghold of Quebec, and in that defeat France lost forever her hold on Canada. The Treaty of Paris was signed, and England at last was at liberty to develop her vast new possession. During the eighty-five years of sporadic raiding known as the French and Indian Wars, almost every village on what is now the coast of Maine had been destroyed or abandoned. At one time only four out of almost thirty remained in existence. Now that peace was established and the Indian menace removed, settlers flocked back across the Piscataqua to reclaim their lost holdings before the forest should have taken them back beyond recognition, or to find new sites and build new homes in the wilderness. It was with this wave of pioneering that the quarantine was finally lifted from the Peninsula.

At that time those parts of New England that were not settled or claimed were ordinarily bought from the Indians by English companies, chartered under English law, and laid out in townships. Any suitable and solvent person or persons desiring one of these townships could apply for a land grant to the proper agency. Maine being a part of Massachusetts, the proper agency in the case of those wanting Maine land was the General Court of Massachusetts, which represented the Crown. In 1764 three men, Francis Shaw, Colonel Nathan Jones and Robert Gould applied for and were given the grant of Township 3, which is now Gouldsboro, and the man-made history of the Peninsula began.

It is a little difficult at this distance in time to determine what exactly were the characters of these three men and what was the relationship and arrangement among them. Going on the evidence of the record and their actions, however, we can make some conjectures about them. They seem to have been three very diverse types. Francis Shaw was a noted Boston merchant of means who apparently looked upon this purchase of Peninsula land as an investment. He never lived there himself, although—as any good businessman would do—he did pay the township a few visits of inspection. His real home was in Boston, next to the home of Paul Revere, and that is where his eleven children were born and where his true interests lay. Two of his sons, however, did settle in Gouldsboro, and lived there until their deaths. One of the two, John, married Sarah Jones, daughter of Nathan Jones, the second of the three original proprietors.

Nathan Jones was a native of Weston, Massachusetts, a pleasant little colonial village on the outskirts of Boston. At the time of the purchase of the Peninsula he was thirty years old, the father of six children, including twins—Louisa and Pamela. Jones was no man to be content with absentee ownership. His purpose in acquiring land was to occupy it and improve it. In 1765 he and his wife Sarah and the children moved lock, stock and barrel to the shores of Jones Pond in West Gouldsboro. The delay after the acquisition of the land is explainable. Their sixth child, Abijah, was born in 1765, and I don't suppose Mrs. Jones, pioneer woman though she was, felt like embarking on so hazardous an enterprise until the baby was weaned,

at least. In the end there were an even dozen children, all of whom lived to become useful men and women except the eleventh, Daniel. He was lost at sea at the age of seventeen.

We shall come back later to the Jones family, because of the three original proprietors of the town they alone are prototypes of the true pioneers. Shaw was an investor, and Gould—

Well, what about Gould, for whom the town was named?

Robert Gould was a surveyor by occupation, a young man of no means, but apparently possessed of enthusiasm and remarkable selling powers. He was, I think, a sort of eighteenth century promoter. In 1761 or thereabouts, in the course of his professional activities, he discovered and cursorily explored the Peninsula. He was immediately possessed of the notion of establishing a town there. He went back to Boston and managed to interest Shaw and Jones in the idea. When the question of his own financial contribution to the project arose he talked the London company of John Lane, Esq., into lending him his share of the money. Lane took land as security, so that on the map of the original survey, which Gould made in 1763, his own name does not appear. The territory is divided into three parts held respectively by Jones, Shaw and Lane & Sons.

Then Gould really went to work. Traveling up and down the coast, he used all his considerable powers of persuasion to induce families to move to the Peninsula, so that soon his name became identified with the area. Long before the town was incorporated it was known as Gouldsborough. I think the name must first have been applied as a joke. "That God-forsaken piece of rock and swamp that young Gould is always ranting about? Yeah—Gouldsborough—heh-heh!"

Be that as it may, it was no joke to Robert Gould. He was in earnest. Family by family, he and the other proprietors managed to build up the population. The Gubtails came, and the Libbys and the Tracys; the Hills and the Spurlings and the Whitakers and others. It was Gould's aim to procure enough citizens to meet the legal requirements for incorporation as a town, which he considered would be a further selling point, and he was not above a certain amount of chicanery to accomplish his purpose. To swell the list of male residents which he proposed to present to the authorities, he induced people to give their dogs such names as Ezekiel, Tobias and Harvard, and then solemnly added these names to his roster. Nobody in Boston ever knew the difference.

But with the outbreak of the Revolution the situation began to deteriorate. No new settlers arrived, and many of those already established moved back to the communities from which they came. Not the Joneses, though. They had too much at stake to abandon lightly. All their eggs were in this basket, and they intended to stand watch over it.

Today, as you turn off US 1 at West Gouldsboro onto Route 186, you coast down a little incline onto a narrow bridge of land between Jones Pond and a beautiful sheltered cove of Frenchman Bay. A brook runs under the road from the pond and empties into the sea. On the right is a quiet pool below a little dam, where there are always white ducks swimming; and I suppose there were ducks swimming there a hundred and eighty years ago, because that is where the Joneses lived. The depression that was once their cellar can still be seen. They farmed the land, fished the pond and bay, built boats, peeled hemlock bark for tanning the hides of the deer they shot, cut pines and sawed planks from them in their little sawmill on the brook, and ground their grain into meal in their own gristmill, the frame of which still exists. The site of their home is beautiful now and must have been even more beautiful then, when there were no roads and the quiet green cup in the forest was accessible only by the sea. They must have had a fine life there, the whole tribe of them, busy all day long with their multiple activities. Even a widowed daughter, Sarah Jones Shaw, lived under the family roof with her infant son, Nathan. It is no wonder that the Joneses were loath to abandon this place.

When the news of the Revolution reached them by way of the crew of a fishing smack they took a reasonable precaution. They hid on an island in the pond their silver and the clock that they had brought all the way from Weston, and then they went about their business as usual. The war was not to them nor to any of the isolated frontiersmen the important and immediate affair that it was to those nearer the center of things. Weeks would go by without their hearing a word about the progress of hostilities. For all they knew, the whole thing might have blown over with their being none the wiser. They were spared the midnight alarums of any Paul Revere.

The war did not entirely pass them by. Once a detachment of British soldiers from a ship that was raiding the settlers on the shore of Frenchman Bay came to the house, demanding Colonel Jones. He escaped through a bedroom window while Mrs. Jones held the door. During the tussle to get it open, the military managed to cut Mrs. Jones's fingers with a bayonet. She and her widowed daughter were making bread at the time, and had the brick oven already heated. The baby, Nathan, was lying in his cradle by the fire.

The story is that the fiendish redcoats threatened to put the baby into the hot oven if the women didn't tell them where the man of the house and his valuables were hidden, and that they were met with proud and stubborn refusal to talk. Probably the outline is correct, but I think things didn't happen quite like that. I doubt if the British really meant to bake the baby. It's more likely that they felt a little foolish, forcing their way into a house and cutting a woman's hand, only to find a simple domestic scene. They probably blustered around while Mrs. Jones tied up her fingers and gave them a piece of her mind. She'd raised six boys to manhood and was used to dealing with the young male of the species. Then when some joker made the threat about the baby she probably lost her patience and told them to take themselves out of there, all of them, before she applied the business end of the broom to them. And they were probably glad to go by that time. At any rate, the baby was not roasted, Colonel Jones was not captured, the silver was not stolen, and the clock is still running in a house in Boston.

The member of the family who had the most exciting war experience was the eighth child, Mary, who was a teen-age girl at the time. She was called Polly, which seems to have been a common nickname for Mary then, since it appears often in old records. Before the war started she had gone to the Provinces to visit family friends. Apparently she was homesick, because when some Gouldsboro neighbors showed up in Nova Scotia she begged a ride home in their boat, with the idea of surprising her family. The boat and all aboard were captured by the British, and Polly and her companions were imprisoned all winter in the fort at St. Andrews. Polly seems to have been a capable young miss, not one to sit with her hands folded. She spent the winter washing out socks and sewing on buttons for the garrison.

I realize that most people then were far too busy to indulge in long detailed written accounts of their day-to-day activities, but the story of Polly Jones is even more maddening than the usual record. An old local history says simply, "In the spring they effected an escape and upon arriving home the Jones family first learned of the daughter's whereabouts as they had supposed she was visiting her friends." Period. *How* did they effect an escape? How did they *get* home? There was no road, and it's a long walk through the woods from St. Andrews to Gouldsboro. Did they thumb a ride on a boat? Who were the companions? What did they do about food? What—? That's the sort of account that drives local historians to drink.

The war was not fought entirely by women and children. The local Revolutionary hero was Captain Daniel Sullivan of the town of Sullivan near Gouldsboro on Frenchman Bay. He was eventually captured and imprisoned on the infamous *Jersey* hulk in New York. Finally he was exchanged, but he died on the way home to Sullivan, probably as a result of privation. His story has a place here only because of the company of militia that he raised from the vicinity. On the rolls are some good Peninsula names, such as Libby, Gubtail, Spurling, Jordan, Tracy, Noonan, Ash, Young and others.

Through no fault of their own, however, the activities of this company were somewhat limited. Three times they marched to Machias in anticipation of some emergency; once they went to Bagaduce (or Castine); and the rest of the time they acted as a protectice force for the inhabitants of the Frenchman Bay area. With the best will and stoutest heart in the world it is difficult to be a hero in the backwaters of a war. The British weren't bothering much about the Peninsula, any more than previous expeditions had bothered about it. They confined their aggressions to rare, small raiding parties; so the Revolution probably had less immediate effect on this territory and its people than on any other inhabited part of the Thirteen Colonies.

Finally the war was over and independence for the colonies won. Then the new Commonwealth of Massachusetts went about setting her house in order. In 1789 she issued an Act of Incorporation making "Gouldsborough, so-called" into "a town by name Gouldsboro . . . vested with all powers, privileges and immunities which other towns of this commonwealth by law do and may enjoy." An Alexander Campbell, Esq., Justice of the Peace, was empowered to issue the warrant to "some principal inhabitant of the said town of Gouldsboro requiring him to notify the inhabitants thereof to meet at such a time and place as he shall appoint, to choose all such officers as towns are by law required to choose."

The principal inhabitant chosen by Mr. Campbell was Thomas Hill, Yeoman, and the place of meeting was the home of Captain Samuel Libby at ten A.M. on Thursday the 23rd of April, 1789. Then and there were the required town officers chosen, including Fence Viewers, Deer Reevers and a Sealer of Leather. Seventy-six pounds and two shillings were voted to be raised for town expenses, and the meeting was dissolved. Gouldsboro was in business.

It wasn't very flourishing business at first. There was a very slim population and very little money. The same men had to double as town officers. Thomas Hill, for example, was one of the Selectmen, one of the Surveyors of Lumber, and the Collector. Nathan Jones was the Moderator and a Road Surveyor. Dr. Benjamin Alline served as Treasurer and Sealer of Weights and Measures. Collector Hill was empowered to collect money for roads and schools; but later, in 1793, it was voted that inhabitants might contribute work or material for these projects in lieu of money, so cash must have been scarce. In 1795 the taxes were for the first time recorded in dollars and cents rather than pounds and shillings, but that didn't make them any easier to pay. Although a few more settlers were coming to the district—the Coles's to Prospect Harbor, the Chilcotts to Ironbound Island, the Clarks to Birch Harbor, and a Negro named Frazier to Winter Harbor, still the number of voters in 1795 was only sixty-six. The metropolis of Robert Gould's dreams was far from a fact.

Then William Bingham and his agent, General David Cobb, entered the picture.

It came about in this way. After the Revolution, the Commonwealth of Massachusetts came into possession of hundreds of square miles of unsettled land in Maine. To raise money she ran a lottery with parcels of this land as prizes. William Bingham, a wealthy and influential Philadelphia banker, drew several townships. This so whetted his appetite for Maine land that he purchased more until his holdings in Maine exceeded two million acres. Among other tracts that he bought were the Shaw share of the Peninsula and the share formerly owned by Lane & Sons, which had been confiscated by Massachusetts at the end of the war. To develop and exploit these holdings properly it was necessary for him to have agents on the spot, and the agent he chose for the Peninsula was David Cobb of Taunton, Massachusetts.

Graduated from Harvard in 1766, Cobb studied medicine, married Eleanor Bradish of Cambridge, and had established a successful practice in Taunton when the Revolution broke out. He entered the Army as a lieutenant colonel in 1777 and so distinguished himself by his qualities of courage, initiative and integrity that he came to the notice of Washington, who appointed him a personal aide. He assisted in the capture of Cornwallis and was commissioned a brigade general by brevet. What is more important, his relationship with Washington progressed into one of personal intimacy, so that at the end of the war he went to Mt. Vernon as a member of the official family. This provided a remarkable opportunity for the young doctor to demonstrate his various abilities, and very soon he was appointed Chief Justice of the Court of Common Pleas of Bristol County, Massachusetts. He was an excellent judge, fair and firm, and from the bench he went on to new political heights until in 1793 he became a member of the Third Congress. In 1795 he was appointed as agent for the Bingham estate, and the following year he moved to the Peninsula.

He found there a rather backward community of settlers scattered thinly along the west and south shores. The central part of the area was almost uninhabited, and the eastern limits, where Corea is now, entirely so. The people were living a life of small farming and fishing, with a little local lumbering on the side—a typical frontier life which probably satisfied them very well. It didn't, however, satisfy General Cobb. He had other ideas for the place, and the energy and authority to try to put them into practice.

Actually, I think, the man was almost an authentic genius. Educated to be a doctor, trained to be a soldier and leader, experienced as a judge and administrator and outstandingly successful in these fields, he had still other facets to his character. He was passionately interested in farming and knew a great deal about it. Soil and forest conservation were not hobbies of his, but principles which he applied far ahead of his day. Commerce and shipbuilding interested him intensely, and so did education and social service. He was, in fact, the founder of Taunton Academy and one of the founders of Massachusetts General Hospital, one of the first hospitals in the Western Hemisphere. Worldly and urbane, he was also a true visionary, with the visionary's fatal inability to recognize and accept facts.

Perhaps it was this blindness to reality that enabled him to see the Peninsula as the site of a great city, surrounded and supported by a rich area of productivity. Or perhaps, having been given a job to do, his natural optimism and sense of responsibility dictated to him an impossibly high standard of achievement. At any rate, he believed that Gouldsboro had a tremendous future as a shipping point for lumber, agricultural produce and fish, and as a mill city and shipbuilding center. He saw the shore lined with great wharves and warehouses, the land covered with prosperous farms, and settlers flocking in from far and wide to share in this bounty.

Almost from the moment of his arrival, General Cobb busied himself in trying to make his dream come true. Roads were his first concern, and on July 19, 1796, he wrote in his diary, "This [the boat] is the only mode of conveyance in this Country as they have no roads. It is a matter of great surprise that People of property and influence, whose wealth must be greatly increased by good Roads, pay so little attention to the subject." To remedy the situation, he laid out a system of highways and rounded up every available man to work on them. He was equally concerned by the wasteful way in which lumbering was conducted, since, after all, he was accountable to his employer. "I am determined that this immense destruction of Lumber shall not continue," he wrote, "if I am obliged to resort perhaps to the worst remedy, a legal process."

He must have been successful, because in a few years Gouldsboro shipped large amounts of lumber to the West Indies. What he failed to consider was the fact that when the immediately available stands were cut off there was no easy way in which the timber of the interior could be transported to the wharves he had built on the bay. In other sections of Maine are great rivers running far inland down which the long logs could be driven, but there is no such natural highway leading back from the Peninsula. His wharves, storehouses and mills fell into emptiness and idleness, and the General turned his attention to agriculture.

It was his plan to burn over the deforested areas, clear them of stumps, and sow rye, wheat and grass seed in the ashes. These crops would be followed by potatoes, turnips and other vegetables until prosperous farms were established. As he said in his diary, "The chief operating reason for my undertaking is the example it will be to this part of the country, in which to their disgrace not a single farmer resides. . . . By seeing a mode of raising their bread, they will add a value to their soil, which at present they conceive of no consequence; they would not accept of the best soil in the World, as a present, if the Timber was off it, thence the burnt grounds which are large in quantity and most of them very good for culture are looked upon as ruined and mere wastes by these fellows, and their information has a baneful influence upon all those who visit here for purchasing and residing. It is of the first consequence that this opinion should be changed and nothing will do it but producing the most damning conviction from the soil itself, which I will do."

On his own farm on Gouldsboro Bay, about halfway between Prospect Harbor and Gouldsboro, Cobb fulfilled his promise or threat. His diary is full of notations like "Ye first cucumbers of our Garden" (August 20), "First peas of our planting" (August 24), and in October, "The Labourers this day finished the Potatoes that they have put into the Hole for the winter. This cellar is closed up and secured against the cold; it contains about two hundred bushels. The rest of the Potatoes are put in the Barn for the use of the Cattle."

The damning conviction that the General was so set on producing extended to fodder. I don't suppose any of us now realizes and appreciates the importance of hay in a pioneer society. Horses and oxen and cattle will not eat maple leaves and pine needles. They *must* have hay. It was the fuel that kept the machinery of the day running, as important then as gasoline is now. Without hay, land transport and the cultivation of the soil was impossible. One of the reasons (in addition to the excellent harbor and the productive hinterland) why the site of Portland, Maine, was considered so ideal was that the many islands of Casco Bay produced such a large crop of hay, easily transferable by barge to the stables and barns of the city. Steps to protect their hay were taken by many communities, such as Mt. Desert Island, which at its first town meeting in 1776 elected a committee to prevent anyone's shipping hay off the island. No town without an abundant supply of hay could prosper; and General Cobb was perfectly well aware of this fact.

There were no natural meadows on the Peninsula. What land was not wooded consisted of barren rock. The only natural supply was the salt hay of the marshes which the settlers cut between tides and carried ashore for storage. This was not considered the best hay for milking or working stock, but it had to serve.

The first thing the General did about the hay situation was to sow parts of his burned-over land with grass seed. Then he turned his attention to the marsh near his house on Gouldsboro Bay. "Went over to view the Great Marshes," he writes. "People were at work on them, stacking and cutting their hay. It is not so well mowed as it ought to be; care must be taken with this marsh and some expense laid out for ditching, etc."

The more he thought about it, the less ditching seemed to be the answer to the problem of the marshes; and he ended by having a series of dykes built to dam out the sea. Almost a hundred acres were thus reclaimed from the tides, and as the salt hay gradually died out on this drier land, the earth was plowed and seed of the best English hay was sown. The land was rich, and a valuable property was developed. In time, when it became clear that the dykes were practical and would hold against the sea, storage barns were built on the marshes, and the area came to be known by the name it carries today, the Dyke Marsh.

But with all his energy and ambition, Cobb was doomed to failure. The Peninsula is simply not endowed by nature with the qualifications necessary for the building of a great commercial center or the developing of an agricultural empire. First the supply of timber gave out. Then more and more people realized that good water power, which the Peninsula lacks, was essential to the industry of the day and moved along to the banks of the Union, Narraguagus, Machias and St. Croix Rivers. Farming was possible, as the General demonstrated, but few cared to or were able to put into the land the enormous amount of time, energy, imagination and money that he did. Even he had his troubles, since he could not control the climate. Time and again he had crops destroyed by early frosts, buildings damaged by gales, or boats wrecked at their moorings by storms.

Finally his health began to fail, and after twenty-five years of hard work at the job he was forced to resign as Bingham agent and return to Taunton. With his going in 1820 (the year of Maine's coming-to-statehood), the Peninsula returned to the slower and simpler mode of life for which it was naturally intended.

Of all the things that General Cobb planned and put into effect, the work on the Dyke Marsh endured the longest. His wharves and storehouses rotted away, his mills fell down, and his fields went back to scrub; but to this day you can trace the broken dykes zigzagging across the marsh. They were kept in repair until gasoline motors took the place of horses and oxen, and many families of the Peninsula still own acres of the dyke land that has gone back to salt grass and to the sea. People there of my age can remember doing what they call "haying the dyke." It was not much fun. The marsh was always hot and breathless in good haying weather, the horseflies were terrible, there was no drinking water except what you brought with you, and there was always danger of a horse's falling into a soap hole, or camouflaged pit of deep mire. But now almost nobody goes to the Dyke Marsh except an occasional Indian to gather sweet grass for making baskets, or those few who are interested in seeing with their own eyes the testimony of another day and age.

Neither Robert Gould nor David Cobb was able to mold the Peninsula into the shape of his dream. It was too stubborn for them, too frugal to give according to their extravagant demands, too set in its own harshly beautiful pattern of rock and sea and loneliness to conform to the elaborate patterns of their eager imagining. It needed a different breed of men to tame it, men whose qualities matched its own.

There is an opinion commonly expressed by summer visitors and other observers that the Down East Yankee, of which generic group the Peninsula people are classic examples, is the result of his environment. The rigors of the climate, the difficulties of wresting a living from a reluctant land, the isolation and the necessity of improvising substitutes for the things they cannot afford to buy are supposed to have made these people tough and durable, independent, ingenious, inflexible and slightly eccentric. The development of these qualities, according to the theory, was necessary to survival.

Actually the thing worked the other way. The lonely Peninsula with its poor soil, cruel winters, icy seas and forbidding coastline didn't form the character of the people. They were that way from the beginning. Had they not been, they would scarcely have come to the Peninsula in the first place, and certainly would never have stayed there. Those who could not take the punishment the country imposed—the faint of heart, the soft, the lazy and the pompous—soon went away to lands of easier living. Left behind was a picked group of the tough, the self-sufficient and the self-reliant, who knew their own limitations and entertained a supreme confidence in their own abilities. They did not demand too much. They didn't want to change the land, but were satisfied with what it had to offer as it was. They were willing to work, to make-do and to do without, and in return all they wanted was a living and freedom to go their own way at their own pace. Operating on this basis, they were able to come to terms with the country. They passed on to their descendants of today not only their stony acres and a well-defined way of life, but all the qualities of character that made them and still make them a breed apart.

In the early days a living was derived about equally from the land and from the sea. Fresh vegetables, eggs and dairy products were things that you either raised yourself or went without. Therefore every family had its own cows, hens and small plot of cleared land on which it raised its own crops. There was time for the cultivation of the soil because the fishermen and lobstermen depended on sails or oars. This limited their working range to the immediate waters of the Peninsula. In the calm of early morning they went out to tend their traps and nets and were back ashore well before the midday breeze came up. Then they could devote the rest of the day to their little salt-water farms.

One of the chores that took up a great deal of their time was the hauling of loads of the knotted wrack, or rockweed, the coarse seaweed so common along the New England coast. Storms piled this up along the shore, and the farmers gathered it to spread on their fields as a mulch and fertilizer. It gave body to the soil and cost nothing but time and labor. It was important enough to farm economy so that rights of way were established by the town across private property for the convenience of those who wanted to get down to the tide line to gather rockweed. Some of these roads may still be used by anyone wishing to haul away the weed, only nowadays nobody ever does. Now it collects in great drifts at the high water mark, and as it begins to steam and rot in the hot sun it smells terrible, like long-dead fish.

One of the features commonly associated with the conventional calendar-art New England landscape is the dry stone wall. These survivals of another day wander in a picturesque manner across almost every pastoral scene. They are, of course, made of the rocks that the early farmers removed from their fields for easier plowing and built into walls more to get rid of them than for any other reason. There are almost no stone walls on the Peninsula, and when I first went to Corea I missed them. So one day when I was waiting for my mail I asked old Dan Young about them.

He looked at me as though he thought I was crazy. "No use building walls here," he said. "We never had anything worth fencing in or fencing out. When we cleared our land we just pitched the rocks in a pile off to the side."

Then he went on to tell me about clearing the fields down on Cranberry Point, where he had been born and lived until he grew up. The clearing took place every spring, when a new crop of frost-heaved rocks lay loose on the surface of the earth. The father of the family assembled all the children—families were large in those days—and took them out into the fields. Then he showed each child a sample stone of the size he was allowed to carry, each according to his strength. The big stones went to the big boys, the smaller stones to the smaller boys and the girls, and the little ones to the little children; and after that each child was responsible for removing all the stones in his bracket. I think that is a fine way to clear a field—making a family project of it, where they all worked together in the pale spring sunlight and stiff salt breeze. You can still see those piles of stones down on the Point, long after the fields have gone back to blueberry bushes, blackberry briars and wild roses.

Everyone in those days owned a boat, just as everyone does today, but then they built their own. In the comparatively idle periods between planting and haying or haying and harvest, most men laid ways on the shore of some convenient and sheltered cove and set their several sons to work on the new boat. It was as normal then for a farmer to be a shipbuilder and owner as it is now for him to own a pick-up truck. These were not great clipper ships like those built at Bath or Brunswick, but just little family schooners for use in fishing or in local trade along the immediate coast, or as a means of transportation from one village to another. The most famous of these boats—perhaps the only really famous one—was the brig *Pilgrim*, built by Captain Jerry Stevens and his brother at Stave Island. It was on this ship that Richard Henry Dana rounded Cape Horn and on which he began *Two Years Before the Mast*. But the one I like best of all was built at West Gouldsboro by Thomas Hill and his ten sons. When he got it done he named it *The Ten Brothers*, which I think is a wonderful name for a family vessel.

Gradually the trade conducted by the little coastwise schooners extended to the growing cities to the west. Loads of barrel staves for the lime industry of Rockland and salt fish for the markets of Portland and Boston were shipped from the Peninsula, and goods for the local storekeepers were brought back. An exchange of commodities was effected which made it possible for men to stop struggling with the meager resources of the land and to turn their entire attention to the rich subaqueous pastures that lay beyond the islands. In 1839 Underwood and Kensett perfected the technique of preserving foods in tin cans to the point where it was commercially practical. They probably never heard of Gouldsboro, but their work was an important factor in establishing the new economy of the Peninsula. Small lobster, clam and sardine-canning factories were built at South Gouldsboro and Prospect Harbor which provided a market for all the seafood that could be caught. Well before the Civil War the whole population had shifted from a semi-agricultural life to one that was supported entirely by the sea; and so it remains, with a few exceptions, down to the present day.

The Young family of Corea illustrates very nicely what took place. In 1812 Joseph Young, who married Sally Tracy of Gouldsboro, moved to Corea—then called Indian Harbor—and built a house on Cranberry Point. He was the first settler of the town, but he was soon followed by six other families of Youngs, three of whom joined him on the Point. The others built homes near the Harbor or over on what is now Crowley Island. For about ninety years they and their descendants occupied their original holdings; but then the whole thing got to be too much for them. They were lobstermen now, keeping their boats in the harbor, since there is no shelter on the shore of the Point. There seemed to be little sense in subjecting themselves twice daily to the long walk across the heath to where their vessels were moored. So they tore down their farmhouses, abandoned their acres, and moved into the village, where they now live in little houses facing out over the harbor. All that is left on the Point are four cellar holes almost hidden by brush, the piles of stones from their fields, and Simeon Young's granite-faced well, from which I draw my water.

Young is the most common name in Corea, but there are quite a few Crowleys, too. I asked George Crowley once when we were out off 'Titm'nan Light in his boat, tending his lobster traps, how his family happened to come to Corea in the first place.

"Didn't have much choice in the matter," he told me in his soft, deliberate voice. "My great-great-grandfather was a British seaman. His ship wrecked over yonder on Outer Bar, a hundred or more years ago, and he was the only one washed ashore. Flotsam, you might say he was. He just never got around to leaving, and none of the rest of us ever see any call to move on, either. So here we be."

George's great-great-grandfather married one of the Young girls, and they had twelve children. Evidently considering that in a family of that size one more wouldn't make much difference, they adopted a thirteenth. This gave them a good running start toward establishing the Crowley name in Corea. They, too, used to run little farms over on Crowley Island; but now they are all involved in the lobster business in one way or another, and live close around the harbor.

Life on the Peninsula became crystallized into a pattern a hundred years ago, and the pattern has changed very little since. Boys went off to the various wars—the Civil War, the Spanish War and the World Wars, but those who survived came back to take up where they had left off. They turned in their guns, put their uni-

forms away in mothballs, drew on their long rubber boots, and
drifted down to the harborside where the boats were coming in,
each under its individual convoy of screaming gulls. Within a few
days they had their own boats scraped and caulked, their gangs of
new traps built, their lobster buoys painted fresh and bright, and
were again busy at the occupation they knew and loved best.

Details changed with changing times, of course. The fishermen
are no longer dependent on sail and oar. Their boats are now
powered with gasoline motors. No longer do the little schooners
put in to the harbors to fill their holds. Instead the big trailer trucks
roar in off US 1 to pick up the crates of lobsters and cases of
sardines.

But nothing can change the sea, and no modern device can be
invented to alter the age-old habits and instincts of its inhabitants.
The same ancient skills are necessary to lure the lobster to the trap
and the herring to the net. No labor law can be enacted that will
dictate the turning of the tide, the path of a storm, or the crawling

of the lobsters so that a man's working day and hours of leisure may be legally regulated. A hundred years ago the men went out when the tides and the weather were right and came in when their work was done. Their getting up and going to bed, the hours at which they ate their meals, and the whole structure of their daily lives were determined by the unchangeable rhythm of the sea; and they still are. They will continue to be as long as the sea continues to be the master and the servant of the people of the Peninsula.

3. The Gay Years

LIFE ON THE PENINSULA WAS AT ITS MOST lively and varied during the four or five decades following the Civil War. At this time all of coastal New England experienced a postwar acceleration in industry and trade which was felt even in this remote area. Commercial activity was not confined as it is today to those enterprises directly dependent on the sea, but was spread over a fairly wide field of endeavor. As a consequence there was employment for almost everyone, no matter what his special training or ability might be. Families were large, and most of the young men and women felt no urge to leave the land where they had been born and brought up and which they knew so well. There was always more work of one sort or another than there were men to do it, so that people from other communities frequently came to the Peninsula in search of jobs, and during these years the population reached its peak. Gouldsboro was, in a mild way, a boom town.

In those days such articles of trade as sugar, molasses, flour, lard, crackers, pickles and many others were invariably shipped in barrels, kegs or wooden tubs. Naturally cooperage, or barrel-making, flourished. Although the heavy growth suitable for ship timbers and masts had been largely cut off the Peninsula, enough smaller stuff remained so that quantities of stave wood for the making of the sides of barrels and of limber poles for the hoops were available. Men—both natives and transient laborers—worked in the woods and the sawmills all winter, cutting, sawing and stacking these staves and poles along the shore. A lively shingle-splitting industry also existed. What wood was inferior for these purposes could always be corded as kiln wood. At that time Rockland and the adjacent territory, because of great local deposits of limestone, became a tremendous lime-burning center, the largest in the United States and probably in the world. Thirty cords of wood were required to fire one kiln, so in order to support the industry Rockland had to go far afield for kiln wood. Enormous quantities were shipped from Gouldsboro. Still another export was cobblestones, an inexhaustible crop from the barren and rocky land, almost free for the taking.

The work of harvesting this bounty was carried on during the winter, when the anchorages were frozen over, the sea was at its wildest, and shipping was at a standstill. The nearest railhead was at Sullivan, and this was too long a haul for horses and oxen, even if rail shipping had not been far too costly for such heavy and bulky products. Therefore all deliveries were made by water. As soon as the landings were ice-free, early in April, fleets of freshly painted schooners and sloops would show up, looking for cargoes and crews. The kiln wood was loaded for Rockland, the staves and poles for Portland and Boston, and the paving stones and shingles for contractors in New York, Philadelphia and Washington. The men, whose winter work in the woods was finished, signed on as members of the crews. They were a versatile group, as competent at sea as they were on the land, and this arrangement provided them with good wages and a chance to see a little of the world. In the fall they returned home on the last visit of their vessel, which usually took place just before Thanksgiving.

The day and hour of the spring sailing was determined by the completion of the loading of the vessel and the state of the wind and tide, and not by the convenience of the crew members, who were sometimes left with unfinished business on hand. Two of my friends in Corea, Amanda Dunbar and Florris Bridges, told me one day about a predicament in which their Grandfather Young found himself. His ship was due to sail from Prospect Harbor, three foot-miles away, at about the time his wife was giving birth to a child.

So he left instructions that when the sloop was sighted beating her way out of the harbor some member of the family should stand on the end of Cranberry Point, where they lived, and wave a large cloth. The color depended on circumstances. As it turned out, they waved a white tablecloth, which meant that a baby girl had been safely born and the mother was well, so he could proceed on his voyage with an easy mind. This was a common device for appraising sailors of the outcome of projects which had been uncompleted when they departed from home, and all colors of signals flew on occasion from the surf-washed ledges of the Peninsula, carrying such diverse intelligence as "I forgive you" to "The sick cow died."

The final trips of the season meant more to the Peninsula than just the return of the men for the winter. All the merchandise—food and clothing and kerosene and grain for the livestock—which was to be sold in the little stores and used by the people until the following spring must be stocked then. The storekeepers had to do some very careful long-range buying to fill the long warehouses that were attached to each store. The goods were hauled up from the wharves by teams of slow-moving oxen until the walls of the storage sheds bulged. Even then there were sometimes errors in judgment so that before April a staple item ran out, and someone had to take the long, slow wagon trip to Sullivan in icy weather over winter roads to supply the lack. The most common deficiency was in hay and grain. Nearly everyone owned horses, cattle and sheep, and almost invariably before the winter was over the supply of fodder was exhausted and more had to be hauled in.

Perhaps because they had so few valuable possessions, men in those days took great pride in their teams of horses. They could excuse any seeming extravagance on the grounds that a good horse was a good investment, necessary to make a living in the woods. Periodically carloads of young western horses would arrive at Plumber's Sales Stables in Harrington, and then a fever of horse buying and trading broke out. Everyone wanted a bigger, handsomer and more spirited team than his neighbor had. Once acquired, the horses were fed and curried until they shone, and their manes and tails were religiously trimmed and braided. Even if a man had to wear patched pants himself, he saw to it that the harness of his team was bright with polished brass ornaments and bells, and the bridles were decorated with big red and yellow tassels.

Some of the older people who lived on the shores of West Bay Pond during their childhoods of seventy or eighty years ago recall as their most stirring memory the return each night of the teams that had been working in the woods. They'd come out of the shadow of the forest onto the pale sheen of the icy pond, darkly silhouetted against the brilliant winter sunset. Manes tossing, bells jangling in the clear cold air, harness creaking, and snow-dust flying in glittering streamers from beneath their eager hooves, they'd race toward the lights of home while the teamsters shouted them on. It must have been an exciting sight, full of color and wild motion, to those who knew so little of pageantry and of the spectacular. I think it still would be, even to a generation accustomed to the offerings of television, where you can see horses running at practically any hour of the day. These horses were different. They were their own; and everybody is entitled to pride of hard-won possession.

In addition to work in the woods and sawmills there were other means of livelihood on the Peninsula half a century ago. There were, of course, the fishing and lobstering, and employment in the lobster- and sardine-canning factories at South Gouldsboro and Prospect Harbor, which we shall discuss more fully later, since they alone of the industries survive today. There was also on West Bay Pond Stream a wool-carding mill. Almost everyone raised his own sheep and sheared his own wool. Instead of carding it themselves, as had been done in colonial days, they took it to the mill, where it could be done better and faster. When the cleaned and carded wool was brought home, the women of the families spun it into yarn for socks, mittens and sweaters. Almost every Peninsula woman of my age could spin if she should ever need to.

There were, however, those fumble-fingers who never could master the skill, or those mothers of large families who could not find the time for it. So a class of specialists came into being, women who were unusually adept at spinning and who made a profession of it. Usually they were older women who had learned the art before the days of the carding mill. Either they never had married or they were widowed and, lacking a supporter, turned their knowledge toward their own support.

They must have had rather an interesting and enjoyable time. Most of them had homes of their own or relatives with whom they lived for the larger part of the year. But as soon as the spring shearing was done and the wool returned from the carding mill to its owners, they made out their schedules. Each would put a few clothes into a carpetbag and start on what amounted to a round of visits throughout the Peninsula. She would stay at each house until the spinning was done, a matter of a few days or even two weeks, when she would be taken on to the home of the next customer. Although she was on business, she was treated more as a guest than as an employee.

There were several reasons for this. There was no question at all of social equality or the lack of it. Everyone was equal, and the spinning woman might be your own cousin or aunt or, but for the grace of God, you yourself. In addition, the arrival of a house guest, in no matter what capacity, was an event calling for the bringing out of the best dishes, the serving of company food, and the opening of the spare chamber with its good bed. Furthermore, since the spinning woman lived intimately with her various clients, she was a wonderful source of information, not to say gossip. Spinning on the expert level does not interfere with talking, and a well-fed and cosseted spinning woman was far more apt to prove expansive than one who felt she was being given less than her just deserts. Last—but far from least—no woman wanted her spinner to report adversely at her next stop on the treatment she had just received.

So the spinners were treated royally and went home at the end of their tour fat and pampered, with pocket-money to last until the next summer. They served not only an economic purpose but a social one. Their arrival at a house inaugurated a short period of festivity, their presence jacked up the table manners of the young, and their company was a boon to many a lonely woman.

The spinner wasn't the only woman to get around; there were

other local women who went outside the geographical limits of the Peninsula and uncharted distances beyond the customs and habits bounding their everyday lives. They went, in short, to Bar Harbor, which is a few short miles across Frenchman Bay but was socially and economically on another planet. In 1844 Thomas Cole, an artist of the Hudson River School, went to Mt. Desert—then a backward fishing island—in search of subjects to paint. Through his pictures and wide acquaintanceship among the very wealthy, the island became during the next fifty years the summer social capital of the United States. Great houses were built, surrounded by beautifully landscaped grounds, and each year people like the Morgans and the Rockefellers came there to spend their vacations. They needed large staffs to keep up their elaborate establishments, and young women from all over the region found employment there. It was very common for Gouldsboro girls to spend their summers working at Bar Harbor, and for some of the young men of Gouldsboro, too, who acted as crew members of the big yachts or as coachmen or hostlers or gardeners and ground keepers in a fabulous scale of living that has almost disappeared.

This seasonal occupation had a more than temporary effect on Peninsula living. The young people came home in the fall with new ideas in their heads, ideas not only about food and wearing apparel and the *nice* way to do things, but about world problems and social attitudes as well. Some of them brought home more material things, gifts from their employers, which they cherish to this day along with their memories of a way of life that was almost unbelievable to them, as it is to me. My friend George Crowley still has a coin left from the days when he sailed on the yacht *Vanda* and was paid off in gold; and his neighbor Forrest Young has a still more valuable prize, his wife Katie, who was born in Hungary as Katerina Platz, and whom he met in Bar Harbor. She had come there from Cincinnati with the family for whom she worked as nursemaid, met and married the young seaman, and has lived ever since in Corea.

Then there was another short-lived but profitable industry which came into being by accident. One day about seventy-five years ago a young woman named Margaret Tracy was walking about in her back yard, which was mostly pine-covered ledge sloping down to the little brook that drains West Bay Pond. She saw something gleaming through the carpet of dead pine needles and scraped them away to discover a bright ribbon running through the rock. This interested her mildly but didn't seem very important at the time. Later, however, chiefly as a means of making conversation, she mentioned her discovery to a man from Cherryfield, William Freeman. He thought it was worth investigating, and almost immediately Gouldsboro found itself in the middle of a silver rush. Shafts were sunk in the Tracy back yard and a crusher erected on the bank of the brook; and prospecting spread all along the shore of Gouldsboro Bay. Nobody became a millionaire overnight, but for thirty-five years silver ore was taken out in profitable quantities and shipped to New York and to England.

Then the vein petered out and the mine was abandoned. The shafts may still be seen, though, in back of the old Tracy house on the Guzzle Road and in the fields on Guptill Point. They are just holes in the ground now, half full of dead leaves and other debris; but to me they are still fascinating. There's something about digging gold or silver or gems out of the earth that appeals to the imagination of even the least avaricious. It isn't that I want a bucketful of silver, especially. It's just that finding it in the ground seems like finding money in the gutter or winning the Irish Sweepstakes—something you hadn't planned on, something unexpected and exciting.

On the Peninsula it is impossible to divide activities into separate airtight compartments and label them industrial, social, religious or what have you. The categories overlap constantly, today as surely as they did seventy years ago, and nowhere is this fact more neatly demonstrated than in the little stores. Each of the tiny hamlets that comprise the Town of Gouldsboro had at least one, a small general store carrying an incredible assortment of goods, and usually combined with the post office.

The first post office was established in Gouldsboro proper in 1799, and the mail came through once a week; but by the mid-1800's delivery was being made every weekday, and the number of post offices was being increased. Indian Harbor was the last to get one, in 1896. Before that, the inhabitants had to walk three miles to Prospect Harbor to collect their mail, a fact which they resented. They also resented being taunted as Wild Harbor Indians. So when they finally achieved a post office of their own they simultaneously killed two annoying birds by having the name of the village changed to Corea, a suggestion of Eva Talbut, the daughter of the first postmaster. No one knows where she got the name, but it is pronounced like the country, Korea.

In those days the mail carrier used horses, and his lot was sometimes not an easy one. Daisy Young, Corea's present postmistress, can remember when her father, Lewis Young, carried the mail. He only had to go to South Gouldsboro and back, but often he left the house at 6:30 A.M. and didn't return until 5:00 P.M. In winter the sleet-laden gales blew so hard across the open and unprotected heath between Corea and Prospect Harbor that he had to get out and walk, leading the horse to prevent its turning tail to the wind. Sometimes even that wouldn't work. In the real blizzards he had to put a crocus sack, which is what they call a burlap bag in Corea, over the horse's head before it would follow into the cutting blast. The Postmaster General expected him to get the mail through or else (the *else* was a fine), and he got it through.

Nowadays the Postmaster General isn't quite so unreasonable. If Holly Myrick, the present mail carrier, finds it really impossible to drive his truck over the deep-drifted road he has to make a written report of the fact and the conditions that brought it about, but that's all that happens to him. Or maybe it isn't a more lenient attitude at all that brought about this change. Maybe it's a simple bowing to the great truth that a man and a horse can go places and do things that a man and gasoline motor can't.

The placing of the post offices in the stores was undoubtedly a governmental gesture toward economy, since none of the villages was large enough or received enough mail to warrant the construction and upkeep of a post office building. The storekeepers were glad enough to accommodate. People coming into the place to collect their mail more often than not make small purchases, all of which add up to a profit. That the store inevitably became a gathering place and mail time a social period was incidental, but nevertheless important. Very soon the storekeeper found himself running an information bureau and employment agency. All the local news came to his ears, and world news, too. After they had discharged their cargoes, the captain and non-local crew members of the schooners, having no other place ashore to hang out, gathered in the store. They sat around the big pot-bellied stove and told what folks up Boston way were saying about the coming election, or gave the consensus of all the ports they had visited on the new tariff bill. If they needed an extra deck hand they told the storekeeper so, and he passed the word along to the next likely candidate that came in. Men out of work automatically went to the store to inquire about possible jobs, and almost always the storekeeper was able to help them. It was to his advantage to do so. An employed man spends more money than one who is unemployed.

The stores were wonderful places. Their heart and center was the stove in the middle of the floor. Chairs were drawn up around it, and even in summer men warmed their feet through habit at its cold sides. There was always a Liars' Bench, too, a long bench against one counter to accommodate the overflow from the chairs. While those who sat on it were not necessarily liars, enough of the idle spent long rainy afternoons there, swapping tall tales, to account for its name. Overhead hung a huge pewter lamp with a reflector, which might burn a variety of fuels besides kerosene: fish oil, lard, whale oil or camphene. Lacking kerosene, lard and whale oil were preferred. Fish oil smelled terrible, and camphene was considered very dangerous because of its explosive characteristics.

In spite of their small size and the large cleared space around the stove, these stores carried enormous and incredibly varied stocks. Shelves bearing overalls, work shirts and gloves, lamp chimneys, patent medicines, twine, thread, tobacco, paint, spices, and cans of food rose to the ceilings. From the rafters hung oilskins, boots, heavy jackets, coils of rope, and buggy whips. The under-counter space was filled with bins of potatoes, onions, corn meal, dried beans and peas and coffee beans, while barrels of sugar, pickles, crackers and flour stood in the corners. Great cheeses, firkins of butter, baskets of eggs, and glass-fronted boxes of store-cookies occupied the counter, along with the glass case containing the penny candy.

If you didn't see what you wanted you asked for it, and almost invariably the owner said, "I've got some of that some place 'round here. Let me give a look." Then he'd go through the small door into his warehouse, and in all likelihood he'd find it. The molasses, vinegar and kerosene barrels were kept in the storehouse, too; and when you brought in your empty can the keeper went out there to fill it for you, jamming a small potato over the spout, in case you had lost the cap, so you wouldn't spill it on the way home. All this was done in a leisurely manner, to an accompaniment of inquiries about the wellbeing of your family and comment on the weather.

But the time when the store really came to life was mail time. At other hours it resembled more a men's club than a place of business. Decent women didn't hang around the store because they were too busy at home, and besides it didn't look well; and the other kind of women, if any, were too much concerned with an appearance of respectability—which is essential in a small community—to risk it by unconventional public behavior. If a housewife ran out of saleratus in the middle of her baking and had to have it at once she usually sent one of the children after it. If she had to go herself she entered in a businesslike manner, eyes to the front, made known her wants in a butter-wouldn't-melt tone, paid for her purchase, about-faced, and marched out. If her own brother happened to be among the idlers she might nod to him; or if her husband were there she could unbend to the extent of asking him what time he'd be home for dinner; but there was no light badinage or playful banter or anything that could be construed as such.

When the mail came, however, a different atmosphere prevailed. As soon as the stage was due the roads came alive with women, children and dogs, all converging on the store. Those who hadn't had a letter in months and didn't expect any came, too. It wasn't the mail that was important, or the fact that this was the hour at which any shopping could be done without danger of criticism. The important thing was that this was the daily opportunity to see people and talk with them, to laugh and joke a little, to get outside the four familiar walls of the house. Even if the mail were half an hour late it was permissible to wait, to loaf around as the men did, enjoying the sociability.

After the mail arrived and had been sorted and distributed there was still a period of ten or fifteen minutes' grace. Most people opened their letters at once, and if there were any items of general interest, these were read aloud and discussed. But even during this comparatively informal interlude there was no mingling of the sexes. The women stayed on their side of the store and the men on theirs. Only a hussy would cross over to the men's side, and there isn't a word bad enough for a female who would sit down on the Liars' Bench. If she felt tired or faint she could lean on the counter on her own side. Nice women knew their place, and so did nice little girls, since even in the lower grades of the schools the boys and girls had their recesses at different times.

This Quaker-like segregation of the sexes is a little relaxed now. At least all the school children play together at recess time. But when I first went to Corea I wanted to buy some fireplace wood. Following the pattern by some blind instinct, since I certainly was a stranger in a strange land, I inquired of Herb Young, the storekeeper, who might have some to sell. He gave me a name, and at mail time I caught up with my quarry in the store. He was sitting on the Liars' Bench, so I—my instinct failing me badly—sat down beside him while we transacted our business. Across the room a line of women eyed me frostily, and when I got home I told my daughter, "Every-one seems to be mad at me today, and I don't think I've done any-thing to warrant it. I only—"; and I told her what had happened.

She was frozen with horror. "Mama, you didn't! Women just *don't* sit on the Bench! You'll *never* live it down." She had got around more than I had at that point, so she knew. Well, never is a long time, and I hope at last, now that the village knows me bet-ter, I've graduated from being disreputable to being merely mis-guided.

The relaxing of the rigid standard dates, I think, from the arrival of the telephone on the Peninsula. The first one was installed in

S. L. Tracy's store in West Gouldsboro in 1892. It was considered a regrettable business necessity, and six residents who felt that they needed it agreed to pay ten dollars apiece, or the deficit at the end of each year, for three years. They never had to pay a cent, since the first year's receipts exceeded sixty dollars. The other stores gradually installed public phones, and a great many families still use them. I do myself, as there is no wiring out to Cranberry Point. These phone booths added to the duties of the storekeeper. Although he was not obliged to do so, he always did answer them and take messages, and he still does.

When the store phones were the only ones everybody used them, and I'm here to tell you from experience that it is absolutely impossible to make a long distance call at mail time. There is too much noise and chatter for you to hear anything over the rather poor connections; or else there is a silence as of the grave just as you are screaming the more personal and confidential passages of your conversation. Therefore anyone wanting to make a call was obliged to make it when the store was relatively empty. This included women, and it was the thin end of a wedge that hasn't really penetrated very far as yet.

The social life of the Peninsula at the time of which we are speaking centered to a large extent around the church. In the early days, the old Gouldsboro Town House, the only public meeting place in the area, was used for worship as well as for town meetings, dances, singing classes and the presentation of plays. In 1872 a church was built at Gouldsboro, and another was dedicated at Prospect Harbor in 1876 or 1877. These were Methodist churches. In 1892 a Union church was erected at West Gouldsboro, and in 1890 and 1902 Baptist churches were completed in Birch Harbor and Corea. Finally, in 1913 or thereabouts, a Latter Day Saints, or Mormon, church was built in Corea.

That's all very easy to write, but the establishment and housing of these churches involved a lot of work. Money was never plentiful on the Peninsula, and some money was needed, although the cost of building materials at the time was not great, and much of the labor could be done by the men and women of the congregations. The first step was the founding of a Christian Endeavor Society or a Sewing Circle or both, which met at any appropriate place in the community, usually the school house. Then the problem of raising funds was given serious consideration. There was little or no help from outside sources. The money had to be extracted from the pockets of the local inhabitants.

To this end, entertainments were given. All of them involved food, since everyone likes to eat and will pay for the privilege—especially in a region that boasts no restaurants or public dining rooms—of eating under special and festive conditions. Baked bean suppers were held, and clam chowder suppers, and lobster suppers. These didn't cost anything much, since the beans, clams and lobsters were native and, in any case, were donated by the workers. Some of the men growled a little about having to hand over half a dozen lobsters which they'd worked hard to catch and then having to pay for the right to eat them, but their wives saw to it that they showed up at the suppers with their money in hand.

Then there were box suppers. A box supper was a little different. Every woman packed into a suitable box a picnic lunch for two. She didn't just take any old shoe box and fill it full of peanut-butter sandwiches and the remains of yesterday's one-egg cake, either. This was a chance to show off her culinary skill, ingenuity and artistic leanings, and no woman of spirit was going to let it be said that her box didn't rank among the top ten, at least. Crabmeat and chicken sandwiches and deviled eggs and dill pickles went into those boxes, and cup custards, and great wedges of moist, dark chocolate cake with thick mocha frosting, and raspberry turnovers and cream-puffs and anything else she made especially well.

But that wasn't the end. She couldn't just wrap it up in brown paper, tie it with a piece of string, and call it good enough The outside of the box was at least as important as the inside, so she went to great lengths to adorn it in a striking and unusual manner. She might cover the whole thing with pink and white crepe-paper rosettes, like a May basket; or she might glue split twigs all over the sides, cut doors and windows, and concoct a pitched roof and a chimney, so that it was a miniature log cabin. Hat boxes could be made into castles or merry-go-rounds, or a collection of various-sized boxes, each one holding one course of the supper, could be so arranged and decorated that they looked like a wedding cake. Oh, there was no end to the possibilities, given a little imagination and a lot of time and patience.

The men didn't have to do anything about a box supper except show up with a free-spending attitude.

On the evening of the affair the boxes were smuggled into the gathering place and piled on a table. No one was supposed to know the identity of their creators, although there was sometimes a little

cheating on this score. With the minister or one of the deacons acting as auctioneer, each box was knocked down to the highest bidder
among the men, who then had the honor and privilege of eating
the contents in the company of the woman who had donated it.
That's where the cheating came in. A popular little minx who was
being courted by several young blades might tell each, in strictest
confidence, of course, which box was hers. This boosted the bidding
to dizzy heights, since the inside track to a woman's heart is not
ordinarily gained by refusing to spend money on her. Boxes sometimes sold for as much as three or even four dollars, which was a lot
of money.

Then there were pie sociables, ice cream sociables, and strawberry sociables. On these occasions you ate supper at home and
went to the sociable for your dessert. Because a wedge of pie or a
serving of strawberry shortcake isn't the same as a full meal, some
sort of entertainment had to be offered to make the affair worth the
price of admission. Sometimes a play was given: "A Slight Mistake," "Elopement of Ellen," "The Noble Outcast," or "My Cousin
Timmy—A Farce." I am unfamiliar with these works, but I am sure
that their tone was moral and uplifting. Sometimes a program of
recitations was presented, like the following, which concluded a pie
sociable sponsored by the Corea church in 1910.

> *Address of Welcome*—by the Minister
> *Song*, "The Story Never Told"—Gladys Rolfe
> *Recitation*, "What Can We Do?"—Kenneth Ross
> *Recitation*, "Stand Up For Your Colors"—Fred Davis
> *Recitation*, "Why We Are Glad"—Harold Young, Colon Perry,
>   Earl Bartlett
> *Song*, "Little Soldiers"—The Primary Kindergarten Sunday
>   School
> *Recitation*, "Ere the Sun Goes Down"—Grace Young
> *Song*, "Plant the Roses"—Minnie Mandy
> *Gramophone Selections*—rendered by Mrs. Mary Ashe

I particularly like the gramophone selections rendered by Mrs.
Ashe. Presumably she owned one of the new marvels, loaned it for
the occasion, and naturally had charge of changing the cylindrical

records. This makes her, I think, the grandmother of the modern disc jockey.

This sociable netted $8.00, which was considered a satisfactory return for all the work and worry involved—the baking of the pies, the hours of drilling the children in their "pieces," the difficult decisions about what they should wear on the platform, and the breath-holding lest they should forget their lines. But it was by such small sums as this that the churches were built, the ministers paid, and the organizations made into vital parts of the community.

Lacking substantial funds on which to draw, the people of the Peninsula used the only substitute for money that they knew—work. Probably it's the only substitute there is anywhere or at any time. They worked on their sociables, but they made real labor into a social occasion. The Ellsworth *American* of March 3, 1911, carried the following modest little item: "The Birch Harbor Baptist Society thanks all who attended the bee and helped build up the church woodpile."

When the Prospect Harbor church needed painting, another bee was held. A friend of mine who attended it described it to me. "I suppose we looked pretty funny," she said, "all us women bobbing around the bottom of the building, slapping on paint wide and handsome and as high as we could reach, whether we knew anything about painting or not. Leastwise, we got the bare boards covered, while the men stood around and joshed us. Soon's we couldn't reach any higher, we quit and let the menfolks have their licks. They put up ladders and painted from the top down to where we'd stopped. By the time they were done we women had got the supper ready and the kids rounded up. We ate out under the trees, like a picnic. Didn't cost the church much, either, only the paint. Everyone brought their own brush and ladder and food. We had some high old time that day, I can tell you. Seems like we don't have the kind of good time we used to have."

The history of religion seems always to have been marked at some point or other by strife and dissension, possibly because people are willing to fight for the things that are really important to them, while they will let minor irritations pass without protest. The

Peninsula was no exception, since their churches were terribly important to Peninsulans. Everything was going along fine until a missionary elder of the Latter Day Saints, or Mormon, church arrived in the area.

Before we go further, let me say at once that by this time polygamy, which to many people is almost synonymous with Mormonism, had been abandoned as a tenet of the faith. Its importance was never as great as the furor it aroused would seem to indicate, and in Maine, where there are a surprising number of Mormons, it was never practiced at all. It wasn't plural marriage that caused the trouble in Corea, trouble bad enough that for years brother refused to speak to brother and neighbor to neighbor. It was something quite different.

When the missionaries first came from Jonesport and from Fall River, Massachusetts, they held their services in the Baptist church. Very soon, however, there was difficulty over conflicting hours of worship; or at least that is the reason given for the rift. Probably jealousy was the underlying cause. The visiting preachers were very persuasive, and their efforts began to make large inroads on the Baptist membership. On some Sundays as many as thirteen or fourteen new Saints were immersed in the harbor near the lobster pound. In a village of that size, the sight and sound of a dozen or more friends and relatives being plunged into the icy waters of the North Atlantic cannot easily be ignored, and the fact that each new convert meant one less Baptist engendered a certain amount of bitterness. The Baptists decided to halt the nonsense by refusing the use of their church building to the Latter Day Saints.

It takes a lot to discourage the Mormons, however, as witness Salt Lake City. They put up a tent and held their meetings there until they could erect a church of their own. This they succeeded in doing, a rather imposing building on the corner across from Herb Young's store. They had forty members, a sizeable percentage of the churchgoing population, and a minister of their own; and for years they flourished. Then, along with a general decline in all religious activity, interest began to lag, so that now the church stands idle, its windows broken and pigeons roosting in the belfry. The members either drive to Jonesport to services, attend the church of some other denomination, or stay at home on Sunday. They still, however, when asked about their religious affiliations, state that they are Mormons. This always surprises me, for some reason. Mormons to me were always something you read about, but never expected to see.

In the heyday of life on the Peninsula, entertainment was by no means confined to the province of the churches. There was plenty of secular social life. There were bees for almost every imaginable purpose—for replenishing a neighbor's woodpile, or painting his boat, or shingling his roof or raising his barn. At these affairs contests were held (a chopping match was a favorite), games organized, and elaborate practical jokes played. The whole family came, from the baby in diapers to the great-grandmother with her cane. Lunches were brought and swapped around, so that an already gala occasion acquired the special glamor brought about by eating food that might not be any better than what you cooked yourself, but seemed better because it was different. Women who hadn't seen each other in weeks had a chance for what was called "a good visit," which means an opportunity to exchange symptoms, recipes and gossip.

Often there were evening parties for no purpose whatsoever except sociability. Sometimes these were card parties, and sometimes games were played—games like musical chairs, spin the cover, charades and hunt the thimble. Three popular games were Sherlock Holmes, which must have been some sort of guessing game, chanticleer and spoons. I haven't the least idea how the last two were played. Then there were special parties. One woman gave a party because the little orange tree she had raised from seed finally, after years of babying along, bore fruit. The fruit was one small green orange, but it was greatly admired, possibly as a monument to her persistence. Another invited friends in to witness the coming into flower of her night-blooming cereus; and still another entertained in honor of her new Victor talking machine.

There were Poverty Sociables, to which everyone wore their most disreputable clothes, and Masked Sociables, where everyone was in disguise. The one I like best, though, is the Mum Sociable. At a

Mum Sociable everybody keeps mum, and whoever says a word has to pay a forfeit. This seems to me to be an excellent idea for making a party a success, as even the most shy and tongue-tied feel an immediate compulsion to burst into speech the minute they are forbidden to do so. Moreover, if you don't happen to feel like talking you can for once keep quiet without being asked if you are ill, offended, or just plain cranky. I don't think I need to add that the climax of every party or sociable was the collation, as refreshments were somewhat elegantly called.

Dances were very common. A Professor Joy ran a dancing class in the Grange Hall at Corea one night a week. He was a little old man who wore glasses on the end of his nose, boarded at Katie Young's house, and furnished his own fiddle music. The charge was fifty cents a couple, and everyone between the ages of about ten to dotage attended. The Professor specialized in the one-step and the waltz. He lined everybody up, demonstrated the steps, and then struck up a tune, counting loudly, playing, and making corrections of individuals all at once. He was a busy man for a while there. But then the formalities were considered to have been observed, and the occasion stopped being a class and became just a plain dance. Most of the attendance could dance expertly already, anyhow, and had just come for fun. They did have fun, too.

When there was a dance at Prospect Harbor a whole group of young people would walk the three miles from Corea, with their best shoes in their hands, to dance the night away. At two or three o'clock in the morning they'd troop back by the light of the setting moon, tired and silly, limping along on swollen feet, laughing and skylarking across the empty heath, bothering no one but the startled deer and foxes. Nobody seemed to consider it foolish to walk six miles and dance sixty more between supper and breakfast. If you were going to have a good time, naturally you expected to work for it.

The Peninsula was a great place in those days for lodges and fraternal organizations. There were the Red Men, the Daughters of Pocahontas, the Knights of Pythias, the Pythian Sisterhood, the Masons, the Eastern Star, the Grange, the Woodmen of the World, the Odd Fellows, the Rebeccas, and many others. Everyone belonged to at least one such organization, and Lodge Night was an important night of the week which nobody missed. The installations of officers were tremendous events, attended by representatives of other chapters for miles around. On these occasions an elaborate marching ritual, the Floor Work, might be performed, an exercise that required weeks of drill. The lodges supplied a need in the lives of the Peninsulans—a need to belong, to participate, a need for color and drama, a need to escape the harsh world around them into a world of make-believe. The only time a woman in her whole life had occasion to wear a real evening gown was at installation, and every woman likes to dress to the teeth once in a while. Then the officers had fanciful titles. The Pocahontas treasurer, for example, was the Keeper of the Wampum. In 1905 the First Warrior of the Pocahontas was Bessie Crowley. I saw a picture of her the other day, and there never was a gentler-looking, sweeter-faced woman. I imagine she *loved* being something as desperate-sounding as a First Warrior, such a far cry from her normal self.

The beginning of the end of the old Peninsula life was indicated by a very small item in the Ellsworth *American* of May 28, 1906. "*Winter Harbor*. A very fine Pope-Hartford touring car was received this week by Dr. A. E. Small, and is attracting a lot of attention. There are several other intending purchasers in this and the adjoining town of Gouldsboro, and soon the appearance of the auto will be a common occurrence upon the roads."

Now I am not one to blame every ill in the world on the automobile. It will, however, have to be accepted as the single agent most responsible for a complete change in the whole American pattern of living. Whether this change has proved desirable or not is beside the point, and we won't discuss it. A great deal has been said on both sides already. Any innovation is inevitably decried by the reactionary element, the stubborn group that resists any change; and there can be no more militant band of reactionaries than those found in small, parochial communities.

These rose at once to challenge the advent of the gasoline age. Automobiles were successfully banned from Mt. Desert Island until

1913, when a patient died who would have been saved had his doctor been able to reach his side sooner than horse and buggy would allow. Isleboro in Penobscot Bay held out a decade longer against the menace, and Bermuda gave in comparatively recently. These were true islands, however, with geography's weight on their side. Gouldsboro, although insular in spirit, is after all only a peninsula, having consequently less perfect control of her destinies. But she put up a good fight.

Three months after Dr. Small's purchase, in August of 1906, the *American* had something to say on the subject. "This correspondent is in favor of an exclusion act for automobiles. Tuesday afternoon Mr. Patton's two-horse team with a heavy load of wood was toiling up Mill Hill when an auto came in view. First they ran back, then sprinted up over a bank into the field. Wood everywhere. Friday night about 5:30, W. M. Pettee's delivery wagon was at the Doyle door, horse facing stable. An auto went by; horse made a circle, locked into a wagon, cleared that and made a dash across the field, landing in a heap on the Hill doorstep with forefeet and head through the screen door. No doubt the inner door being shut prevented his landing on the dining-table. Saturday morning E. J. Robertson's new red auto arrived in town, causing commotion all along the way."

There actually was a petition for a law excluding cars from the roads of the town presented to the legislature, but the madness was spreading. By May of 1907 there were two more cars on the Peninsula, a Ford and a Waltham-Orient. Worse, the summer people at Grindstone Neck were arriving by automobile. There was no way of stopping them, except by law, since the roads were public thoroughfares to which their taxes, too, were applied; and the law was never passed. There was too much sentiment against it as more and more advantages of motor transportation were discovered. By 1912 the battle was really over, and the inevitable accepted. In February of that year W. F. Bruce of Prospect Harbor attended the Automobile Show in Bangor, setting the seal of public approval on internal combustion.

But it took Frank Sawyer to finish the matter in style. I must tell you first about the Sawyers. Frank's father, Abraham, was a Jewish pack-peddler from Jonesport who had changed his Hebraic name to Sawyer almost as soon as he arrived in this country. He walked the roads of Eastern Maine with a pack on his back, selling ribbons, ladies' gloves, thread, needles, hairpins and other knickknacks and notions. He was always welcome at the houses of the Peninsula because he was a pleasant man with a fund of songs, jokes and stories, and because he carried a more varied and unusual stock than did the stores, whose business he didn't compete with, but only complemented. Soon he acquired a pushcart, which he himself pushed uphill and down-dale in all kinds of weather, and along with it the nickname Pushcart Sawyer. Even after he worked up to a span of handsome horses and a big enclosed wagon he was still known as Pushcart. By this time he was carrying suits, coats, dresses, yard goods and what-all. His cart amounted to a traveling drygoods store.

In the course of time Pushcart retired in favor of his son Frank, who was perhaps an even better merchandiser than his father. The clothes he sold, so I am told, were as stylish as anything you could find in Bangor, and much cheaper; and if you couldn't find exactly what you wanted in your size he'd get it for you and bring it the next time he came. The clopping of his big horses' hooves along the roads was a signal for women to drop whatever they were doing, shake the egg and bait-bag money out of the old china teapot, and give themselves over to an hour's pure pleasure in examining Frank Sawyer's miraculous stock.

Then in 1915—but let's let the *American* tell about it. "Frank S. Sawyer, the traveling merchant so well known throughout Hancock County, has purchased a Reo auto-truck for his moving store. The top of his big wagon will be taken from the present running gear and mounted on the truck. The truck has a guaranteed capacity of two tons, and a speed of eighteen miles an hour. It has solid tires, double treads on the rear wheels and single on the front. The top will be wired for electric lights, supplied from the regular storage battery. Mr. Sawyer expects to mount the top on the truck to-day, and will be on the road in a few days. The truck will enable him to cover his route more frequently or to extend it."

I suppose it did, for a while, but now his marvelous Reo has gone the way of Pushcart's pack. Women drive themselves to Ellsworth now if they need a new spring coat.

All the old industries are gone. The silver mine petered out, no one raises sheep any more when it's so much easier and cheaper to buy good yarn, and most of the great estates of Bar Harbor have been sold or were burned in the terrible forest fire of October, 1947. Smoother and better street surfacing has taken the place of cobblestones, and the use of steel and Portland cement in building has crippled the limeburning industry, so that there is no more demand for kiln wood. Almost everyone uses asbestos shingles nowadays. Modern packaging in waterproof paper, cardboard cartons, tin cans and steel drums has made a real barrel almost a curiosity. With the decline of the demand for these exports and the coming of the heavy-duty trailer truck, the lovely coastal sloops and schooners vanished from the harbors of the Peninsula. Through no fault of their own, but only because of changing times, the Peninsulans have been deprived of their once varied economy and all of the advantages that went with it.

The same thing has happened in other places, of course. In fact, that is the common history of all of New England and the Northeast, a history of outgrown or outdated industries being replaced by newer and more ambitious projects. Up to the point of Frank Sawyer's Reo, the story of the Peninsula and the lives of its people differs very little from the story of any other area. But from that date on other places progressed because they possessed additional resources or were strategically situated in positions of importance to commerce. The Peninsula has remained almost static, except for its population, which has regressed and is each year becoming smaller. All it ever had, tucked away off the lanes of trade, was rock, wood and the sea; and nobody wants the rock or the wood any more. So the people have been driven back to the first New England industry, the fisheries, and to the simple way of life that dependence on the sea dictates all over the world.

4. The Meadows of the Sea

BEFORE I BEGAN SPENDING LONG PERIODS OF time on the Peninsula I knew a great many facts about the sea. I knew that it was salt, that it covered over seventy percent of the earth's surface, and that all life had originated in it. I knew that its tides were controlled by the moon, which with irresistible fascination drew two balancing waves around the globe, so that twice daily on countless far-flung beaches of the world the waters advanced and retreated. I knew that it has always been the source of a tremendous food supply. I knew that it has served throughout the centuries sometimes as a barrier, sometimes as a protective moat and sometimes as a thoroughfare, with the result that the course of history has been determined to an appreciable extent by the degree of man's mastery of the sea. I knew the sea personally as a pleasant playground during summer vacation months, and through literature and art as the scene of terrible ordeals and epic struggles or the inspiration of beautiful poems and pictures. I knew that it has been loved and hated, feared, used and even worshipped.

All these things I knew, and more; but I hadn't the least understanding of what it means to live with the sea constantly and to depend on it completely. I knew that the salt in the blood that flows through the veins and arteries of each one of us is a legacy from the dim past when all vital organisms had their being in the sphere of the ocean, so that we all—whether we recognize it or not—carry about with us always and wherever we go elements of the ancient sea. But I never understood until then how close a kinship could be established with it. I never understood that men and women could feel toward the sea almost the same emotions they might feel toward a strict but loving mother or a moody, unpredictable father. I didn't know that the sea could be regarded not as a force of nature or an interesting geographical feature, but as a prerequisite to existence, as necessary as air.

One day I was describing to an old lobsterman my home in the woods, Forest Lodge. I told him about the long, lovely lakes stepping down like terraces from level to level between the mountains, about the narrow valleys with their short, tumbling rivers, and about the dark shelter of the forest where one moves always in dappled, dancing shadow. He listened and nodded from time to time.

Finally he said politely, "Must be real nice, but I dunno's I'd like to live away from the sea." He looked about him at the restless void of water stretching away unbroken to the horizon, at the lacy fringe of surf breaking on the reefs, at the treeless heath and the granite ledges, honed keen by the constant wind, and upward to the inverted bowl of the unobstructed sky. His eyes came back from their limitless journey through space and brilliance to fasten themselves with something like fear on my face. "I—I dunno's I ever *could* live away from the sea," he said, a little helplessly.

That is the way the Peninsulans feel about the sea.

Yet the sea is not kind to them. It offers them nothing of warmth and comfort, of repose, of easy gain or future security. It demands everything a man has to give—his time, his thoughts, his whole strength, all his vigilance and skill. In return it promises only hardship, danger, even death, and a bare living; only these things and personal freedom of thought and action and a philosophical tranquillity of spirit as undisturbed by the world's alarums as the depths of the sea are undisturbed by surface tempests. To the Peninsulans these recompenses are worth the cost. They realize perhaps better than anybody that freedom and peace are never gifts. They must be earned not once, but every moment of the free man's life.

The lobsterman's day begins before dawn. "We pry up the sun

in the mornin'," they will tell you, laughing a little. They rise when the east is barely flushed and the morning star glitters bright over the ocean. The land is hushed and dim, and the wind which will come up with the sun to blow all day long is still. The sea is almost calm. In the quiet air the wood-smoke of breakfast fires rises straight and unwavering as the men in their hipboots and oilskins plod down to the harborside. Nobody talks much. It's too early to be sociable. In silence each unties his punt from a longlegged wharf and rows out to where his own boat is moored, riding lightly with its bow to the tide. He climbs aboard, ties his punt to the mooring, and runs a practiced eye over his gear. Then the predawn stillness is shat-

tered by the roar of a score of powerful engines coming to life, and the gulls rise in a protesting cloud and circle, screaming and mewing, over the harbor. One by one the lobsterboats slip through the narrow passage between the pink ledges to the open sea, their wakes following in confusion along the channel's edges. The sun tips over the horizon, and the boats are gone except for a far, diminishing throbbing in the air. The gulls subside, and the land is quiet again in the level light.

Long, long ago the Down East shipbuilders established for themselves a reputation for building the best and loveliest vessels in the world. In fact, Maine clipper ships have been called the most beautiful objects ever made by American craftsmen. The little lobster-boats of the Peninsula are in the same tradition, a tradition which requires that utmost efficiency for a specific purpose be combined with beauty. There is nothing showy about them, and nothing superfluous. Most of them are white, for easy visibility, and the average length is about thirty-five feet at the water line, a size that can be accommodated in the tiny harbors and tortuous channels, that is safe in a rough sea, and that can be handled easily by one man. But a lot of loveliness can be packed into thirty-five feet of boat if the builder knows what he is doing. There is style in the lines of the lobsterboats and grace in their sheers. They delight the eye with their balance, having just enough beam and freeboard for stability without clumsiness. They have an air about them of trim competence. They look dependable and just exactly right.

The best way to learn about the lobstering industry is to go out in one of these little boats on a summer's morning. This involves getting up pretty early and is a project that should not be undertaken by anyone who is subject to seasickness. Sturdy as the boats are, there is still quite a bit of rolling and pitching and a pervasive odor from the overripe fish used for bait. Since seasickness is something which I have to date been spared, and since I like to get up early if I'm not *obliged* to, going out with the lobster fleet is one of my favorite summer diversions. I know George Crowley best of the lobstermen, so usually I have gone with him.

I meet him in the chilly predawn light at his nephew Twink Crowley's lobster car over on Crowley Island, which is reachable by a causeway. Twink—or Myron—Crowley is a lobster buyer, which means that he is licensed to buy lobsters from the boats and sell them to the city wholesalers. He is a big, sunny-natured bear of a man in his thirties who started life as a lobsterman himself. I like Twink. He answers silly questions with saintly patience, and he is one of the gentlest and kindest of fathers to his small children that I have ever encountered. He's called Twink because, when he was two years old, his mother colored a little dress of his with the home dye of that name, and he was so proud of it that he went about pointing to himself and saying "Twink." He outgrew the dress long ago, but never the name.

His place of business consists of some low, ramshackle buildings on the bare ledges of the island, a high-posted wharf with a gas pump for the fueling of the boats, and the lobster car. This is a submerged wooden tank, about fifteen by thirty feet in area and three feet deep, which floats just below the wharf. In the covered top are trap doors through which the lobsters may be dropped for storage into the water-filled compartments below. This top also serves as a landing stage, since it rises and falls with the tide, so that sometimes you can jump down onto it from the wharf and sometimes you have to climb down sixteen or seventeen feet of slippery ladder. Guy Francis, across the harbor from Twink, is also a lobster buyer, and so is Don Anderson, although he buys ground fish, too, and sells marine supplies and sea clothes. It tells a lot about Corea that the hamlet can support amicably three healthy establishments that depend on the sea for their success, but only one small store dealing with the demands of the land.

The afterdeck of George's boat as he swings in for me is piled with traps that he has had ashore for repairs, and the open cockpit is crowded with bait tubs, coils of line, a box of bait bags, freshly painted buoys, and the empty kegs which he hopes to fill with lobsters if he is lucky. I step forward into the shelter of the half-cabin, open to the starboard side and to the stern but warmed by the motor nevertheless, and stand beside George to gaze ahead through the spray shield. As we clear the passage and veer to the southwest the decked-over bow, until then as steady as rock, starts a gentle lift and drop above and below the horizon line, and the needle of the compass above the wheel trembles to the north. Spray spatters the glass of the shield as the motion increases, and the sound of the motor drops a tone. The sun looks over the rim of the world, and the last pursuing gull turns back to shore. We are at sea.

Being at sea in a lobsterboat is very different from viewing it from the decks of the *Queen Mary* or from the shore. You are almost as close to the water as a swimming gull, close enough to look upward at curling combers, close enough to change dramatically all perspective. It's perfectly beautiful out there in the early morning. The arrowy light strikes across the waste of broken water, shining clear green through the toppling crests of the waves and leaving the troughs in deep purple shadow. To the east the ocean is a shimmer of gold, and to the west a bright blue, laced with whitecaps. The land is a low line in the distance with the village picked out sharp in the sunlight, each house tiny and distinct and the spire of the church a white exclamation mark. It looks like an elves' village. The breeze, following the sun from the other side of the earth, is crisp and unbelievably clean, like no other air you ever breathed. Everywhere are the multicolored buoys which mark the location of the traps, red and yellow and blue and orange, so that the surface seems strewn with confetti. Stone Horse Ledge spouts like a geyser, sending sun-shot spray thirty feet high.

"Purty, ain't it?" George comments and slows for his first buoy. As the noise of the engine fades the soft insistent whisper and sigh of the waves as they march endlessly past fills the ear. The whistle buoy moans near at hand, and further away the gong buoy clangs plaintively and musically. With a boat hook, George neatly picks up the line attached to his buoy, passes it over a pulley and around a drum attached to the motor shaft, and moves the gearshift. The line tautens and reels inboard, sluicing sea water prodigally, the boat lists slightly as the trap leaves bottom, and the business of the day has begun.

A lobster trap is a sort of wooden cage, shaped like a Quonset hut, with open ends. The sides are made of laths fastened to spruce bows which the men cut from the sparse woods of the Peninsula and bend to the proper curve. Flat stones are placed in a compartment in the bottom to overcome the natural buoyancy of the wood, and the ends are fitted with funnel-shaped nets called heads. In the center of the trap, between the small ends of the funnels, a twine-mesh bait bag full of decomposed fish is suspended. This lures the lobster into the funnel, a passage he can easily accomplish; but once in, he can't find his way out of the narrower opening. The lobsterman removes him by opening a small hatch in the top of the trap, at the same time replenishing the bait.

It's a very simple type of trap; and the interesting thing to me is that the model used today is the same as the very first traps. No improvements have been made or can be made unless lobsters change their tastes and habits. Because the supply of spruce bows is dwindling, some men now make box-shaped traps out of light-dimension stock, but the fundamental design remains the same. There is disagreement about the square traps, some claiming that they haul harder and some maintaining that they don't. Everybody agrees, though, that they are easier to make, stack better on a boat's stern, and are less likely to fall overboard.

A good trap represents a cash outlay of about ten dollars. When you consider that the average lobsterman runs a gang of between a hundred and fifty and two hundred you can see that he has a sizeable investment in traps alone. In addition, there is the investment represented by his boat, a matter of three or four thousand dollars at the least, and the constant operating cost of gasoline, bait, upkeep of the boat, replacing of lost or broken gear, paint for buoys, new heads and bait bags, the five-dollar charge for a lobster-fishing license, and what-all. Sometimes a sudden storm, moving in before the men have time to shift their traps further out from shore or to bring them in, destroys seventy or eighty percent of them. This is a very serious loss in a business which operates always, on the lobsterman's level, with a conspicuous lack of financial reserves.

I don't know how much outlay of time each trap represents. Before a man can even start building one he has to collect the materials. Most Peninsulans make outings of these expeditions in search of trap-bows and ballast rocks. Whole families, armed with axes, troop off into the woods to cut the spruce branches; or they pile into the boat, their lunch in shoe boxes, for a trip to Ironbound Island, where the action of water and frost has broken the ledges into ideal small, flat segments like flag-stones. They have a good time on these excursions, which are the sort of family project for the family welfare that has become slightly anachronistic in the modern world.

The men build their traps on days when it is too foggy or stormy to haul, but the women knit the trap heads and tie the bait bags whenever they have a spare moment. I love to see them work. They sit in their kitchens, facing a window, and their hands flicker in and out of the mesh attached to the sill like swallows flying. It's fussy, exact work, but half the time they don't even watch what they are doing. Their eyes look out over the sea, or watch the flight of a bird, or turn to your face as you talk; and all the while the shuttle darts in and out and the work grows to quick completion. It's a fascinating performance, so swift and adept.

While we are on the subject of equipment we might as well consider the buoys. These are blocks of wood, either oblong or torpedo-shaped, painted distinctively to show ownership of the traps which they mark. Each man has his own combination of colors—red-and-white or blue-and-yellow, for example; and any man caught hauling a trap not his own is liable to legal punishment. Both traps and buoys must be marked with the lobster-fishing license number of the owner. Immersed constantly in salt water as it is, and exposed to the sun, the paint on the buoys fades rapidly and must be renewed fairly often. This is a job that can be done by the children, some of them quite small, who usually receive a little pay from their fathers—three or four cents a buoy, perhaps. Very early, therefore, the young learn two valuable lessons: that money is something for which you have to work and that each individual has a responsibility to the group of which he is a member.

The children also go about collecting empty bottles—pop bottles, beer bottles, grape-juice bottles, any bottles of pint to quart capacity. Wooden stoppers are whittled to plug them tight, and they are attached to the lines that run from buoys to traps at a point about eight feet from the buoy. It used to puzzle me to see, at low tide, each bright buoy accompanied by a floating bottle; but now I know the reason why. At high tide the bottles are submerged as the lines run straight to the floor of the sea; but as the tide ebbs they rise toward the surface, picking up with them any slack that might otherwise snag on the rocky bottom and hinder hauling. It's a simple, ingenious device.

As you can see, the energies of the entire village have been directed to making possible such moments as the one when George and I paused at his first buoy, attached the line to the winch, and leaned over the starboard gunwale to watch the trap swim cumbrously into the light and air.

No matter how many years a man has been lobster fishing, or

how many traps he hauls in a day, he still—so they tell me—feels a surge of anticipation and excitement each time he lifts a trap into the boat and bends to see what it contains. Rarely is it empty. He hopes, of course, that it will contain lobsters of legal size. Failing that, there will almost certainly be other sea life—an eight-inch starfish, a codfish or skate, a cluster of spiny sea urchins, a sea cucumber or a sea mouse, odd creatures that I find inexhaustibly interesting. George does not. He regards them with indifference, if not disgust, and throws them overboard with a fine gesture of disdain. If I want to take some ashore in a bucket for further examination he's tolerant, but far from enthusiastic. He's seen too many queer fish to get all starry-eyed about one more ugly devil of a sculpin.

The lobsters are something else again. They are his living—these weird, grotesque creatures with their cunningly contrived and jointed plates of armor, their great, awkward claws, and their evil eyes looking out from the narrow green helmets. He removes them from the traps gingerly, grasping them about their bodies to avoid the viciously snapping claws and tails, and applies the metal rule that determines their legality. The measure is taken from the eye to the beginning of the tail, and to be within the Maine law it must be between three and one-eighth and five inches. The smaller ones must be thrown back to grow and the larger ones for purposes of propagation. Eggbearing females must also be released. The keepers he puts into a keg.

But it makes a difference which keg. A large percentage of the catch is destined for Massachusetts markets, and according to Massachusetts law a lobster may not measure under three and three-eighths inches. Therefore there is a Maine keg and a Massachusetts keg. And that's not all. As a lobster grows, his shell—which is really his skeleton, carried on the outside—does not grow with him. So periodically he must shed it and grow another, better-fitting one. While this is taking place, he is for a short time without protection and an easy victim of predators, including his own kind. These "shedders," so soft and defenseless, must be kept in a separate container where they will be safe until they become

hard again. Finally, there are the "dumbies," those that are not perfect specimens but lack one or both claws. Sometimes the member
was lost in a fight, but oftener the lack is the result of a peculiar
defense mechanism possessed by the lobster. In times of danger he
can at will drop off, or "shoot," a claw. This is supposed to con-
found the enemy, and it doesn't hurt the lobster, who in time grows
a new one. Until that happy day arrives, though, his market value
is less, so he is kept in a separate keg, to be sold to those who intend
merely to make lobster Newburgh or salad.

The catch, if any, safely disposed, George rebaits the trap and
throws the whole set overboard. The bait is ideally small herring,
called brit, which the fishermen catch for themselves in weirs—pronounced "wares"—that they maintain over back of the Peninsula
in Gouldsboro Bay; or they may buy bait from the sardine factory
in Prospect Harbor, where there are usually damaged fish not fit
for canning. If these sources fail, redfish has to be imported from
Portland, and the lobstermen go about remarking bitterly that the
bait dealers are the only ones who make any money in the business.
But, redfish or brit, it all looks and smells the same, which is terrible.

I never can figure out how the lobstermen find their traps. There
are no signposts on the ocean, and any sightings and cross-sightings
taken from the distant shore are necessarily liable to wide error.
There is nothing but water on the south and east, and the land to the
northwest is hazy and indistinct. The buoys that looked so big and
bright drying on the rocks ashore now are nothing but pinpoints on
the immensity of the sea, easily overlooked among the watery hills
and valleys. And yet George will say, standing on the engine housing to peer over the cabin and steering with his feet, "I've got
twelve in a bunch along here somewhere." How does he remember?
The exact location of each of two hundred traps in an area of thirty
square miles is quite a lot to carry in your head. Yet he and the
other men move surely from point to point in the chartless waste,
picking up traps, rebaiting them, shifting them further offshore or
nearer to a submerged ledge, with never a sign of doubt. They
must be equipped with inborn radar.

The day wears on. The sun climbs higher, and the sea turns

milk-blue in the distance and dark emerald near at hand. We circle in near Schoodic Point and then far out again to 'Titm'nan Light, where the keepers are sitting on the rocks fishing with hand lines. Off the entrance of Dyer Bay by a rock called The Castle we have our mug-up, or lunch, consisting of sandwiches, bananas and tea. A passing lobsterman waves, shouting something we can't hear, and we wave back.

"Ellis Bishop," George says, although I don't know how he can tell at that distance. "Know his boat," he explains. "He's got ship-to-shore. See his aerial? Pretty handy rig, if you're in trouble. Though we got along without it the sixty-odd years I been lobster-in', and without fathom-meters, too. We just figured out the depth and kind of bottom by guess and by gorry. Got along without engines and winches, far as that goes. Depended on sails and hauled by hand and made a livin'." He broods for a moment and then adds, "But 'twas damned hard work."

"Sixty-odd years is a long time," I remark rather obviously.

"Yep. Sold my first lobster when I was ten. Got ten cents for it. Course, I'd caught plenty before that, but selling one give me ideas. Started my career—such as 'tis—in a rowboat. Then I gradu-ated to a fluke—one mast, she had, and two jibs—and finally I got me a power boat. Seemed like the last word in luxury and conven-ience at the time; and now look. Lobsterin's still lobsterin', though. It ain't easy, but it's better'n cuttin' wood, which is the only other thing I know." He squints into the sun. "There's Harry Wasgatt goin' in already. Must be takin' his wife shoppin' to Ellsworth this afternoon."

"I suppose you know his boat, too."

George looks at me in mild surprise. "Wal, I see it every day."

I point to what is no more than the flash of the sun on a spray shield at the farthest horizon. "Who's that?" I ask.

"Babe Crowley," he says promptly. "Can't see that far, but that's where he's due to be about this time of day." I give up and retire to the stern, where I sit on the edge of the afterdeck, dangling my feet, half drugged with sunlight and the crisp salt breeze and the lazy, continuous motion.

We start a wide, slow sweep along the outer edges of the little Sally Islands. The sea is dark, dark blue now, and the land a black bar against the golden sky. "That's the last of 'em," George says, tossing overboard his final trap. "Guess you ain't no Jonah. We'll be gettin' in in good season."

I look at my watch and am astonished to find that it is only a little past noon. I feel as though I had been on a long journey to a far place. George turns the bow landward and, while I hold the wheel steady, starts cleaning up the boat, tossing overboard the remains of our lunch, the dregs of the bait tub, and those of my treasures that have lost their pristine freshness. Immediately and out of nowhere a great congress of gulls assembles, wheeling over us and diving to snatch the refuse before it sinks. We enter Western Island Channel, and George takes charge again, easing the boat through the narrow way. Ahead of us Kenneth Young is just crossing the bar that guards the harbor, and behind us is a whole convoy of boats, each with its trailing white scarf of gulls, coming home like sheep to the fold. The land on either side of the harbor passage embraces us, and we circle slowly until Kenneth has finished unloading his catch. Then we too tie up at the lobster car.

"How was it outside today?" Twink asks; and George says, "Good."

Good? I think. It was wonderful. It was like being outside time and space and life itself. I had come to the Peninsula from the woods, from all the small towns in which I had lived, seeking simplicity and peace and room in which to find the self that somewhere had been lost. I thought that there I had found the place for which I was looking—the simplest, cleanest, openest place in the world. But I knew now that nowhere on the land was there peace like the peace outside, where neither time nor the pressures of life existed. I could not stay out there forever. Nobody could, and indeed it was not desirable that one should. It was enough to know that it was always there, the quiet and the emptiness, always waiting across the low threshold of the harbor to encompass and heal the troubled heart.

"Want to see a blue lobster, Louise?" Twink asks. "One of the boys just brought it in. It's in that crate." I look, and it really is bright blue, an odd and unnatural sight. Lobsters are supposed to be green until they are cooked, when they turn scarlet. "They come that way once in a long while," Twink explains. "Feller over to Prospect caught a white one last winter, an albino. Nothing wrong with them at all. Just freaks." He starts weighing George's catch and transferring it by hand—because lobsters break if you dump or pour them—through an open hatch in the lobster car. They'll stay alive and healthy there in the sea water until one of the big refrigerator trucks comes down from Portland or Boston, when they will be crated and taken away, eventually to be served, for a pretty penny, in the better hotels and restaurants.

I tell Twink that I'd like to buy two of George's lobsters—*George's*, I emphasize, as they are personal acquaintances; and he tells me all right, wait for him up in his office and he'll be with me as soon as he gets through with *them*. He indicates the three or four boats idling off the car, waiting their turn. So I climb the long ladder to the wharf, go into the shack that serves as an office, and sit down in an overstuffed armchair that has seen far better days. On a shelf in the corner Twink's radio is muttering away to itself, tuned to the short-wave band that picks up the fishermen's ship-to-shore messages. A disembodied voice with a Down East twang is saying, "Yep, I can see him from here. He's got a trap in tow. Cal'late he's movin' it further out."

"Picked up a floatin' trap myself this mornin'," another voice says. "Bottom's some stove up, but barrin' that she's a good one. Got new nylon heads to her. Can't find no markin's, but she looks like a Nova Scotian. Kind of a long way from home."

"You goin' in now?" asks the first voice. "Tell my wife I'll be late. Wasn't plannin' on haulin' my whole gang today, but she's smurrin' up to the so'thard, so I figure I might as well finish up while the weather holds."

They're still out there, I think; still out there in all that space and brilliance and peacefulness; and I wish I were still out there, too.

That is what lobstering is like in the summer. I have never been out in the winter, but I have seen the boats leave and return, and I know all I need to know about it, or intend to know. It's cold, miserable work during the months when the sun is far to the south and the northern days are short and bitter. Sometimes the quiet water of the harbor is frozen over at dawn, in spite of its saltiness, and the ice must be broken by placing the feet on opposite gunwales of the punts and rocking them violently to and fro, a rather precarious business.

A young friend of mine, Vincent Young, fell overboard recently while engaged in this activity. Since he was fully clothed in hip-boots, several sweaters, and oilskins at the time, and since the freezing point of salt water is well below thirty-two degrees, I was horrified. "Great grief!" I exclaimed. "It's a wonder you didn't drown! Or freeze to death. Or at least have a heart attack. It must have been an awful shock to your system. Are you *sure* you shouldn't be home in bed?"

He looked at me with amusement. "Oh, I felt myself goin', so I was prepared," he said, as though that fixed everything up fine, including the temperature of the water. "Besides, if I went to bed every time I took a dousin', I'd spent the most of my life there. I got a family to support." And that was that. Prepared? I can only think he meant mentally. What else?

The ice is sometimes as thin as the panes of a window, and then it is called window-glass ice. This is the worst kind, because it can slice through the hull of a boat like a knife through butter. Then thick plank shields called breaking-boards are lowered around the bows to protect them, and the boats go around and around the harbor and up and down the channel, so that the wash will break up the perilous ice.

On mornings so cold that the harbor has frozen, the whole surface of the sea is concealed by rising wreaths and spirals of vapor through which the boats thread their way, now looming dark and distinct, now dim and ghostly. This is not fog, but steam rising from water that is warmer—cold as it may be—than the air. It's called arctic smoke. It condenses and freezes on the cold surface of a boat, completely sheathing it in ice. Then the men move slowly and carefully on the glassy decks, each motion planned and studied. It's bad enough to fall overboard in the harbor. It would be hopeless to go over the side on the open sea, with no one near and no possibility of climbing back in over the glazed sides. Even if a man could keep afloat for a time he would have no chance of survival.

He'd see his boat, the motor still pulsing evenly, draw relentlessly away from him, eventually to founder at sea or to be shattered on the ledges or smashed to kindling wood by the surf. Then the cold would strike into his blood and bones, and he'd sink like a stone. There'd be nothing to tell where he lay among the canyons and cliffs of the floor of the sea. It's an end which will not bear thinking upon, but which must always be borne secretly and fearfully in the mind of a lobsterman.

To seafaring folk the weather is always important, but in winter its importance is magnified so that it becomes a constant preoccupation. There are so many days when it is impossible to haul that even half a day—even a few hours—of reasonable winds and tides is seized upon eagerly. Before he rises in the morning, while it is still pitch dark and he is steeped in sleep, the lobsterman knows what lies in the immediate future. His mind may be drugged with drowsiness, but it reaches out with subconscious antennae to catch the significant signals. Is there a rattle of sleet on the window or a drumming of rain on the roof? He hears it without knowing that he hears it, and goes back to sleep again. Is it too quiet, so that a slow-paced dripping from the eaves sounds loud and insistent and a dog's bark is strangely muffled? Without opening his eyes, he knows that the world is swaddled in a thick blanket of fog, and there'll be no hauling today. His ear is pricked always, even in his sleep, for the dull roar of the offshore rote or the sound of the bell buoy off Cranberry Point and the whistle buoy near Western Island.

If the wind is in the north or northeast they can't be heard at all, or only faintly and intermittently; but if the wind is in the southwest—a good weather sign—the sounds drift loudly and clearly through the village, so that they seem almost to be under the very windows of the houses. The whistle buoy, known as the Groaner, consists of a cylinder that moves up and down in a sleeve with the motion of the waves, forcing air out of the top or the bottom with each plunge, and giving forth a noise very much like that of a cow mooing. If this sound is very loud and very frequent it reveals not only the quarter of the wind but also the fact that a short, heavy crosschop is running. A slow and stately groaning indicates a long, lazy swell.

Any shift of the wind to an ill quarter or change in the sound of the surf brings the lobsterman up standing out of the soundest sleep, alert to his first concern, his boat. The harbor at Corea is protected from all storms except a really bad southeaster, which can roll the breakers in over the bar and through the passage violently enough to tear the boats from their moorings and pile them on the beach. When such a storm breaks in the night, lights spring up all over the village as men, warned by their inward monitors, rise hastily and dress. Immediately, cars start converging on the harbor and spacing themselves all around its perimeter from Don Anderson's wharf to the end of the road on Crowley Island. They are parked so that the headlights shine out over the water and onto the moored boats. Most of them have spotlights as well, bought in anticipation of this very emergency; and the lights move constantly from boat to boat, seeking out any strain or weakness. If a boat breaks loose or an anchor seems to be dragging, a dozen punts put out from shore to the rescue. Each boat is everybody's boat on nights like this.

On these rare nights the harbor is eerie and beautiful, like a trolls' carnival. Almost never is it illuminated, but lies after sundown in deep obscurity. Now it is ablaze, with the boats shining unearthly white in the headlights and tossing and tugging at their bonds while the restless spotlights weave a golden web to hold them. The shadows of men working and watching along the shore are grotesque and black, leaping hugely across the water or shrinking to nothing. The air is full of blown spray and spume, and out of the vast and noisy darkness beyond the limit of light great ghostly crests rear one above another, and the ledges tremble with their trampling. It's a wild and lovely scene, full of fluid motion and glancing brightness and savage clamor.

No weather sign escapes the lobsterman, whether he seems to be paying attention or not. A red sunset is a good omen for the next day, while a bloody dawn is a danger signal, as is a mackerel sky or a sky full of mares' tails. A wind that shifts against the sun is not to be trusted; shortly it will shift back again. If the rain comes before the wind a long storm is in prospect, while if the wind comes first the storm will be of short duration. Fast-gathering clouds indicate a quick-breaking spell of weather, but if the clouds crawl slowly over the horizon there is yet time to do a day's work before running for shelter. "Short warning, soon past," the lobstermen say; "long foretelling, long last." Upon such lore depend their livelihood and sometimes their very lives.

I have said that I don't know what it's like outside in the winter, but I have formed a fair idea from being on hand at Twink Crowley's lobster car when the boats come in. They are later than they were in the summer. The tardy rising of the sun delayed their morning departure, and the need for caution, coupled with the difficulty of manipulating gear with cold-numbed hands, has slowed progress all day long. The early-setting sun almost touches the edge of the heath, and the harbor lies in gray shadow, all colors muted and subdued, although the sun still casts a pale, cold glow over Western Island and the tumultuous sea beyond. One by one the boats, weighted with ice, labor across the bar, each with a white bone in her teeth and a wavering pennant of gulls blowing behind her. They carry small triangular riding sails at their sterns now, to hold them steady against wind and tide. Slowly they circle, tired boats manned by tired men, while from the shelter of the office shack I watch their beautiful, precise maneuvers. There are no false moves, no commotion, no running about and shouting. These men are professionals of the sea, plying their trade under the most difficult circumstances with the quiet competence that marks the professional in any field; and, like all true professionals, they would consider praise for their skill gratuitous and insulting. They're supposed to know how to bring a boat in, and they do know how. Almost absent-mindedly they jockey for position and come up alongside the car as accurately as though they were on tracks. They know their business.

"How was it outside?" Twink asks; and they answer, "Not bad," or "A mite dusty." But their hunched shoulders and their faces, pinched with cold and exhaustion between the turned-up mackinaw collars and turned-down ear flaps, belie their words. Slowly they lift out the kegs, only partly full now, and slowly climb onto the car, beating their arms about their bodies to restore circulation.

"Why do you do it?" I asked two of them one bitter day as they passed me to where their cars where parked. They walked like old men, although Lewis Conley is only thirty-five and Junior Jordan in his middle twenties.

With the enormous natural courtesy of all the lobstermen, they stopped to give me a considered answer, although I knew they were exhausted, half-frozen and eager to get home. "It's the thing I know best," said Lewis. "It's the only work I can do where I can be my own boss." The last was the operative clause.

Junior looked out over the darkening sea, empty now except for the questing winds. His blue eyes went a long way, and then, lively and sparkling, came back to me. "Because I love it," he said simply.

He was the youngest of the deep-water lobstermen, but he was speaking for all of them. Every man in Corea except four holds a lobster-fishing license. One of the four is Herb Young, the store-keeper, and the other three have retired from the sea because of their great age. Even boys of nine or ten set traps along the shore from punts or skiffs, saving their lobster money for the day when they can buy their own lobsterboats and go outside. Any other future would be unthinkable to them. They have been born into an international citizenship beyond the citizenship determined by the arbitrary and limited boundaries of the land. They are citizens of the sea, far easier there than they are ashore, and they may be recognized as such wherever they are encountered. They carry about with them a quality that is the hallmark of their first allegiance.

This quality is a little hard to define. It is, as best I can describe it, an air and bearing of individual dignity that is almost regal. I do not mean to imply that the lobstermen are free from the faults common to mankind. They have their meannesses and cowardices, their vices and failings, just as the rest of us do. But they seem less lost and confused in an increasingly chaotic age than any group I know.

They conduct themselves, sometimes in rags, almost as though the universe belongs to them so indisputably that they have no need to assert their ownership. They are completely at home in their world.

I think that this is the result of their successful adaptation to loneliness. All men are lonely. That is humanity's tragedy: that only very briefly and for only a few moments in a lifetime can each individual penetrate the isolation that surrounds him and enter into true communication with his kind. What breaks and ruins many people is the desperate attempt and inevitable failure to communicate with their fellow men. In the futile struggle they divide themselves into bits and pieces, blindly assuming that the failure lies with themselves and that if they can only change themselves, if they can only discover the common mold and fit themselves into it, their

terrible solitude will end. Eventually the individual is shattered into so many fragments that nothing of value remains, and he is lonelier and unhappier than ever.

The lobsterman inherits not only the spiritual loneliness that is the birthright of every man, but he is exposed as well to a simpler and more rigid kind of loneliness: actual physical isolation from others for most of his waking hours. Once he has left the harbor he is completely alone, his own keeper, dependent on his own skill for survival and upon his own inner resources for companionship and comfort. He accepts loneliness as a fundamental fact of life and learns to live with it. He doesn't try to change himself. There is no need or incentive to do so. Thus he remains an integrated person and is at least lonely in good company. On the empty wastes of the sea he learns the technique of dealing with loneliness on the primitive, physical level; and, once this lesson is learned, any subtler and more complicated kind of loneliness that he may find ashore holds no terrors for him. He is in all respects his own man, equally in control of the small kingdom of his own boat, the disposal of his own time, and the self that he recognizes surely as his own.

His is the original type that settled this country, the pioneer stock that was not afraid of loneliness and hardship, that wanted only room and the right to be themselves. When others started impinging upon them they pushed the frontier westward until there was no frontier left, no other place to go. Then they died out or adapted, which is the same. There are only a few, last, beleaguered strongholds of them left in such places as the Peninsula, along the last frontier, the pathless prairie of the sea. There they will cling, independent, self-reliant, self-sufficient and free, until they too are engulfed in the great wave of progress. They seem a little misfitting and strange in the modern world. Or perhaps they alone are not misfits on a planet designed for man and man's use and enjoyment.

The lobsters are not the only harvest that the sea offers to Peninsulans, although the crop is not as diversified as once it was. Once the flats that are exposed at low tide were rich with clams, and clam-digging was a profitable occupation. Now there are so few that nobody bothers with them, unless they want just a quart or two for their own use. Their scarcity is the direct result of a complete lack of conservation methods in clamming, but the same cannot be said about the mackerel, huge schools of which used to visit the New England coast periodically. Suddenly they simply stopped coming, and no one, not even the scientists who make it their business to investigate these matters, knows why. They think that perhaps environmental changes have affected the mackerel's ability to reproduce in these waters, but they're not sure. In the meantime one of the favorite topics among the fishermen, as they sit around the store talking on foggy days, is the mackerel: where did they go and will they ever come back? Once in a while a few dozen are caught in the herring weirs, but there aren't enough of them to ship to city markets. The men take them home to their families, give them to neighbors, or peddle them from door to door in the villages.

Next to the lobster the herring is the fish most important to the economy of the Peninsula. The comparatively small numbers caught in the weirs (wares) are used for the bait on which the lobster industry depends. These weirs are set in shallow bays and coves, and they look like net fences strung on a circle of tall poles. The herring swim into the watery corral and can't get out again until someone dips them out with a hand net on a pole. The weirs need constant attention, because seals, sharks and dogfish—a species of harmless shark—frequently follow the herring into them, eat their fill, and then escape by the simple expedient of tearing holes in the net. There's nothing much that can be done about the sharks and dogfish, but when the seals get too bad the men take turns lying out nights and shooting them. The sealskins aren't worth anything now, but when George Crowley was a young man they used to be taken home, tanned, and made into vests. No blade about town was a really sharp dresser unless he flaunted a sealskin vest. It was the mark of the sporting character.

By far the larger numbers of herring are destined to become sardines, since domestic sardines are nothing more or less than small herring boiled in oil and canned. The sardine factory nearest to Cranberry Point is at Prospect Harbor, about a mile and a half across the long bay to the west. Therefore all day long, looking out the windows of the cabin or sitting in the sun on the rocks of the Point, we can see the big white sardiners plying to and fro between the factory and their fishing grounds off in the general direction of the Bay of Fundy. They are broad-beamed, businesslike boats, carrying crews of four or five men. We don't pay much attention to them on their outward voyages, except to wave to the crews if they're near enough inshore; but when we see them coming home we start listening for the factory whistle.

The sound of this whistle drifts easily over the open bay and level moor, and it is an integral part of village life. Even visitors like us depend on the one blast at seven in the morning and the one at twelve noon to set our clocks. Two blasts means that the boss is wanted in the office, a fact of no particular interest to anybody outside the factory. But when the blasts run up to three, four, five or more, everyone starts counting. The incoming sardiner has radioed ashore the size of the catch in her hold, and if it is more than the permanent skeleton staff of packers can handle, additional shifts of workers are needed and are so informed by the whistle code. Women from all over the large area that lies within earshot are on the roster of extra packers, and each knows by the number of blasts whether her shift is wanted. At the sound of the factory whistle everybody stops whatever she is doing—hanging out the washing, changing the baby, baking a cake—and listens. The village is suddenly as quiet as Armistice Day at eleven o'clock.

Then there is a flurry of activity. The unhung wash is bundled into the basket for another day, or the baby is entrusted to the care of a sitter, or the cake is abandoned. The women quickly change into clean cotton dresses and hurry to the store, where the factory bus will pick them up in a few minutes. There is a holiday air about the gathering. This is an opportunity to earn a little extra cash in a community which offers few chances for women to pick up their own pin money; but, more than that, it is a break in the sometimes dull routine of their lives. Going over to Prospect to pack is as much a social event as a paying job.

The scales of the billions of little herring involved in the sardine business used to be thrown away, but now they are regarded as a valuable by-product. They are removed by a scaling machine and used in the manufacture of the cheap artificial pearls sold in ten-cent stores. In fact, the pearl business is becoming almost as big and important as the sardine business, from which some weighty observation about feeding vanity versus feeding the body could probably be made, but I'm not the one who's going to make it.

There are other kinds of fishing on the Peninsula, too. In Gouldsboro Bay boats drag for sea scallops, the shells of which are sometimes as large as plates. A bag of rope net held open by a metal ring is dragged slowly along the bottom of the bay, collecting scallops as it goes. The edible muscle is removed aboard the boat and the shells are thrown back into the bay, a conservation practice required by law, since the microscopic spawn like old shells to fasten upon. The season is limited to the first four months of the year, and some of the lobstermen change to scallop dragging during this period. It's slightly easier and about as profitable, and the little lobsterboats can be used for the purpose.

Dragging for ground fish—flounders, dabs, cod and haddock—is a separate and independent business, requiring a large boat called a dragger and special equipment. A weighted net with wings which funnel the fish into a net bag is dragged slowly along the bottom, picking up whatever comes into its path. The draggers work fairly well offshore, and on summer days you can see them, patiently plowing back and forth over the pastures of the sea. They can be distinguished from the trawlers, which also catch ground fish, by the tall masts and derricks necessary for hauling the nets aboard.

The trawlers drop overboard long lines, or trawls, from each of which dangle a hundred hooks on "snoods," or drop-lines. The ends are weighted to keep them on the bottom and are marked by buoys so that they may be located when it's time to pick them up again. Each trawler fishes about eight lines, each of which is baited ashore and coiled in a tub. Baiting eight hundred hooks is a tiresome and dirty job, but some women make a business of it, as it pays well. After the trawl has been on the bottom about an hour or so, by which time all the fish that are likely to be caught have been caught, it is wound inboard by a winch, the fish being taken off the hooks as they come over the side. Nowadays the catches of both draggers and trawlers, which formerly were salted and dried, are mostly sold as fresh fish or are sent to freezing plants to be processed as frozen fish.

Occasionally a whale is sighted off the Peninsula, but no one troubles him. The Peninsulans are not in the whaling business, so he passes as merely an interesting phenomenon. And occasionally people—but not the men who have worked all day fishing for a living—go down to the harborside with drop-lines and fish off the wharves for fun. I've done it myself. Pollock are the fish most commonly caught, small gullible fish so stupid that it is almost impossible not to catch them. They'll grab anything, including a hook baited with stale doughnut or even a bare hook. They're good to eat, although a little bony.

Wresting a living from the sea is far from easy. She guards jealously what is her own and demands full payment in time and energy. But once in a while she casts up unexpected gifts. Most of the houses of the Peninsula contain today articles dating from the wreck of the *Lucy P. Miller* over a half century ago on what is called 'Titm'nan Backside, or the outer shore of Petit Manan. The *Lucy P.* carried a general cargo, which means that it included everything from jackknives to pianos; and as soon as word arrived that she was aground and breaking up, every boat on the Peninsula went to the scene and loaded to the gunwales with items of the doomed cargo. Families in Corea today are still eating off dishes from the *Lucy P. Miller* and sitting on leather cushions from her cabins.

"What did your family get?" I asked Marcia Spurling when she told me about it.

"That was before my day," she said, "but my mother could still get mad at my father twenty years later whenever she thought about it. You know what he brought home? A whole boatload of lamp chimneys and raisins! My mother could buy all the lamp chimneys she'd ever need for a nickel apiece, and the raisins were all completely ruined by the salt water. I guess she was some old disgusted, now I want to tell you!"

I must say that my sympathies were with Marcia's mother.

All sorts of things are continually being washed ashore and picked up by those who patrol the water's edge, which is nearly everyone, including me. You can always find good pieces of wood for any building project you have in mind, and less good pieces which are suitable for fireplace or stove. There are traps that require only a little work on them to make them serviceable, and sometimes useful articles that have fallen off passing boats. I have a wooden bailer, worn to the texture of gray satin, that I picked up at Shark Cove and now fill with bouquets of wild roses; and a homemade clam basket of weathered laths that I found near the Devil's Oven and that is just right to hold books and magazines; and the cork floats from nets make wonderful candle holders. Once my daughter Dinah found a note in a bottle, which filled her with wild elation until it turned out that it had been cast adrift only the day before by Condon Rogers, the granddaughter of the Gratton Condons over on Crowley Island, whom she knew anyhow. But it *might* have been from a handsome youth held in durance vile on a sinister yacht.

During World War II great quantities of butter and lard were picked up during one period. It was perfectly fresh and good, having been refrigerated by the icy water, but no one was very enthusiastic about it. It could have come only from some ship that had been sent to the bottom by enemy action, and its finding made everyone uncomfortable. It was a terrible feeling, one woman told me, having it brought home so vividly that ships were sinking and men were drowning just over the horizon, and you going about your business in ignorance all the while.

Some of the best harvests came during Prohibition days. This part of the Maine coast has always been a haunt of smugglers and bootleggers. It is close to Canada, and the ragged, broken, dangerous coastline has made it child's play for a small boat, expertly maneuvered, to ghost through the net of the Law. Even before national Prohibition, bootlegging was fairly common, since Maine was a dry state before anyone else ever dreamed of such a thing. In fact, Maine invented Prohibition, establishing the first total abstinence society in the world in 1815 and following it up with the first law prohibiting the manufacture and sale of spirits in 1846. For a long time any law restricting commerce in alcohol was known everywhere as a Maine law.

I find this rather puzzling, since from earliest days Maine has always been a hard-drinking state. In colonial times the first public buildings to be erected in a new community were usually the tavern and the church, in that order. Almost any of the great clipper ships was built with the aid of enough rum to float her. Tots were always issued to the shipwrights several times a day as part of the contract, and on special occasions, such as the hanging of the anchor or the stepping of a mast, there were double tots. Everybody drank. Farmers depended on jugs of hard cider to see them through the haying or a difficult calving, and ladies depended on a glass of sherry to settle their nerves. Rum, whiskey and fine wines were important items in a trade that carried Maine ships all over the world, and the consumption of them seemed fitting and natural. Nevertheless, the uneasy and puritanical idealist that dwells under the hard, practical, fact-facing hide of the paradoxical Downeaster wouldn't rest; so Maine had Prohibition.

Naturally, it didn't work very well. Even on the Peninsula, where there is less drinking today than I have encountered in any other part of Maine and where there was never much drunkenness, the law acted as a challenge rather than as a deterrent. A hundred years ago, so they tell me, the *Strumpy Tucker*—a little bootlegging sailboat from Canada—was slipping regularly and unobtrusively in and out among the islands and harbors all up and down the coast. Forty years ago a lobster-buying smack, the *Speedwell*, used to call at Corea every week to pick up the lobsters that had been collecting in the pounds. Her owner, Captain Burns, was an accommodating man and would do errands in his home port of Boston for anyone so desiring. He almost always had two or three requests to bring back bottles of whiskey, which was sold legally in Massachusetts. This may not have been breaking the law, but it was certainly evading it.

During national Prohibition bootlegging took a new lease on life. Leaky old vessels long past their seaworthiness were hauled off the beach to participate in this remunerative trade. Some of these, in danger of foundering in the rough seas off the Peninsula, jettisoned parts of their cargoes for safety's sake; and some, being overhauled by revenue cutters, threw the whole works overboard for the sake of a clean slate when searched. Much of this contraband washed ashore on the strong tides, and almost everybody engaged in the business of salvaging it. Even teetotalers joined the game. After all, the booty could always be sold. It was fun while it lasted.

But the sea that surrounds the Peninsula is more than a means of making a living and a giver of occasional gifts. It is more than a conspicuous work of nature. It is a presence and climate that forms the characters of the people, influences their thinking, molds the shape of their lives, and dictates even their most intimate relationships.

The other day I had occasion to call on a young woman who lives with her husband and two small children in a huge housing development outside a large city. I could not help contrasting family life in this example of what may be modern living in its most exaggerated form with family life on the Peninsula, which follows the pattern first laid down, probably, by the cave man.

In the development, all the houses are exactly alike, and the lives of the people are pretty much alike, too. All the husbands are young, and they all commute to jobs in the city where the disposal of their time is commanded by somebody else. They are gone from what I suppose they call their homes from early morning until evening. All day long that enormous area is peopled with only women and children, to me a most unnatural state. The father is virtually a stranger to his offspring, since they are usually in bed by the time he arrives home, cross and frazzled. The child's upbringing is left almost entirely in the hands of his mother, and his life has almost no variety in a woman-ridden world of identical houses and small, barren back yards. Actually it has very little meaning, either. Everything is reduced to a dull level of conformity in which there is nothing new and interesting to see or do or learn. I came away feeling depressed and more than a little apprehensive for their future.

It's different on the Peninsula. The children there may not be as well housed, dressed or fed, but at least everyone's home is particular and not like anybody else's. Each child's yard is the whole various and beautiful countryside with its woods and ledges and heaths and shingled beaches, and all that it has to offer the inquisitive young mind. Moreover and especially, the child lives in the constant society of both men and women who are free from regimentation to devote themselves to him. Fathers know their sons and daughters and spend a great deal of time with them. The sons, as soon as they can walk, are initiated into the secrets of their fathers' occupation. One boy I know, Jack Young, started lobstering when he was seven years old, a fact in which he takes a great deal of pride, since his father Kenneth was ten before he started and his grandfather Dan all of twelve. The three Young boys—Jack, Kenneth and Dan, who is eighty-five—do a lot of the kind of kidding about their respective careers that is unheard-of and impossible on a housing development where sons have no comprehension of their fathers' work and grandfathers are legendary figures lost in the mists of some small town in upstate New York. In more sophisticated communities, most boys, as soon as they can legally drive a car, acquire jalopies. These serve no useful economic purpose and are usually a menace to the life and limb of both their owners and the general public as well. The only doubtful value they may have is as an outlet for adolescent energies and repressions and as a means of escape from the crushing boredom of what is neither a family nor a circle in any real sense. Boys on the Peninsula don't go in for jalopies much. Instead, they own small boats called peapods, from which they set traps along the shore. They take as much pride in their boats as their urban counterparts do in their hot rods; or more, since these boats have real value. They contribute substantially to the family income and give their owners stature on an adult level in the community. Through them, energy is directed to a purpose, and a boy with a purpose and the means of achieving it is not very likely to be troubled with dangerous repressions.

The lives of the little girls, too, have meaning. They also participate, painting buoys and knitting bait bags, and they derive great satisfaction from being obviously useful citizens. Once I asked a very small girl who was laying out lengths of tarred line on the surface of the road, "What are you doing?"

She glanced up at me briefly and said with some impatience, "Helping my father." I can't tell you the world of pride there was in her tone.

On another occasion I was wrapping a package for mailing and having difficulty getting the cord tight enough. A ten-year-old girl who was watching me finally said, "If you'd wet the string first you'd have better luck. It'll shrink up when it dries and be taut as a fiddlestring."

"Where'd you ever learn that?" I asked; and she told me, with all the composure of a member in good standing of a respected guild, "Oh, all seamen know *that!*"

The girls don't go out to sea and haul as the boys do. It's much too hard work for them. But even here they are not excluded. On fine days they often go along for the ride, of course; but, more than this, a father often designates one of his traps to be Linda's trap or Nancy's trap. Anything that is caught in it belongs to her and is put into a separate bucket, and the proceeds from its sale—forty or fifty cents, perhaps—is hers. This is a custom that has been going on for a hundred years or more, and I think it is a nice one. It's good for a little girl to know that she has a father who is working especially for her when he's way off on the horizon, hauling her trap and attending to her lobster.

This is what it means, then, to live constantly with the sea. It is to observe century-old customs because they are still valid; to follow a pattern of living whereof the memory of man runneth not to the contrary; to rest secure in a world that is unchanging because nothing can change the presence that dominates it. And nothing will change that world so long as the Peninsulans keep their faces turned eastward to their sea.

5. The Face of the Land

Now I would like to tell you about the land which this sea so jealously embraces: not about the villages or the people or the roads or anything else of late arrival, but about the great and patient Peninsula itself. It is a land that I cannot consider without emotion. Already I have fallen into the pathetic fallacy of endowing it and the sea that surrounds it with human traits. I know perfectly well that the sea is incapable of jealousy and the land of patience. Of course they do not feel. It only seems to me that they do, because I myself feel so strongly about them.

There is a pristine quality about the Peninsula, a quality of being unused and unhandled, that makes all other places in which I have lived seem by comparison old and tired and trampled into submission by man. In the Old Bay Colony area of Massachusetts, where I spent my childhood and many of my adult years, the grass is domesticated, spreading in velvet lawns under orderly plantings of trees. Even in the wild mountain and lake region of Maine where I lived the seventeen years of my married life, the ugly slashes left by the lumbering operations spoke of man's exploitation and despoliation. Here on the Peninsula the evidences of man's occupancy exist, but they have about them a temporary air of existing only on sufferance. It seems as though at any moment the tide might rise higher, the wind blow stronger, or lightning descend from the sky to destroy all trace of this latest and least successful experiment. It is a land still unpossessed.

This feeling of recency is not entirely a matter of my emotions and imagination. Actually, as coasts go, this one is very young. Ten thousand years or so ago—which is, speaking geologically, a short time—the Peninsula, along with the rest of the coast of Maine and of Nova Scotia, was a range of hills and mountains standing well inland beyond a broad plain that bordered the sea. Short rivers tumbled down the mountain gorges and meandered across the level piedmont to the ocean. Then the polar icecap started its ponderous and inexorable expansion and advance; and under the tremendous weight of the great glacier the shell of the globe cracked at a point somewhere near Long Island, so that all of the territory northeast of the fault tilted down. The whole coastal plain and many of the lower foothills and plateaus disappeared beneath the sea, which rushed up the river valleys, encircled the higher hills, and crashed against the faces of what had been mountain crags. In all probability the whole Peninsula, with the possible exception of Schoodic Head and the positive exception of six-hundred-foot Mt. Cromer, lay beneath the surface of the ocean.

When the glacier finally retreated and the enormous pressure was relieved, the resilient crust of the earth responded by rising slightly. There have been found on Mt. Desert Island and Isle au Haut sea beaches and marine fossils at an elevation of over two hundred feet, incontrovertible evidence that the sea once lapped at that level. But the land could never resume its old position. The damage was too great. The wide plain remained a continental shelf, some parts of which lie under a thousand feet of water, the long valleys are winding estuaries and deep bays, and the hilltops are the countless islands and reefs that ring the land. Some of the submerged territory, however, including the Peninsula, did regain the open air to become what geologists term a *drowned coastline*.

I like to think of the Peninsula on that day of its rebirth, for the eons that it took for it to emerge from under the vast waters into the light of the sun were only a day in time. Up it came, a great prairie of solid rock, polished and scoured by the abrasive action of the glacier and washed clean by the currents and surfs that had poured and pounded over it for centuries. No soil remained on it, and no vegetation except the brown pastures of rockweed, knotted wrack and devil's aprons. Slowly it rose, like a big, shaggy dog, with the water streaming from its ragged coat of weeds and the small fish and crabs and lobsters scurrying in alarm to the safety of the rejected sea. Clouds of gulls came screaming out from their haunts and breeding grounds on the higher ledges which had never been drowned, to pick and quarrel over the urchins and mussels that lived quietly among the weeds; and the great blue herons sailed majestically over, trailing their extravagant legs and peering down their long bills at the sea life landlocked in water-filled depressions of the rock. It must have been a great day.

Then the Peninsula rested, steaming in the unaccustomed sun. The seaweeds dried, turning first to malodorous rubber, then to brittle black paper, then to dust. The captured pools of sea water evaporated, leaving an encrustation of salt in the cups, great and small, that had held them. Springs of fresh water which had never failed during the ages of submersion, when their flow was lost in the sea, continued to issue from sources deep within the earth to form little streams and ponds. Torrential rains of summer and driven snows of winter washed away the salt and dust, so that the true structure of the Peninsula was revealed in all its skeletal strength. It was bleak, perhaps, but it was beautiful. For a long, long time the glacier and the sea had been at work tempering all harshness of line. Now the rounded contours of the bare pink granite flowed sweetly and gently each fold into the next, as they do today. The land had been given that very rare thing, a chance to obliterate the lumber of the past, to destroy forever and past remembering old errors and encumbrances, and to begin anew to make of itself what it could.

The beginning was necessarily modest. There was not much to work with toward establishing forests and meadows and heaths. But all the time in the world lay ahead, so the Peninsula could afford small beginnings. First came the lichens, spreading themselves in intricate patterns over the rock—the sage-green, scarlet-tipped rock lichen, the deep orange splashes of the wall lichen, and the tough green fabric of the lichen known as rock tripe. Doggedly they worried away at the surfaces of the ledges, dissolving by means of an acid secretion infinitesimal bits of rock to make the first deposit in a soil bank. Their discarded parts, disintegrated and washed down into hollows by the rain, swelled the account until in the low damp places enough organic matter had collected to give a roothold to the mosses, the spores of which drifted in on the wind from the higher land. Low and plushy, gray and yielding, or coarse and rank, these mosses crept slowly out of their original tiny holdings, venturing further and further over the rock, each generation nurturing itself on the mold of the generations before, until there was enough soil to support grasses and ferns, small vines and low bushes, seeded by the winds and the tides and the birds. All over the bare granite a green carpet was spreading, insignificant as yet, but full of promise.

Other agents were at work simultaneously. In every little cove and catch basin along the shore the tides cast up all manner of debris—shells, leaves and branches, uprooted seaweeds, the bodies of birds and animals and fish—which rotted away into compost. At the head of each sheltered inlet a small beach of gravel, sand, pebbles and pulverized shell was formed, out of which soon grew the various salt-marsh grasses and weeds. Over the centuries the gulls deposited tons of guano on the Peninsula; and, flying high, they dropped millions of sea urchins, blue mussels and crabs onto the rocks well back from the shoreline, to crack the shells for eating and to add, inadvertently, to the treasury of soil. The algae in the waters of the ponds died and sank to the bottom to form a rich silt for reeds and water lilies. The rock itself, exposed to sun and wind and rain and to the great power of frost, crumbled to contribute to the store. And in this new soil a greater and greater variety of plant life grew, the seeds and spores riding in on the winds, on the tides, on the coats of deer and foxes and rabbits, in the maws of birds, until thickets and then forests were established on the land, each one of which added yearly to the deepening blanket of loam.

I have written as though this process went on concurrently all over the Peninsula. It didn't, of course. The higher, central parts of the land rose from the sea first and were ready to start their regeneration centuries before the fringe areas had achieved the light of day. Therefore they were well advanced, probably supporting full-grown pines, fir and spruces, while other parts were fathoms under water. That is what makes the Peninsula so fascinating. You can see for yourself, taking no expert's word for it, every step of the evolution from barren rock to shady wood and flowering meadow. In twenty minutes you can move through eons of time and observe exactly what happened and is still happening.

The best way to do this is to drive onto the Peninsula over the Pond Road, which roughly bisects it. Here you will be as far away from the sea as it is possible to be, out of sight and often out of sound of it, although there will always be gulls coasting overhead to remind you of its nearness. Aside from the presence of the gulls, you might easily be in the midst of any New England countryside. There are small farms, open fields sloping down to the shores of Jones Pond, lilac hedges, maple groves, and stands of fir. The country is gently rolling, and there is nothing to show that close beneath the surface of a flourishing truck garden lies the ancient and eternal rock.

But within a very short distance—for it is only nine miles by this route from US 1 on the mainland to the furthermost tip of the Peninsula—the country changes. It becomes more open and airy. The trees are smaller and the grasses coarser and sparser; and larger and larger areas of bare ledge are evident. This is newer land, land that emerged more recently from the sea. The change becomes progressively more pronounced as you turn off at Prospect Harbor and proceed across the Big Heath to Corea, and beyond Corea the half mile or so to Cranberry Point, which is the newest land of all. It struggled up from the depths only yesterday, geologically speaking, and the work of rebuilding is barely well begun.

The Point is a fresh, untarnished place, open-faced and unsubtle. It is hard to believe that it is a part of the same anatomy as the apparently old and firmly established terrain back on the Pond Road; but you need only to look east to the islands to see that this is true. The islands are miniature counterparts of the Peninsula, having the same basic structure and having undergone the same ordeal. The one most easily viewed from the Point is Western Island, which is an excellent example. It's a small island, steeply sloped and fairly high, shaped rather like a whale. On the summit, which came out of the ocean first, is a crest of wind-bent fir trees. All around this copse is a belt of low bushes, diminishing gradually into a broad area of cranberry vines, briers and grass. Lower are the mosses, then the lichens, then a wide band of barren rock plunging into the ocean. Below the mean-tide mark are the beds of kelp and rockweed, exposed at low tide. There is even a diminutive heath on the island, a small saucer scooped out of the rock by glacial action, filled with decayed organic matter and rain water, and sustaining various flora; which is all that the biggest heath on the Peninsula is: just a large, shallow bowl full of detritus and watered either by rain or by springs.

Looking at Western Island from across the strait, you come to understand the framework of the entire Peninsula. The contour of the bare rock disappears beneath the cover of verdure, but your mind's eye can easily follow it to where it reappears at the other edge of the green. It is very apparent that the soil supporting the growth is superficial, just a skullcap covering the bald ledges. So it is on the Peninsula as a whole, with Cranberry Point analogous to the newer area between the scrub-line and the sea.

Perhaps that is the reason why the Point made such an immediate and deep appeal to me: that it is new, that it is the perfect natural example of a fresh beginning. Undaunted by a catastrophe that had destroyed the accumulations of its preglacial existence, it is rebuilding on the old and essential foundation of bedrock. I found myself in instant empathy with the place, found myself entering at once into the feeling and spirit of the long, low tongue of land. I, too, through a series of personal losses, failures and disappointments in myself and others, had been submerged in a troubled sea of bewilderment and discouragement that had washed away many of my former faiths and certainties. It was with increasing effort that I tried to present the self that had become known as mine to the world. We all, through the years, unconsciously and unintentionally build a façade of manner and attitudes behind which to hide, but which slowly grafts itself onto us, until self and façade are indistinguishable. Only when a personal cataclysm reveals the falseness of the front are we left dismayed to consider what is behind it, to ask ourselves the frightening question: "Who and what am I?"

It is a question almost impossible to answer among familiar surroundings and in the climate of old relationships. There one finds oneself responding automatically to the accustomed influences, to the sweet and fatal seductions and unplanned blackmail of friends, to the pressure of opinion, to the picture of oneself that has been created and must be lived up to. Only by disassociating oneself entirely from the past, by casting off the hampering agglomerations of previous knowledge and experience, may one hope to get down to the bedrock of one's own character, whether good or bad.

The attempt to weigh oneself and one's standards and values, I had already discovered, is a dangerous business. It takes an extremely strong and detached mind to consider itself constructively, and that kind of mind would probably never have fallen into the morass in which I found myself. To the average mentality such as mine, self-analysis quickly becomes self-absorption; and a descending and tightening emotional spiral is created which ends in self-pity, the least worthy and most destructive of human feelings. I wasn't exactly sorry for myself when I arrived at Cranberry Point, but I was too close to being that way for comfort. The Point cured me of that.

For there are some people who can live without wild things about them and the earth beneath their feet, and some who cannot. To those of us who, in a city, are always aware of the abused and abased earth below the pavement, walking on grass, watching the flight of birds, or finding the first spring dandelion are rights as old and unalienable as the rights to life, liberty and the pursuit of happiness. We belong to no cult. We are not Nature Lovers. We don't love nature any more than we love breathing. Nature is simply something indispensable, like air and light and water, that we accept as necessary to living, and the nearer we can get to it the happier we are.

From the moment that I first set foot on the sparse soil of the

Point I have felt closer to the earth than in any other place of my experience; and it is a feeling that increases with further acquaintanceship and knowledge. Perhaps that is another reason why I so love the Peninsula: because I feel here as much a part of a colossal scheme as are the tides and the winds, the small flowers underfoot and the birds passing overhead. I feel as though I belong.

The cabin on Cranberry Point is a marvelous place for one like me who often doubts her competence in the complicated structure of the society of her own kind, who sometimes feels that she would have been more at home in the world had she been born in a nest or a burrow. It is made of logs, with a huge fieldstone fireplace, and it is low and weathered and unobtrusive. Its roof and great chimney are covered with lichens, like an outcropping of the ledges. In fact, I believe—since it is unoccupied for much of the year—that the birds and beasts forget that it isn't a ledge. Foxes trot within six feet of its windows, swallows nest under the eaves, gulls perch on the roof, and rabbits raise their families beneath the floor. And I, going about my business within, watch them from the windows as they go about their business without; just as they undoubtedly watch me from covert and copse when I walk abroad. We don't bother each other. We merely observe each other's antics with what is probably about equal interest.

No human being, of course, can ever enter entirely into the world of the wild things. Too many centuries of training in self-consciousness and in adherence to superimposed artificial patterns of behavior prevent his ever attaining complete identification with those whose conduct is characterized by a total lack of affectation and a complete absence of deviousness. I would be the last to advocate that the race of man abandon suddenly and simultaneously its carefully wrought structure of conventionalities and its system of curbs and strictures, and start acting like animals. We have at our disposal far too many means of wreaking havoc and far too much imagination and inventiveness in fashioning others to make such a program, even if it were possible, anything but catastrophic. We behave badly enough as it is without inviting further trouble.

However, it is—to me, at least—fascinating to observe wild animals when they are unconscious of observation, to take one short step over the border into the land of blamelessness, to discover that they and we have enough things in common so that once in a while, briefly, our worlds overlap. It is not only interesting, it is refreshing and heartening to learn that we still retain a lien on innocence.

Unlike humans, wild animals are never doing anything of which they are ashamed. Therefore the observer, even when using powerful field glasses, is never made to feel like a Peeping Tom. Then, too, they never display any of the less attractive human traits, like jealousy, spite, or purposeless cruelty; and they never act spoiled. Only domesticated animals, tainted by human companionship, are ever jealous, spoiled, or made to feel guilty. Wild animals always behave ethically according to their undisputed standards, and they wouldn't know how to go about spoiling themselves or each other.

I don't know which is my favorite wild animal. One day it was the deer, because a doe and twin fawns stepped out of the bushes across the little cove in front of the cabin and stood like statues gazing out to sea. Through my glasses I could see the bright coin spots on the fawns, who must have been very young indeed. They made a perfectly charming group on the ledges, with the deep blue sea behind them and their coats red in the sun.

Finally the doe wheeled and walked back to cover, followed by one of the fawns. The other still stood and stared, bemused by the piling surf, oblivious of or disobedient to whatever means a doe has of giving orders to her offspring. The doe waited for a moment at the edge of the thicket and then stamped back to where the fawn lingered and gave him such a rough shove with her nose that he staggered. Very definitely she was saying, "When I speak, young man, you *mind* me!" I laughed out loud. I've had occasion to convey the same idea in my own manner to my own young, and I knew just exactly how she felt. For a moment we were not doe and woman, but two mothers sharing a common annoyance of motherhood.

Some days I like rabbits best, when I see them come out from under the cabin to nibble clover, rise suddenly onto their haunches, their long ears turning like radar detectors to check for enemies, and, their minds relieved, saunter with a peculiarly awkward gait to the next clover patch. When rabbits run they are as smooth and fast as greyhounds, bounding over the rocks in prodigious leaps, ears flat on their shoulders as a streamlining measure; but when they walk they huddle along like old women.

I like them best, though, when they come out just before sunset and play tag, chasing each other, turning and reversing the chase according to rules of their own which I have not yet figured out, and having a fine time, not for love or food or enmity, but simply for fun. The rabbit is the accepted prototype of the timid and trembling, so that we speak of an insecure person as a scared rabbit of a man. It makes me feel better about rabbits to know that their lives contain lighthearted enjoyment as well as fear.

Actually rabbits aren't as full of nervous apprehensions as are chipmunks. Chipmunks go about borrowing trouble. Here on the Point, where there is little soil, most animals den in crevices of the ledges instead of digging burrows; and that's what chipmunks do. At the extreme end of the Point is a high ledge facing the open ocean to the south and west; and on days when the sea is running high that is the best place to go to watch it come crashing in from the West Indies. My visiting sister and I went over there one day to see the surf. We were sitting quietly on a rock when a chipmunk raced almost over our feet. She herself was not more than three inches long, and in her mouth she carried by the nape of the neck one of her young, who could not have measured an inch. Tail rigidly upright, eyes glassy with terror, she disappeared into a crevice about ten feet from us, deposited her child, and tore back the way she had come to another crevice about five feet from where we were immobilized with amazement. Three more times she made the trip, until all her litter had been transferred from the danger zone to a zone which she, in her addled way, considered to be safe.

Now if, with the instinctive wisdom that animals are supposed to possess, she had simply sat tight, we would never have known that she and her family existed. All she succeeded in doing was to call attention to herself, and it was just her good luck that Alice and I are not bring-'em-back-alive-or-dead types. We dismissed her behavior as erratic, concluding that she was probably a very young mother, unused to responsibility and therefore jittery.

The next day, and the next and the next, the same thing happened all over again. Between our visits she'd move her family back to the old homestead, but as soon as we showed up she'd go through her evacuating routine all over again. She was wearing not only herself, but us also, to a frazzle. Finally we had to find another rock to sit on. We couldn't stand being cast as menaces, even by a neurotic chipmunk.

It seems, however, that she was typical. I told the man who came to fix the water cistern about her stupid behavior, and he said, "Ayuh, they'll do it every time, the durned fools." Chipmunks just aren't very bright, I guess.

My long-term favorites among the animals of the Point are the foxes. They're so very handsome with their red coats and black points, and so very intelligent. They handle themselves gracefully and efficiently, they're independent and self-sufficient, and they have a sense of humor. I have no means of determining the fox population of the Point, but it must be fairly large. I seem to see foxes wherever I turn. It's a good place for them. The ledges provide warm, dry dens, and the hundreds of acres of uninhabited land are their undisputed domain. I don't count as a disputant. For a few days after my every arrival they give me a wide berth, but after a week I'm an old and harmless story. When I went back to the well for water this morning I saw one in the Bridges' old sheep pasture. He looked at me and I looked at him. Then he turned his back on me, sat down, and scratched his ear. I suppose that is the fox method of demonstrating social poise and *savoir faire*, if not contempt.

I wish they would treat my dog with equal indifference. Since I am alone much of the time out here at the dead end of a grass-grown track across the moor, with no telephone and no neighbors, I bring my black collie, Caro, with me for company and to act as a sort of Sister Anne, to warn me of approaching callers. He's not a protector, since there is nothing to protect me against; but I like to know in advance when people are coming, so that I can pull up my socks and put on some lipstick. The flaw in this arrangement is that Caro warns me not only of the rare bipeds he sights, but also of the much more frequent quadrupeds. It's a bit deflating to have rushed to powder your nose and change into a clean shirt, only to discover that all that was for a woodchuck. However—

One year I arrived in early May to find that a vixen had denned among the ledges over across the gully by the cabin, at a distance of perhaps two hundred feet. I'd see her sunning on the rocks with her family playing about her; and occasionally the pups would wander over into what I call my front yard, although it is just an area of granite, patched with moss and grass and tiny flowers, between the cabin and the sea. When this happened, Caro would rush out with a great roaring and bellowing, and the little foxes would evaporate.

't didn't take them many days, however, to discover that he is an old dog, afflicted with arthritis, so that even I can run faster than he can. This was all they needed to know to set them on a course of deliberate dog-baiting. They'd come over, the whole bunch of them, for fun and games with Caro. They'd tantalize him into chasing one of them, then another would cut across the path of pursuit— as children do in the game of cross-tag—until the poor old boy didn't know whether he was coming or going. His bark would become hysterical, his tongue would hang down to his knees, and I'd have to go out and get him before he suffered a stroke.

It's still going on. The foxes are half-grown now and have other interests in life, like rustling their own meals and learning the ways of the world; but every now and then they still come over and sit in the front yard, looking at the cabin and projecting the silent invitation: "Yoo-hoo, Caro. Come on out and play!"

Foxes at work are fascinating. A few weeks ago I was looking out the window doing what I fondly call thinking, when I saw a movement in the short spring grass on the further point. Abandoning my mental efforts, I seized the field glasses and brought into near focus a big dog-fox flat on his belly to the earth. His attention was riveted on a large crow, picking around the jetsam left by the retreating tide. Clearly the fox had ideas concerning the crow, and in my opinion his ideas were foolish. Crows are among the craftiest of the birds; and besides that, there lay between prey and predator not only ten feet of close turf, but at least seventy feet of naked shingle and beach as well. The fox, I felt, was wasting his time.

In the next half hour, my respect for foxes soared. Inch by inch, with a patience and muscular control that was incredible, he worked his way out of the grass and onto the tide strip. He lay for moments completely immobile, so much a part of the tawny sand that when I took my eyes off him I had trouble finding him again. I never saw him move, but after an interlude I would realize that he had somehow advanced three, five, seven, ten feet. Finally, with infinite care, he gathered himself for the kill. There was a burning arc of red, an explosion of black fury, and the fox trotted gayly into the bushes, head up and steps high to keep from tripping over the limp body of his victim.

I felt like cheering, it was such a striking display of extraordinary skill. I'm a fool for competence in any field. That's why I like foxes. They're competent.

My least favorite animals are porcupines. They are incompetent. They're also stupid, slow, destructive of property, and a danger to my dog. The only interesting thing that I know about them is that in some states they are protected by law because they are the only animal that an unarmed man lost in the woods and starving can overtake and kill for food. They tell me that the flesh is quite palatable. I've only seen two in my years on the Point, which suits me very well.

I've never seen a snake on the Point, although I'm sure there must be some here. The reason is, I suppose, that they do not fill me with the atavistic aversion and fear which afflicts many people in their presence. I have never lived in a locality where there were poisonous snakes. Therefore I am not snake-conscious. It is the thing we fear that we see in every shadow. I fear fire; therefore I smell smoke where there is no smoke. But I don't fear snakes, so I don't see snakes where there probably are snakes. My only experience with them on the Peninsula—but that is another story.

Until I came to Cranberry Point I was never particularly interested in birds. The *idea* of a bird is fine, combining as it does all the poetic elements of song and flight and freedom and beauty; but in actual practice I always had found birds to be silly, brainless, noisy creatures with rather dirty habits. A few—the thrushes, some of the sparrows, the catbirds in mating season—produced lovely music, but most of them just squawked or chittered in a very irritating manner. Anybody was welcome to my share of the birds.

I have had to revise my thinking on the subject. There is something to be said in favor of the birds, after all. I doubt if I ever become a dedicated ornithologist, but I find myself giving more and more time to watching our feathered friends.

The most common and obvious birds on the Peninsula are the herring gulls. They are extremely handsome, almost two feet long, with dove-gray mantles, black wing-tips and yellow hooked beaks in sharp contrast to their over-all snowy whiteness. I've known them all my life, in a distant sort of way, and I've always conceded their picturesque value to the seaports and harbors of New England. But it wasn't until I came to the Point and sat like a troglodyte in my cave of logs, unseen but seeing, that I came to understand them better and to like them.

Here I see them, not showing off for tourists, but living their private lives as they were intended to be lived. They sit on the ledges and oil their feathers at high tide, and at low tide they scour the exposed pastures of seaweed for mussels, crabs and urchins. Given too tough a shell to crack, they soar high and drop it, usually on a rock but sometimes on my roof, closely following the falling object to earth to guard it against highjackers because there is always some smart aleck who would rather steal his brother's dinner than go find one of his owr. When such a raid is successful the air is filled with cries of righteous indignation. Then the offended party sulks on a rock for a few minutes until his naturally philosophical temperament triumphs, when he sets out to find another tidbit.

Gulls are more teachable than I would have thought possible for bird-brains. I used either to burn or to bury my garbage, but one day, pressed for time, I threw some sandwich trimmings and stale doughnuts out onto the ledges, planning to attend to them later. Within minutes, the gulls were on the spot, scavenging like mad. Now they wait for the daily handout, and what surprises me is this: I can come and go empty-handed nineteen times a day, and they will ignore me, but the twentieth time, when I have my scraps in hand, they come flocking in from all directions, screaming and mewing and calling each other names, to snatch the broken bits of yesterday's biscuits before they touch the ground. I'm suddenly the center of a maelstrom of great white wings, fierce yellow beaks, and hoarse, sweet cries. It's a little daunting, but it's exciting, too.

Gulls like to fly. They fly in order to get places, but they also fly for the fun of it. There are, a little way from the front door of the cabin, a few stunted fir trees, perhaps eight feet tall. When the tide is high and there is no scavenging to be done and the gulls are bored with just sitting around, they fly figure eights in and out of the firs for absolutely no reason whatsoever except the satisfaction of completing the slalom course successfully. Then they go back

and sit on the rocks. And I have seen, on windy days, individual
gulls experimenting with air currents, practicing the art of gliding,
of using to best advantage the up and down drafts. Only the hum-
mingbird, I am told, can fly backward; but I saw a gull make a rear-
ward landing. He wasn't flying, it's true; he was gliding. But he
did land backward with great accuracy on the six exposed inches of
a tide-washed boulder. It was a very stylish performance.

I am as conscious of the swallows as I am of the gulls, because I
live intimately with them. Ours are cliff swallows, and they choose
to regard the cabin as a cliff, building their pouch-shaped nests
under the eaves. They are blue-black, with rosy breasts, and they
are a very restless tribe. From dawn till dark they are on the wing,
taking short, swooping flights from their nests and back again. They
chatter continually, even when flying, but their chatter reaches a
crescendo with each safe return from these excursions, so that the
rooms are filled constantly with their light and happy voices. It's a
pleasant sound against the deep roar of the surf and the sighing of
the wind.

There are less pleasant features connected with having them for
close neighbors. Unfortunately, one of their nests was directly over
the kitchen window, so that every morning my first act of the new
day was to wash the outside of the glass, because who wants to
view the lovely panorama of the islands, while doing the dishes,
through a murk of swallow droppings? On these occasions I would
tell myself that I was going to climb up and tear that nest down.
I'd get out the stepladder and arm myself with the putty knife, and
then I'd look up and behold the two little faces of the householders
gazing trustfully down at me from the small openings at the top of
the pouch. My heart would fail me, and I'd put the ladder and the
knife back where they belonged.

Then one August the matter was taken out of my hands. It had
been a peculiar day from the beginning. There was no wind at all,
in itself a rare thing on the Point; but a great surf was running, what
they call here an "old" sea, the edge of some distant and violent
storm. All day long it had piled in tiers onto the ledges, running
far above the high-tide mark into the grass and bushes. The gulls

flew low, their mewing subdued and anxious, and the dog refused to amuse himself, but stayed close to my heels. Just before sunset, as my sister and I were eating our supper, we heard a dull thud, and a cloud obscured the dining-room window. The swallows' nest over the kitchen had fallen down of its own accord, in the dead calm, and had completely disintegrated into a puff of dust.

It was on that day that I came to a partial understanding, for the first time, of the influence of signs and portents on primitive man. Even my sister and I, who fancy ourselves as intelligent women of some worldliness, were halfway under the spell of the day. We would not have been surprised, after the swallows' nest fell down for no good reason as a climax to hours of strange tension, if something perfectly dreadful had happened: an earthquake, or a tidal wave, or the end of the world. In fact, we almost expected it to happen, but it didn't.

What became of the dispossessed swallows? At first they couldn't believe their bad luck, but kept flying back to the site of their nest, fluttering confusedly under the eastward eaves. Then they tried unsuccessfully to move in with their more fortunate friends under the southern eaves. Then they went away.

The following spring I arrived on the Point ahead of the swallows. It seemed very quiet without them. Suddenly, in the middle of the brilliant forenoon of May 14, a wreath of them, like leaves blown by the wind, whirled under the cabin eaves where their nests had been each year. The lucky ones set up housekeeping at once in their old homes, but those whose nest had fallen down were not dismayed. They began immediately to build again, bringing with infinite labor and patience the tiny beakfuls of mud and saliva of which their gourd-like nests are constructed. I should have discouraged them right then by tacking a piece of screening over the area, but, fascinated by their activities, I let the moment pass. So again I have to include window-washing in my daily routine of chores.

I read in a book that the great blue heron nest only, in this region, on an island off Mt. Desert which has been set aside as a sanctuary. Therefore when I saw them wading and fishing at low tide on the ledges in front of the cabin, I was very careful to do nothing to disturb or offend them. They'd come a long way, I thought—these beautifully plumaged, four-foot birds—for a meal, and the least I could do was to act the considerate hostess.

One Sunday Grattan Condon—an artist by profession but like me a beachcomber at heart—rowed me out to Sheep Island, one of the little Sally Islands that guard the Peninsula. We were going to explore it and pick up whatever we could find in the way of interesting driftwood, shells, pebbles and other debris. Penetrating the tangled growth that covers the crest of the island, we stumbled on a heronry. In the tops of half a dozen dead trees were platforms of sticks on which roosted half-grown blue herons. Hearing us thrashing around in the underbrush below, they were doing their best to simulate dead branches, thrusting their long necks and slender heads straight into the air and swaying convincingly with the on-shore breeze.

So much for what you read in books! Hereafter I shall be less tender of the sensibilities of visiting blue heron. It's less trouble for them to fly here from Sheep Island than it is for me to go to the village for my mail.

A bird that interests me particularly is the raven. They are black birds, very like crows but twice as large, with shaggy throat feathers where the crows have sleek necks, and a true croaking call where the crow articulates clearly "Caw." Ravens coast with horizontal wings, while crows bend their wings upward when gliding. The reason that ravens interest me is purely intellectual. They have been used repeatedly in literature as symbols of disaster and harbingers of doom. Two centuries before the birth of Christ, Plautus wrote direfully in *Aulularia*: "It was not for nothing that the raven was just now croaking on my left hand." Seventeen hundred years later, John Gay observed pessimistically:

> That raven on yon left-hand oak
> (Curse on his ill-betiding croak:)
> Bodes me no good.

And everybody knows about Poe's raven, who, when entreated to take its beak from out the writer's heart, quoth "Nevermore."

My ravens aren't like that at all. A pair of them live over across the gully in a hackmatack tree, and they are much more sinned against than sinning. When they go down to the shore to scavenge a meal, the gulls gang up on them and chase them away; and when they try to pick a few strawberries in the front yard, a very small sparrow who has a nest in a bush there rises wrathfully and attacks them. Because she is so much quicker and more maneuverable in flight than a raven, she is able to maintain a position at the back of her victim's neck, pecking viciously at his head. This is understandably disconcerting, and the poor clumsy raven flees in disorder, croaking dismally, to the safety of the hackmatack.

Even in their family relationships ravens are ill-starred. One evening I saw all the gulls streaking out to sea to follow a lobsterboat into the harbor, and the sparrow was apparently busy elsewhere. So the ravens ventured timidly down to the shore, where they scratched around for a while on the clear coast and then sat side by side on a boulder. It was a lovely time of day, with the sun casting long rays of level golden light over the ocean, and the surf slow and gentle. The romance of the hour affected the ravens, and they started what would have been in any other birds billing and cooing. They sidled awkwardly up to each other and began bashfully to stroke each other's necks. I was touched by this display of affection, until they fell off the boulder. Carried away by their emotions, they moved too near the edge and over they went. After a moment's stunned silence, they picked themselves up off the shingle and flew sadly home, their mood destroyed.

I feel sorry for them. They may croak all day in yon left-hand hackmatack, if it's any comfort to them. Nobody here takes them seriously. The only lore connected with them has to do with the weather. If you see a raven flying north it's going to be warmer, and if he's flying south it will turn cold. That's what they say here, but nobody believes it.

Then there are the wrens and finches and robins and a dozen kinds of sparrows. There are many varieties of ducks, and there are the loons who puzzle the gulls by diving at a distance and suddenly surfacing in the middle of a complacent group and causing great consternation. There are the eagles, who pose on dead stubs, looking noble; and the curlews who come in late August, filling the air with their flute-like whistling, to eat their fill of blueberries before continuing their migration south; and the flocks of little pipers flying fast in close formation almost at water-level, presenting first their dark backs and then, as they wheel in a tight turn, their lighter undersides, so that a pinch of silver-dust seems suddenly to blow across the deep blue of the sea. There are the double-crested cormorants, huge birds almost three feet tall, who stand for ten minutes at a time with their wings stretched to full five-foot extent, drying their feathers. It makes your arms ache in sympathy to watch them. And there are the sea pigeons, plump little birds so tame or stupid that you can walk almost to within touching distance of them as they peck about the rocks; and many, many others.

I am alone on the Point. The only houses within sight are on Crowley Island, way over on the other side of the harbor entrance. I never hear the sound of neighbors' voices calling, of car doors slamming, of radios turned high, of any human activity. When the wind buffets the cabin, riffling the shingles, and the surf rolls endlessly in; when thick fog reduces my world to a small circle of moisture-beaded grass and ghostly bushes; or when day is done, and the boats are all safe in harbor, so that the sea stretches wide and empty to where 'Titm'nan Light hangs like a low star in the eastern sky—then I could feel lonely and forsaken, were it not for the animals and birds. Their ways differ from mine, but we all live and breathe, eat and sleep, rejoice and despair on a common ground that we all love. I cannot be lonely, aside from the inherent loneliness shared by all mankind, with this myriad life about me.

The wild things have done more for me than to provide me with a bulwark against loneliness. The first lesson to be learned, if you wish to see them at their natural best, is to be still. You must sit very quietly for a long while, until to them you seem a part of the earth. It is a strange thing, but soon this physical stillness expands into a quietude of mind and spirit, so that you are lapped in an almost palpable peace. The breeze comes in off the sea, scattering diamond spray, and the salt grasses toss. Bees hum about a wild rose bush. A flock of pipers skims along the water's edge, a field mouse scurries across a rock, and over all the sun shines down sweetly. It is then that at last, dimly and with a feeling of tremendous discovery, you begin to understand the meaning of the words: "Be still. Be still—and know that I am God."

Once, a long time ago, I saw an ancient and beautiful tapestry on the wall of a museum. I have forgotten what it depicted—a lady and a unicorn, perhaps, or an armored knight with a white wolf-hound—because I was so enchanted with the ground on which these figures walked. With infinite pains the tapestrist had woven a turf composed almost entirely of tiny flowers starring the short grass. They were so minute, so varied and so perfect that they held me spellbound, and I thought that surely these must be the Elysian Fields, for nowhere on earth could such a thing exist.

I was wrong. It does exist on Cranberry Point. The soil here is so shallow that the basic covering is largely moss and lichens, interspersed with patches of stubby grass; and all through this cover, so modest that you must look closely to see them, are blossoms. In the spring there are deep purple, almost stemless, violets, and the furry white paws of ladies' tobacco—which here is called pussyfoot—and the white stars of the wild strawberry, and the dandelions' blazing suns. Tiny blueberry bushes not more than two inches tall are covered with pink waxen bells, and the cranberry vines put forth their diminutive rose-and-white lilies. There's yellow cinquefoil, and woolly gold-heather, and white bunchberry, and delicate lavender toadflax; and growing in impossibly thin and gravelly soil is the goldthread, each white blossom shy and lacy, but present in such numbers that the ground seems to be covered with a sprinkling of snow. The roots look like skeins of fine gold thread, which accounts for the name, and they were used by the Indians, because of their astringent properties, for the staunching of minor wounds.

All of these blossoms and many others are, because of the harsh conditions under which they grow, much smaller than average examples of their various genera. They are miniatures. Each part is microscopic, and yet each part is complete and without flaw. Such meticulous perfection on such a reduced scale is awe-inspiring. It makes you realize that size and flamboyance are nothing.

I'm not a passionate botanist. My delight lies not in pigeonholing an obscure species, but in all the attendant circumstances of finding even so ordinary a thing as the first daisy of the year: the looks of the sky that day, and the color of the sea, and the way the wind lifts the light branches of the birches, and the whole frame of the occasion. Nevertheless, I do make a rather unsystematic attempt to identify the plants of the Peninsula that are unfamiliar to me, simply because I like to know the names of things. A scholarly friend of mine tells me that this is a common attitude of mankind, based on an age-old superstition that calling a thing by name renders it powerless to harm you; so that back in Old Testament days one encountering a lion said, "Lion, lo, lion art thou and thy riddle lieth bare before me." Thus exposed, the lion presumably slunk away, defeated.

He may be right, but I think that there is a little more to it than mere superstition. To me it's a matter of reassurance. Finding a seashell or flower or bird the like of which you have never seen or heard described before, you are for the moment disoriented. You wonder whether you can believe the evidence of your senses, a very disturbing doubt. Then, finding that the object has a *name*, you regain your balance. Enough other people have traveled before you and observed the same phenomenon that it is accepted as existing and meriting a label of its own. You are not alone in this situation, you realize with relief, and the universe becomes again an orderly place in which you can feel reasonably secure. Or so it seems to me.

My system leans heavily on asking questions and reserves the chore of thumbing through reference books as a last extremity. Even by this sloppy method, however, I have learned some interesting things. I learned, for example, from a man who has one on his property, that if a balm-of-Gilead tree grows in your dooryard your house will never be destroyed by fire. Furthermore, he went on to tell me, a friend of his who also owned a balm of Gilead applied to his insurance agent for a reduction of rates, arguing that he was already at least partially insured by the presence of the tree. The soulless corporation refused his request, so in a huff he went home and chopped down his tree. Very shortly thereafter the house did indeed burn to the ground. I can show you the ruins.

I learned also that my instincts in regard to the really spectacular rugosa that are scattered all along the shore of the Peninsula just above the tide line were correct. These great, sprawling bushes bear enormous pink, red or white blossoms, very much like roses. They smell like roses, too, and are extremely showy and beautiful, but somehow they never seemed to me to belong here.

As it turns out, they don't. They have arrived within the memory of persons younger than I. When Bar Harbor changed so quickly from a simple fishing village to the summer social capital of the nation, the owners of the newly established great estates set about beautifying their grounds by importing various ornamental shrubs, among them the rugosa. These hardy bushes throve so well that soon they had to be restrained by extensive pruning. The cuttings were thrown into the sea and carried by wind and tide to the Peninsula, where they took root. Now they're all over the place, rejoicing in their escape. They're lovely, but I like the little indigenous dwarf wild roses better.

I learned about the alpine bearberry, a low moss-like evergreen that covers the ledges with a thick, springy carpet and is perhaps as instrumental as any plant in converting barren rock to productive soil. But its usefulness doesn't stop there. By steeping the fine, narrow needles and small black berries in hot water you can make a tea that is equally effective as a spring tonic or as a poultice for infections, cuts or abrasions. I must admit that I haven't tried this yet, but I fully intend to when occasion arises.

Then there's what is locally called rattlebox, and I'm going to have to call it that, too, since I can't find it in any flower guides. It is an insignificant plant, six or eight inches tall, bearing on its slender stem narrow, opposed leaves and flowers that consist of small yellow petals springing from a large, pouch-shaped calyx. The whole blossom looks rather like the head of a green parrot with a yellow beak. By mid-July it is done blooming and goes to seed. The petals fall off, and the whole plant turns reddish brown and becomes sere and lifeless. It's even less impressive now than before.

But if you are lying on the ground, as I often am, you grow gradually aware of a faint, fairy rattling all around you that seems to spring from nowhere and everywhere. The air is full of it—a dry and wispy sound that is inescapable. It's eerie but rather charming, this ghostly accompaniment to the sound of the surf and the mewing of the gulls. It's the seed of a million rattlebox, shaken in their pods by the wind; and it's a sound that will haunt you forever, in your quieter moments, once you have heard it.

To me, the two most interesting plants found on the Peninsula are the sundews and the pitcherplants, probably because their carnivorous habits appeal to a deplorably morbid streak in me. The sundews grow over on that part of Cranberry Point that looks and feels like a wasteland of the moon. It's a large barren tract surrounded by a fence of gnarled trees, most of them dead and skeletal, and it is always full of the sound of the surf and the tolling of the bell buoy near the Old Woman. It's a strange, unearthly place, eminently suitable for such strange plants as the sundews.

These are tiny, with a short stem bearing small white flowers rising from a little rosette of round, reddish leaves. Each leaf is hairy, and each hair is tipped with a drop of syrupy moisture which sticks to your finger if you touch it. When the sun strikes across a large bed of sundews this moisture glints and glistens, so that the ground seems to glow and shimmer. It's a pretty sight, but beauty is not the purpose of the intricacies of the sundew. Small insects, attracted by the glitter and by the blossoms, swarm carelessly about them and sooner or later find themselves stuck in the glue on the leaves. Then, very slowly, the leaf folds about its prey like a tiny fist and devours it. When the process of digestion is completed the leaf opens again and lies in wait for another victim.

I know that the whole process is purely mechanical, but there is something so apparently premeditated about it that it seems to be directed by a rather evil intelligence. It's a little frightening. I'm always thankful, after a visit to the sundews, that they don't put forth leaves six feet in diameter. In that case, nobody would be safe.

The pitcherplants are found over on the Big Heath back of the cemetery or on the small heath near Mill Cove. The blossoms grow on tall stalks, and they don't look like flowers at all, but like abstract and surrealistic impressions of flowers. They are bronze and green and red, and altogether difficult to believe. The leaves, too, are bronzy-green with delicate red veining. They're six or eight inches long and shaped like small pitchers with gracefully fluted lips. They stand erect and are always half-full of water, drawn from the earth or collected during rainfall. I'm told that during dry weather birds drink from the pitcherplant leaves, but I've never seen it done and I don't know whether it's true or not. The pitchers were designed to be traps for insects, which fly in and can't get out again because the inside surface of the leaf is covered with short bristles, all point-ing down, which prevent exit. So the insects fall exhausted into the water, are drowned, and are then digested by the plant.

I don't know why the pitcherplant's murderous ways bother me less than do those of the sundews. Possibly it's because their role is passive, while the sundews take aggressive action. Or it may be that I admire their bizarre and highly stylized appearance so much that I make subconscious allowance for lapses in behavior. Hand-some people often get away with what approximates murder? Why not handsome plants?

For a long time nobody could tell me the name of what I con-sider the most beautiful wild flower I have ever seen anywhere, and I was forced by this lacuna in local lore to consult a flower guide, which didn't list it at all. Identifying it now became a challenge, so I wrote to the University of Maine, which is very helpful in these matters, and was told that it is sea lungwort, known colloquially as oyster leaf. I'd like to know where this colloquialism obtains. Here it is known colloquially as "That blue and pink flower that grows along the shore."

Everything about it is beautiful: the large, oval, silvery-green-gray leaves; the trumpet-shaped flowers which are pink when they open but turn to a clear, pure blue within hours; and especially the habit of growth. The stems lie along the ground, radiating from a central taproot so symmetrically that the plant is a perfect disk, sometimes as much as four feet in diameter. The stems bear leaves along their entire lengths and the blossoms grow in clusters at the

tips. I can't tell you how heart-lifting it is to come across, on a bar
ren and gravelly beach, one of these great doilies of silvery greer
edged with a wide lace of pink and blue. You'd have to see it foɪ
yourself.

When first I came to the Peninsula my visits were limited to
summer time. Each year I spent three months here, and after a
while I grew to believe that I knew the place well. I had seen, I
thought, about everything: the pearly sheen of the sea just before
dawn, the violet play of lightning on jade surf during a midnight
thunderstorm, the breathless hush of high tide at noon, and the
boisterous whoop-and-holler of a three-day so'easter. I'd seen weeks
of diamond-clear weather and sat out eight days of solid fog which
had drifted down from the fog-factory, as the Bay of Fundy is re-
ferred to locally. I knew most of the people, I was familiar with
most of the fauna and flora, and I'd learned where to go digging
for clams and where to go looking for sand dollars. I was practically an authority on the place—or so I thought.

Actually I hadn't even begun to learn all there is to know about
the Peninsula, and now that I have spent each season of the year
here I know that I never shall learn it all. One lifetime is not
enough. As soon as one face of the land becomes almost familiar,
the season changes and a new face is presented, and you have it all
to learn over again. As autumn approaches, first single maples on
the heaths and then all the maples everywhere turn scarlet, and the
carpet of low blueberry bushes changes to a crimson that is almost
purple. The birches and poplars and hackmatacks become trees of
beaten gold leaf, and the tops of the rowan trees bow under their
load of orange berries. There is so much color everywhere that
light seems to come less from the sky than from a radiant earth, and
the glory is almost too much to be borne.

The birds and animals alter their ways in the fall of the year.
Foxes bark all night at the moon. The gulls abandon the inscribing
of their evanescent geometry against the sky and settle in great numbers on the blueberry barrens, pecking industriously and looking
oddly domestic, like a flock of barnyard fowl. The swallows gather

in preparation for their migration south. I have often seen them in other places strung like notes on a bar of music along telephone wires; but here there are no wires. Instead they use dead trees as assembly points. I can think of few things more decorative to a landscape than a weather-silvered dead tree full of swallows, etched boldly against the lemon and apple-green of an autumn sky.

The Peninsula lies across one of the several great migratory lanes of North America, so in the fall wedges of high-flying wild geese go over. Their strangely disturbing honking drifts down from the rarified cold heights, and domestic geese in barnyards listen and look up and, standing tall and trying vainly to take flight, answer in desperate appeal. Or great companies of lesser birds arrow in from the north and settle on the rowan trees, which are called roundwood berries here. Their twittering fills the air, and when they rise again, the rowan is stripped of all its fruit. The wrens and robins and sparrows depart, leaving behind only the gulls and ravens and crows.

Winter, too, is beautiful in a quieter, subtler way. The open ocean takes on a steel-hard brilliance, and the partly frozen coves and channels with their bare half-tide ledges are intricately marble-ized in black and white and deep blue. Nor is the land colorless. Red stems and the bleached gold of grasses thrust up through the snow, and where the wind has swept the ledges bare, lichens show olive and green and orange and garnet. The firs and spruce are black against the glittering sea. The voices of the gulls are still now, and they sit hunched on cakes of ice; but the ravens croak louder than ever. As the tide goes out the fragile shell-ice in the mouth of Beaverlily Brook falls and splinters on the rocks with a crystal, elfin ringing.

In 1957 I arrived at the Point early, when winter was past but spring not yet begun. The land was dead, its great bones and gentle contours showing through a tattered shroud of brown twigs and matted grass. But within a day or two a breath of green touched everything, a green so faint and tender that it seemed illusional. Then the alders shook out their powdery catkins, and the leather-wood bushes—which I had known in summer as coarse, uninteresting shrubs, the bark of which was used by the Indians as cordage—became masses of fragrant, pale yellow blossoms. Suddenly everything frothed into bloom at once: the violets and dandelions in the stony fields, the blue flags in the swampy places, and—all along the roadsides and in the woods, looking like tall angels in shining white —the shad bush and the sugar pear. I never saw so impetuous a spring anywhere. If you turned your back for a second you were in danger of missing something. I decided then that spring was my favorite season on the Peninsula.

That's what I think about every season here while I'm living it. They all go by so fast that I'm always left with questions unanswered and lessons unlearned. I always shall be. It doesn't matter. I don't particularly care about having a headful of information, anyhow.

Children sometimes say, to indicate that they can repeat a lesson perfectly by rote, "I know it by heart." Used thus, the expression is meaningless. There are great gaps in my information about the Peninsula and many things pertaining to it of which I am completely ignorant. Nevertheles, I know the Peninsula by heart. That's the way I have known it from the first moment when I, a stranger, set foot upon it. That's the only way it can be known—it, or any other place on the face of the globe. No matter how many facts you may gather or how much intelligence you may bring to bear on the study of any locality, unless you know it *by heart* you'll never know it at all

6. The Sober Years

ASIDE, POSSIBLY, FROM A DESERT, NO LAND could be much simpler than the Peninsula. There are only the ledges, the heaths and the scanty scraps of woods, held loosely in a frail net of narrow roads, the sea, and the wide sky. There are no magnificent cataracts, no towering mountain ranges, no plunging gorges to impress the senses and awe the mind. There is variety, but it is a variety contained within an original tight pattern that precludes the stupendous and bizarre. Nothing exists to distract from the clean functionalism of the place, so that in the end the great simplicity comes to be recognized for what it is, as actual and awesome a phenomenon as the more obvious Niagara or Everest.

Whether as a reflection of this countryside, or as a result of their means of livelihood, or because of qualities handed down from their ancestors, or for purely economic reasons, the people's lives are simple, too—almost as simple as they were a hundred years ago. The effect of the automobile, which has served to complicate life elsewhere, has been balanced by the fact that where there used to be a number of ways by which a man could earn a living, now there is almost nothing but the fishing and lobstering, augmented by a few jobs in service stations and stores and by roadwork. Consequently, the population is suffering a slow decline as those who had no heart for the sea have forsaken it and, lacking other occupation locally, have moved away to other places. In 1955, for example, there were sixteen births in Gouldsboro and twenty-seven deaths. Fifteen of the deaths occurred to persons over seventy years of age, to persons who had lived here always and knew this as their home which they could not possibly leave. Very few newcomers have arrived to make up the population deficit.

All over northern New England there are ghost towns, or towns that are almost ghosts, coming to life only briefly in summer when they receive the annual transfusion of tourist blood. The Peninsula hamlets are not like that. Although the population is decreasing, this is only a trimming away of the superfluous, who would have been of no particular value here anyhow, no matter what successes they may achieve elsewhere in other lines of endeavor. There remains the hard core of fishermen, the self-reliant prototypes of their early ancestors. They can survive and they will survive, being dependent only upon themselves and their skills, as they and those who went before them have always been. They pick up a few dollars—a very few, since this is not tourist territory—from the summer people, but they could get along without them. They know how to trim their sails to the winds of adversity, to jettison the unnecessary; in short, to simplify.

The fundamental physical aspects of living are about as simple as they can be. I don't mean that modern gadgets don't exist. Almost everyone has a radio, for instance; but a radio is no longer a luxury or a toy, but a necessary adjunct to modern living, even on the Peninsula. It has become incorporated into our whole scheme, so that without a radio we are lost. The Civilian Defense tells us to keep tuned for instructions as to what we are supposed to do next in the current air-raid drill; and the Weather Bureau warns us to keep listening for reports on the progress of the latest hurricane. We'll just have to accept the radio as very nearly essential, and the Peninsulans do so accept it.

But they use it as an essential. They listen to the news and the weather and fishermen's reports and then turn the thing off. I have seldom entered a house to find the housewife sitting with her hands folded, enthralled by the tribulations of some soap-opera heroine. She has other things to do and troubles of her own to worry about.

And I have never been into a house where the radio did chance to be running and been told to sit down and *hush*, as has happened to me in some other places. The Peninsulans hold the possibly primitive view that even trivial encounters with a corporeal neighbor are more valuable and interesting than listening to disembodied voices talking nonsense out of the ether. It's a harking back to the days when the sound of a voice and the sight of a face other than those of the members of the family were real events.

I have described the lobsterman's day, which isn't an easy one. His wife works hard, too. This is no fishing locality of poetic romance, where the women walk up and down the strand, gazing out to sea, wringing their hands and singing sad ballads. They're at home, up to their ears in housework. Some houses have running water, but many do not. Sometimes there isn't even a pump in the sink. The water must be carried in pails from a well or spring. It takes a great many pails of water, lugged in and heated on top of the stove, to do the weekly laundry for a husband and several small children. Yet from the clotheslines of Corea billow some of the whitest washings I have ever seen. The brilliant sun and the stiff salt breeze may be partly responsible—and one woman told me that there was nothing like hanging out in a good thick fog to bleachen-up your sheets; but most of the credit should go to what is known as elbow grease, or plain old-fashioned scrubbing.

Washing machines and vacuum cleaners and electric toasters exist on the Peninsula, but more women than not do without them. They are luxuries to which a lobsterman's income does not usually run. With a broom, a mop and a scrub brush, with a washboard, a pair of galvanized tubs and a set of old sadirons, and with a big kitchen range for heating the irons and for the endless cooking, the women of the Peninsula get through their work in good order.

In fact, I'm not so sure that they're not better off than many city housewives of my acquaintance who have completely electrified homes. In theory, these lucky women push a button and read an improving book while the gadget does their work for them; but it doesn't always work out that way. Things go wrong with gadgets. Then the housewife humbles herself before a service man who promises as a great favor to come next week and look at the automatic washer. In the meantime the dirty clothes pile up, the repair man doesn't come, and she has to make out as best she can by rinsing out a few things in the bathtub. A civilization that breaks down is much worse than no civilization at all, because it leaves you with nothing, not even the opportunity to use your own native abilities. Nothing much can go wrong with a tub and washboard. With them, you know where you stand and exactly what lies ahead of you. The backs of the Peninsula women may ache after they've finished a two-weeks' wash, but their nerves are still steady and their pride intact. That's worth a lot, to proceed under your own steam, asking favors of no one.

My visiting sister once said to me, "At first I thought all the kids around here looked exactly alike, but now I see that they really don't. It's just that they are all so scrubbed-looking and brown and cheerful, and all their hair is bleached by the sun, and they all wear clean old dungarees and T shirts. It's just that I'm not accustomed to such a uniform appearance of health and cleanliness in the city children I see."

That seems to me to be the perfect tribute to the endless diligence of the women of the Peninsula. And somehow they all seem to find time to knit bait bags and trap-heads, to tend dozens of houseplants, to crochet bedspreads, to piece quilts, and to give a coat of varnish to the worn place on the living-room floor.

Nor does their work stop at the thresholds of their homes. I've seen women on ladders, painting the window trim, and women at woodpiles, splitting kindling, and women pushing lawnmowers, jealously grooming their tiny, hard-won lawns. A man, they will tell you, can't be in two places at once, and take good hauling weather like this, "he" is outside. Women keep small flocks of hens and tend little vegetable plots and lavish attention on their flower gardens; and if you admire a particularly spectacular perennial border, its owner is more likely than not to tell you deprecatingly, "Well, it's something to keep me busy." Being kept busy is an end in itself, which seems to me to be an attitude with points in its favor. Busy people are seldom unhappy or bored or prone to get into trouble. Idle people are apt to be any or all of those things.

Everybody on the Peninsula is busy. That's why, I think, that most of the faces you see are serene, nobody has ulcers, and men and women of sixty-odd are considered to be at their working prime, with wisdom and experience compensating for the slower pace enforced by the years. It's *important* here still to be able to do a creditable day's work. It makes you Somebody. The saddest thing that can be said of a person is "Cal'late he's hauled his last trap" or "Guess she's scrubbed her last floor." It sounds like an epitaph, and it is virtually an epitaph, although the subject of the discussion may continue for a decade to walk around in the sun and rain. He is not despised for his idleness, but greatly pitied as having been deprived of a part of man's birthright.

Of course nobody can or wants to work all the time, and on the Peninsula, as elsewhere, nobody does. Not many people possess TV sets, the nearest motion picture theater is in Ellsworth, thirty miles away, and there are no concert halls or legitimate theaters at all, except briefly in summer. Then repertory groups and vacationing artists present plays and recitals up along the coast to the west and over on Mt. Desert Island, but these are outside the Peninsulans' world. They're too expensive, for one thing. Nobody can afford to spend three dollars apiece for a single evening's entertainment, with bait and gasoline and pot-warps costing what they do. Furthermore, they are strictly summer-people forms of diversion, where the average Peninsulan would feel out of place—albeit inwardly amused—surrounded by white flannels, dinner dresses, broad *a*'s, and comments like "Rahther provocative, don't you think?"

How then, with no packaged forms of entertainment available, do the people of the Peninsula fill their leisure?

Well, as in bygone days, the focal point of each day except Sunday is mail time, which in Corea is just before noon. From eleven o'clock on, the standard question is "Has the stage come in yet?" The "stage" nowadays is Holly Myrick's International truck, but it's entirely suitable that the old term should be retained from the past, along with the old flavor and social importance of mail time. Going to the store to see if there is any mail for you is now, as it was fifty years ago, a device by which you get to see everybody and to learn what's going on in town.

I like mail time. The men sit on the Liars' Bench, talking about the threat of a lobster strike if the dealers won't meet their asking price of thirty-five cents a pound for shedders, or quietly consigning to the lower regions the Bar Harbor-Yarmouth ferry, the big *Bluenose*, guilty of bringing into the market tons of cheaper Nova Scotian lobsters. There should be a law about the *Bluenose*, the consensus runs. The women stand in groups chatting, and dogs and children mill about. As I come in with my own dog at my heels, the three-colored, double-pawed cat on top of the candy case huffs up to twice her normal size and spits viciously at Caro—a matter of form, since she knows very well he can't reach her and wouldn't if he could.

One of the women asks, "Blueberries ripe down to the Point yet? All right if I come down and pick a few quarts?" and I say yes to both questions.

"Mail's in," Herb informs me, "but 'tain't sorted yet. They're still peckin' it over"; and indeed I can see the postmistress, Daisy Young, and Holly Myrick busy behind the partition of glass-fronted boxes that divides the post office from the store. Herb goes on, "There was a telephone call for you from New York. Claim they want you to call back when you come in. Got the number wrote down here." He hands me a torn scrap of paper, and I decide

I might as well place my call right then and there. "Doubt if 'twill be any use," Herb says. "Feller said he was goin' out to lunch and won't be back till 'round three."

"Three!" one of the women exclaims in shocked tones. "My, they must eat an awful big lunch in New York!"

Then Daisy calls through the wicket, "Mail's ready now," and we converge in an orderly manner on the distribution window. No, mail time hasn't changed much in the last half century.

Neither has the function of the store. It's still a social center, employment agency, and service and information bureau. I never leave the village for any length of time without stopping at the store to tell Herb where I'm going and when I'll be back. He then conveys this intelligence to anyone who may be looking for me. I've found a man to fix the pump, returned a borrowed book, received and accepted a dinner invitation, delivered a sundew plant to Hortense Condon, and determined the proper cooking time for goose-grass greens, all through the good offices of the store.

It provides another service new in my experience. I used to see occasionally, leaning against the wall near the door, two or three or half a dozen of the brightly painted buoys with which the lobstermen mark the location of their traps. They never all belonged to the same man—they were of different shapes and colors—and they changed from day to day. I assumed that Herb was venturing into the gifte shoppe business and selling them to city slickers to take home as souvenirs. I'd seen this practice in operation in the more effete communities up the coast to the west. Tourists will buy the oddest things; and I didn't blame Herb for turning an honest dime if he got a chance. Finally, out of curiosity, I asked him how much he charged for them.

He gave me a reproachful look. "By dear, them ain't for sale. Them belong to the boys." The boys, around here, are the lobstermen, be they aged sixteen or sixty. "Them things take a lot of time and money to make. Must cost close to a dollar apiece, time they're whittled out and painted and marked. So if a feller finds one floatin' around loose he picks it up and brings it in here. Sooner or later the owner'll claim it."

In my walks around the shoreline of Cranberry Point I frequently had found almost new buoys, probably cut adrift by the *Bluenose* and cast up by the tide. In my ignorance I had failed to realize their value. Sometimes I carried them home because they were pretty; and sometimes I left them where I found them. Now, if they're any good at all, I too take them to the store. So far my salvage efforts have certainly not contributed appreciably to the economy of the village, but they've done a lot for me. Every time I add a buoy to the collection behind the store door I feel less and less like a summer visitor and more and more as if I belong.

In the evening the store is still definitely a men's club. While there is no stated rule excluding women, there's no doubt in anybody's mind that at this time of day woman's place is in the home, or at least not in the store. I drive past and see through the big windows all the lean, brown coastal faces, shadowed and serious in the soft light, and I wonder what the men are talking about so gravely. I'll never know. On the one occasion when I had to invade the masculine privacy an absolute dead silence fell, the kind of silence designed to push me right straight back out the door. It was perfectly courteous treatment, but only my great need prevented me from retreating on my hands and knees.

I had discovered at dusk that one of the tires of my jalopy was almost flat. It would be flat by morning, when I was supposed to meet my sister at the Bar Harbor airport. I've changed tires in my life before, and I thought I could do it again; but I couldn't get the lugs started, the tire was getting flatter by the minute, and the light was draining fast away. I finally gave up. There was enough air left to get me to the store if I set out at once, I thought, and maybe Herb could suggest someone who would help me.

The silence settled as I entered and continued throughout the recital of my woes to Herb. Then, without a word, two men rose. "You got a jack and a spare?" one asked from the doorway; and in about three minutes the job was done.

"I can't tell you how much obliged I am," I said. "How much do I owe you?"

The younger, Ernest Woodward, looked surprised. "Why, nothing," he told me. "Glad to help you out."

"I know," I said. "But I was really in a jam. If there'd been a garage here I'd have gone to it, and they'd certainly have charged."

He started loading my tools and tire into the back of the car with an air of finality. "No law I ever heard of against giving a hand to a neighbor," he said. And that was that.

I've kept strictly away from the store after supper ever since. This business of segregating the sexes in public places after six P.M. may be slightly archaic, but I'm happy to string along with it while the equally archaic notion that one freely and cheerfully helps a neighbor in distress also survives from a pioneer society.

Only the stock of the store has changed in the last half century. You can still buy rubber boots and rope and lamp-chimneys there, but the wonderful variety exists no longer, because no longer is the community entirely dependent on the local emporium. The automobile has made it easy to get to Charley Small's supermarket up on US 1, or to Ellsworth, with its chain stores. Instead of the pickle barrel there is now the white enamel freezer full of ice cream and Birdseye products, and the big refrigerator with its dairy produce, fresh meats and soft drinks. The shelves are loaded with standard brands of canned and packaged foods. There's a rack of postcards, too, which Herb uses as his business barometer in summer. If he sells a lot of postcards, then he knows that trade is good. If the cards fail to move, then money is awful tight and it's time we changed Administrations.

However, there are limits to the concessions Herb will make to progress. I went in one day and asked for a package of ready-mixed flour, thinking to make myself some hot biscuits for supper. Herb told me with some disapproval, "I don't carry that stuff. No call for it 'round here. 'Round here, the women, they stir up their own biscuits. No *body* to them ready-mixes, we hold 'round here."

"In that case," I said, "I guess I'll eat just plain old bread and butter."

"No need for that," Herb told me. "You got flour down to the Point, ain't you? And shortenin'? All you need then is baking powder, and I got plenty of that. Won't hurt you a mite to mix up a batch of biscuit. Somethin' to keep you out of trouble."

"You think I need keeping out of trouble?" I asked.

"By dear," he said darkly and obliquely, "don't harm anybody to keep busy."

He placed a can of baking powder on the counter with such an air of authority that I meekly accepted and paid for it. What's more, I used it.

On Sundays there is no mail, but, as in the olden days, there is church. Each village boasts a church, but none of them is large and rich enough to support a full-time minister. Instead, they share ministers. For years, the Corea church was disused, and it was necessary to go to Prospect Harbor for services, to one of the churches about which the Rev. Margaret Henrichsen tells in her book, *Seven Steeples*. But now the young minister from Steuben, a little further Down East, comes over at two o'clock each Sunday afternoon to lead the righteous in worship.

At a few minutes before two the bell in the steeple sounds its summons, and people start climbing the hill to where the little white building, firm on the highest ledge in town, looks out over the harbor and the sea beyond. The bell has an unusually sweet, clear tone, and I can't tell you how good it seems, even to such a Laodicean Christian as I, to hear its voice drifting out over village, harbor and heath after so long a silence. It makes Sunday seem like Sunday once again, like the Sabbath day of my childhood. This feeling is underlined by the fact that Herb closes the store for an hour on Sunday, so that he too can attend. On other days it is open from early morning until as late at night as any of the men want to sit around and talk.

The first time I ever went to church in Corea was during the winter. The knife-edged wind was pouring down from the northwest, snatching the light snow that covered the ledges into the air and blowing it in wreaths and swirls out over the steel-gray harbor. The faces of the worshipers hurrying up the hill were pinched with cold in the thin sunlight, and altogether it was a bleak and desolate scene. I hoped, but without much conviction, that the church would be adequately heated. I didn't see how it could be, really, thrust up there on the top of the rock in the full sweep of the wind, with no protection on any side.

I underestimated the faithfulness of the men whose duty it was to start the wood fire in the morning and keep it going until church time. A wave of warm air met me at the door, and I saw that the top of the box stove at the back of the room glowed a rosy red. I'd always wondered, in summer, why the stoves in country churches were placed as far away from the chimneys as possible, so that a long and ugly stretch of black stovepipe ran the entire length of the interior, detracting from and marring the simplicity and austerity that characterizes New England places of worship. Now I understood why. Heat radiated not only from the stove but from every inch of the long pipe as well, so that every corner of the building was warm and comfortable.

But the warmth I encountered was more than a physical matter. Where I come from, a person puts on his Sunday face and manner, along with his Sunday clothes, when he attends the church of his choice. He goes quietly to his pew, sits down, and speaks—if at all— in whispers, and then only to the members of his family. Here it was different. People visited back and forth across the aisles, talking and laughing in normal tones. Several persons turned as I entered, and they all waved to me, calling "Hello, Miz Rich. Nice to see you," or "When did you get here?" or "How long you plannin' on stay-in'?" It was a wonderful atmosphere to enter from the bleakness without, very warming to the heart and spirit.

The bell sounded its final clangor and was still. Mrs. Young, the mother of the twins, took her place at the parlor organ and began playing a soft prelude to worship. Immediately all conversation ceased and all faces, turning to the front, grew serious and attentive. The young minister, who had been at the door greeting arrivals more in the manner of a cordial host than of a pastor, walked down the aisle to the pulpit. Now his face was grave, almost stern, and he seemed years older. He faced us for a moment in silence, and then with great dignity he welcomed us to the House of the Lord.

There were not many people there, and the little building was unadorned by candles or flowers or any of the appurtenances of worship to which I was accustomed elsewhere. Most of the congregation were dressed as on weekdays. A few women wore hats, but many of them had tied kerchiefs over their heads or were bareheaded. Only the men looked unfamiliar to me. I had seldom seen them hatless before in the years I had been here; but now, in respect for the time and place, they had removed their visored caps. Surmounting each bronze weathered face was a smooth white forehead, startling in contrast; and I realized suddenly that this was the true brand of the seaman, a hallmark impossible to counterfeit.

But in spite of the lack of pomp and the everyday aspect of the gathering, at the end of the hour I knew that I had been to church. There was an unmistakable atmosphere of true religious devotion throughout the entire service. No one was there to show off her new clothes, or to improve his business connections, or for any other reason than to acknowledge God and to receive help and strength from Him. The wind howled outside, the blown snow rattled against the windows, and from the windward side of the Peninsula came the muffled and angry rumble and mutter of the offshore rote; and within the warm shelter of the room the lobstermen who would tomorrow face again the biting wind and all the perils of the winter sea sang fervently

> Rock of Ages, cleft for me.
> Let me hide myself in thee.
> Unknown waves before me roll,
> Hiding rock and treach'rous shoal.

It was a hymn which they understood, and they sang it with a conviction that was moving and impressive. It would take a far more cynical mind than mine to remain unaffected in the presence of such obvious faith. The Peninsula churches, small and poor though they may be, are truly living churches.

Just as Sunday afternoon is church time, Thursday afternoon is library time. The nearest public library to Corea is at Prospect Harbor in a beautiful little gray-and-white building across from the store. Hanging in the small vestibule is a framed copy of the 36th verse of the 9th chapter of the *Acts* of the Apostles:

Now there was at Joppa a certain disciple named Tabitha, which by interpretation is called Dorcas; this woman was full of good works and almsdeeds which she did.

The Dorcas Society of Prospect Harbor, whose object is to raise money for various worthy local projects—in short, to do good works and almsdeeds—shares quarters with the library. The room on the left as you enter is the library, and the room on the right is the Dorcas room; and since the Dorcas Society meets weekly on Thursday afternoons, two birds are killed with one stone by designating that as library day as well. It's a practical arrangement. The building needs to be heated only once a week, and the librarian does not have to sit twiddling her thumbs between borrowers, but spends her free time working in the Dorcas room.

I'm fairly well acquainted with a number of public libraries. Since life without something to read is inconceivable to me, I have always upon moving to a new community immediately sought out the nearest library. Of all that I know, I enjoy the one at Prospect Harbor most. The selection of books is not great, since funds are limited. Much of the collection is the fiction that summer people have left behind when returning to the city—light love stories and whodunits, chiefly. That doesn't bother me, though. This is one library that I patronize less for the books than for the company I encounter there. I pick three detective stories at random and a book about the plants of northeastern America, and then go in to visit with the Dorcases.

A nicer bunch of women I never met. You can hear them laughing way out on the road where you have parked your car, and you can't believe that a group that is having such a good time is getting any work done. They are, though. There is always a quilt on the frame, with four or five women busy at the thousands of tiny stitches necessary for the quilting. Someone is always at the sewing machine, making aprons for the annual sale. Women are cutting wool into strips while others braid it and still others sew it into rugs. Everybody looks up and greets me as I come in, but nobody stops what she is doing. "Sit down," they say. "What's new over in Corea?" And their fingers continue to fly. I have a good time with the

Dorcas Society, but they make me feel lazy and useless. All year long they manufacture articles for the August sale, and as soon as it is over they start right in again working toward next year's sale.

Once when I went in there they had on the frame a quilt that I admired tremendously. The name of the pattern was Hearts and Flowers, and it was exactly what it sounds like: a delicate patchwork of hearts and flowers, all done in pastel shades. It was perfect for a young girl, and I wanted to buy it for a coverlet in my teenage daughter's bedroom; but it was already sold, they told me.

"We'll make you one like it, though," they assured me. "Or at least, we won't, but the Ladies' Aid will."

"Are you sure they will?" I asked, being unacquainted with the Ladies' Aid. "I want it *exactly* like this. Are you sure I can trust them?"

The building rocked with laughter, and finally Harriet Noonan explained. "The Ladies' Aid is the same group as this. The only difference is that we meet on Tuesdays in the Aid room up the road. Don't worry. It'll be all right." And it was. But I felt twice as lazy and useless as before, knowing that those women gave two afternoons a week, instead of one, to good works.

Almost everybody belongs to one or more fraternal organizations. Besides the Dorcas Society and the various Ladies' Aids, there are the Masons and the Knights of Columbus and the Pythian Sisters and others, just as there were years ago. The weekly meetings, along with mail time and church services, are fixed events which pin time down by the corners, so that it retains a definite shape. But there is still quite a lot of slack to be taken up, although not enough for all the things one wants and plans to do.

Summer is the busiest time, partly because it is the season for outdoor activity and partly because the population is augmented by the handful of inlanders who choose to vacation in this unlikely spot. In some other coastal areas where I have summered, life was carried on at two definite levels, that of the summer people and that of the natives. The two groups did not mingle socially. It's not like that on the Peninsula. The few outlanders are mostly considered as friends, and the feeling is reciprocal. Those who come back here year after year do so for only one reason, because they

love the place. They must of necessity be persons of simple tastes, interested in and delighting in the same things that absorb the natives. Barriers of diverse background, or of occupational and financial inequality, cease to exist in this community of interest. While the natives provide services such as laundering, selling fresh vegetables and fish, and doing repair work, these services are rendered and accepted more as favors than as menial employment. The fact that a woman has cleaned your cottage or a man has repointed your chimney does not stand in the way at all of your going on a picnic or to a fair together, or of your children being bosom cronies. This is an excellent state of affairs by which both parties profit, since each has much to offer the other of viewpoints, philosophies and information.

Long as the summer days are at this high northern latitude, they are never quite long enough, even though everybody gets up with the sun. Here that's pretty early, well before five in the morning. There's no nonsense about sunrise here, no having to wait for it to climb over mountains, buildings or trees. When it's time for the sun to come up, it comes up, hoisting itself clear of the watery eastern horizon, its rays shining levelly across the wastes of the sea and into the village windows. There's no nonsense, either, about people's rising. When the sun is up, it's time everybody was up; and everybody gets up. By five-thirty the whole Peninsula has breakfasted and is well started on the day's work.

This seems to me to be a very sensible way to live, although I can see that it wouldn't be very practical in some places. What's the use of getting up at four-thirty when the office doesn't open until nine? But here everyone works for himself and can make his own schedule. Nobody is going to catch a train or punch a time clock or submit to any other man-made regulating of time. Clocks mean nothing. You arise when it is light, eat when you are hungry, and go to bed when you are tired. If you're going to be up and doing for sixteen hours of a day, as most of us are, it doesn't make much difference which sixteen hours you choose, except that no portion of the day is quite like the first three hours after sunrise. The world looks so fresh and new then, with the sea all gold and blue and white, the grass bright with dew, and the air crisp and invigorating. You can put a whole day's work behind you in those three magic hours.

This sounds like a very disorganized and haphazard way to live, but it isn't. A natural discipline and intrinsic rhythm establishes itself, free from the strains and tensions of clock-watching. You have a sense of abiding by broad universal laws rather than of being bound by narrow and arbitrary rules. You feel free of bondage and yet secure in an order that governs the rest of the world around you—the march of fogs from the sea, the mating of foxes in the spring, the migration of birds in the fall. The pendulum of the clock has nothing to do with you, nor have its sweeping hands. Only the great pendulum of the tide can drive you away from the sand bar where you have been gathering blue mussels; only the slow hand of the declining sun can call you home from mulberry-picking on the heath. You experience the sense of wellbeing that comes from complete harmony with your surroundings, and you find it good.

Summer activities are multiple, but you can't often plan them in advance. Too much depends on the tide and the weather. You can't plan a picnic for a week from Tuesday, because by then the world may be blanketed in fog, or a three-day northeaster may be whooping and roaring. Picnics are conceived and executed on the same day.

My favorite picnic spot is Outer Bar Island, perhaps because it's not easy to reach. When there's an unusually low run of tide it's possible to get over there by walking across the exposed sand bar to Inner Bar Island and then scrambling ankle-deep in cold water along a rocky reef to Outer Bar. But you can't stay very long. The minute the tide turns you have to start back. If you wait too long you're going to be stuck out there for twelve hours, or until the next low tide; that is, unless you can attract the attention of a passing lobsterman who will take you off. If you plan to stay long enough to build a fire, boil lobsters and explore the island, it's necessary to go with a friend who owns a boat.

In my case, the friends are the Condons, and once a year at least we go over to Outer Bar with Josephine Stewart, who was a Crowley of Crowley Island before she married, and who owns half of Outer Bar. Of the six islands in the Sally archipelago, Outer Bar is much the best. Eastern and Sally are little more than bare ledges; Sheep and Western are crested with almost impenetrable copses of spruce and are rock-bound, providing no decent landing place; and Inner Bar is too small to be really interesting. But Outer Bar has everything. I'd love to build a house there and live in it if there were any way of getting off in winter, when the high seas lash it continually. There is a small beach on which to land, a little forest of pine and spruce, sheltered, open fields, patches of raspberries and gooseberries to pick, and at the seaward end great ledges over which the surf crashes, sending up lofty wind-blown geysers. There is even a sort of Roman bath among the ledges, a sixteen-by-twenty foot pool in the pink granite containing about three feet of water. This water is changed by every high tide. Between times the sun warms it sufficiently so that bathing in it is a pleasant experience. The same cannot truthfully be said of ocean bathing here, which comes more under the heading of an ordeal than a sport or pleasure. The water is so cold that your extremities remain numb for an hour after emerging.

But perhaps the real reason why Outer Bar so appeals to my imag-

ination is the stories connected with it. It is the island on which
George Crowley's great-grandfather—the British seaman who married one of the Young girls and established the Crowley name in
Corea—was washed ashore. But there was another seaman less fortunate than George's ancestor. About a hundred years ago his body
was washed up on Outer Bar. Since there had been no wreck along
this coast in a long time, he probably fell or was pushed from a passing vessel. The local authorities made a reasonable attempt to establish his identity and find his kin, but they failed. So the body was
buried on Crowley Island near the end of the sand bar, in what was
at the time an apple orchard.

The coast along here changes very fast, and within a decade or
two what was an orchard became a sand dune. In the course of the
transformation the skeleton of the stranger came to light. It was
buried again, a proceeding that occurred fairly frequently over the
next fifty years. By this time the bones were so familiar an old story
that even the children regarded them in a casual manner. When
Jo Stewart was a child, one of the games she and her friends played
when they were bored with everything else was to dig up the bones,
pile them on the shore, and try to put them together the way they
belonged. When they got tired of the puzzle, they buried it again
until the next time. She says she never had the slightest feeling of
revulsion; in fact, she guesses she assumed that all children, everywhere, naturally had a skeleton to play with, as a part of growing
up. It never occurred to her that it had once been a man.

But I can't help wondering what kind of man he was, and where
he came from. Did someone, somewhere, wait a whole lifetime for
him to return home? And more than anything, I wonder how he
would have felt about having the strong white bones that had carried his flesh and spirit about the world through times of hardship
and times of joy serve as a game for little boys and girls, playing
in the thin sunlight and crisp salt breeze on a bleak and surf-loud
northern coast. I hope he would have been pleased.

Once the Condons and Jo spent a whole afternoon trying to find
the skeleton again, but they couldn't. Either it had finally disintegrated to dust or been washed out to sea in a winter gale. I still

think about it, though, every time I walk along that stretch of shore. In the summer of 1957 there was another wreck on Outer Bar. It happened on an August morning when the fog was so thick that I couldn't see the little trees growing within thirty feet of the cabin windows. I could hear the surf, though, crashing on the shingle, and the wind was blowing hard and gusty from all directions at once. Most of the lobstermen stayed in harbor that day; but old Sam Colewell, who has taken his various boats in and out among the islands and channels for most of his seventy-odd years and knows the area like the back of his hand, went out in his *Ida B.*

He said later, in the store, that he was baiting his trawl and waiting to hear the moan of the whistle buoy, since he couldn't see beyond his bow, as a signal to change course into the channel between Western and Outer Bar. He'd done it scores of times. But the tricky wind deceived him, and he heard the whistle and struck the ledge off Outer Bar simultaneously. The impact ripped the bottom out of the *Ida B.* and she started to fill. He had no time to think; he did automatically what the years at sea had taught him to do: put her full speed ahead and rode over the ledge and up onto the end of Outer Bar on the next tremendous comber. Then he scrambled ashore. It was a miracle, everyone agreed, that he lived to tell the tale. As it was, he had to sit the tide out in the dense fog for five hours until he could wade ashore and report his loss. It must have been a long and dismal five hours.

I don't think any inlander can realize what it means in a fishing community when a man loses his boat. There is always the thought in every man's secret mind, "It could just as easily have been me." Every man responds as he hopes others would respond had it been he. That afternoon, as soon as the fog had thinned, the entire lobster fleet converged on Outer Bar to salvage what they could. They took out the engine of the *Ida B.*, and the little galley stove, and all Sam's gear, and carried them high on to the ledges, out of reach of the tide. Then they removed all the windows that weren't broken, and all the hardware and fittings, and added them to the pile. It was a good thing that they did, because the next high tide smashed the stripped hull into kindling wood.

Grattan Condon and I went out there the next day to look for good pieces of driftwood, which he uses to make frames for his marine paintings, and we came upon the salvage. It looked pathetic there on the bare rib of granite against the immensity of sea and sky: a few coils of line, some unmatched plates and cups, a rusty stove, a wooden bait tub, a heavy-duty battery, and some odds and ends of metal. It seemed so very little to show for a lifetime of hard work.

"It's too bad," I said. "Poor old man. I wonder what he'll do now. It'll be hard for him to stay ashore."

I underestimated the breed from which Sam Colewell springs. He never even considered staying ashore. Within a week he had acquired an old but seaworthy hull, installed his salvaged engine in it, and fitted it out with his rescued oddments. Within two weeks he was back at sea.

Summer is the time for all the big projects. One of the biggest a year or so ago was the auction for the benefit of the new school building. It had been decided at Town Meeting to close all the little one-and-two-room schools in the various hamlets and build a good consolidated grammar school at a central location halfway along the Pond Road. The school was built along modern lines, so that it at once became known as the Glorified Chicken Coop, and is still so known. Money for equipment over and above the bare necessities was lacking, so it was decided to hold an auction to make up the deficit. It was to take place in August at the Gouldsboro Town Hall up on US 1, a good time and place, since in August US 1 is crawling with tourists, few of whom can resist a country auction.

For weeks the committee in charge combed the Peninsula for donations. Anything in your cellar, attic or shed for which you had not found a use in the past three years, you were told, you probably never would find a use for, so you might as well put it in the auction. Never mind if it wasn't much good; it might be just what someone else was looking for. Those who had no old furniture, bric-a-brac or braided rugs to spare—and many Peninsulans need every stick they own—donated services. For example, a woman would engage to do a family washing for two weeks at whatever price the auctioneer could run the bidding to, or to baby-sit for four hours, or to supply a household with cut flowers from her garden for a month. Local artists gave pictures and the owners of the cannery at Prospect Harbor gave fifty cases of sardines. By auction day the Town Hall was crammed with articles too numerous and various to list.

The affair lasted from nine in the morning until eleven at night, and it was one of the best auctions I ever attended. The whole population was there, and hardly an out-of-state driver had strength of mind enough to go whizzing past this fascinating spectacle. The auctioneers were local men—one of the selectmen, the stage driver, the proprietor of one of the stores—and they really threw themselves into their act. I bought a two-gallon stone Bennington jug and a case of sardines, and I nearly bought a little old rosewood desk; but just when I thought it was mine a Cadillac with New York plates pulled up. I can't compete with the kind of money Cadillac owners possess, so I lost it. I'm not bitter. It was in a good cause.

I met Holly Myrick, one of the auctioneers, in the store at mail time next day and asked him how much money was realized. "Just about twelve hundred dollars," he whispered.

"Good. Is it a secret?" I whispered back.

"No. But I ain't been able to speak out loud all day. Wore my voice out that last hour at the auction. One thing—we won't have another for fifty years at the least. The whole Peninsula's picked clean as a whistle. I doubt if you could find a spare common pin on it."

And I guess he was probably right.

A fixed event of the spring is Armed Forces Day. There is, out on Schoodic Point, a Naval installation devoted to radio, radar and other means of communication. I guess. It's all highly hush-hush, and during the rest of the year you get a very cold scrutiny from the armed guard if you even slow down when passing the high gates. This is a small base of about two hundred men. It was formerly at Otter Creek, over on Mt. Desert Island. During the First World War, when methods of communication were less well developed than they are now, there was a great deal of difficulty in keeping in touch with Europe. Periods of silence would occur at the best and most powerful stations. A man named Allesandro Fabbri discovered, however, that clear reception was always possible at Otter Creek, so that a twenty-four-hour-a-day contact with Europe could be maintained. It was the only place in the Western Hemisphere where this was possible. The Navy awarded Fabbri the Navy Cross for his services and established at Otter Creek a station which proved invaluable.

In the interim between wars one of the Rockefellers who had a summer place on Mt. Desert declared himself willing to give a very large sum of money for the improving of the island in the way of establishing bridle paths, park areas and things of that sort. Otter Creek was in the middle of the planned project, so Mr. Rockefeller prevailed upon the government to move the base over to Schoodic just across Frenchman Bay, where the reception was equally good He partly financed the move, so the change was made. But that concerns us little now, except that the installation has expanded over onto the heaths above Corea, where there are tremendous towers, sinister-looking, barn-like buildings, and a large sign, KEEP OUT! I don't know what they do out there on the heath, but, whatever it is, they sometimes manage to foul up completely radio and TV reception in the village.

On Armed Forces Day security measures go into abeyance for one afternoon, although I suppose the really top secrets are kept under wraps. The base is open to the public, and people like me, who have been dying to know what's behind that high fence, seize this opportunity to find out. It's quite an occasion. You are welcomed aboard (the Navy is doggedly nautical, even when "aboard" is a fenced area of ledges and spruce trees) by a group of officers and assigned as a guide an enlisted man who has obviously been drilled and *drilled* in manner and procedure. Everything is spit and polish and terrific courtesy as you are shown the motor pool, the living quarters, the mess, the hospital, the shops, and finally the various instruments of communication. It's very interesting indeed, although the Navy and I had a slight skirmish in the shop, which is equipped with the best and most impressive of power tools. The gentleman who had been told off to explain these tools to dopes like me finished his exposition of the drill press by stating that you could even bore square holes with it.

That I couldn't let pass. "Wait a minute," I said. "You can't bore a square hole with a round drill. Or if you can, I'd like to see how it's done."

He looked stunned. I'll admit I do look the housewife type who would be more at home with an egg beater than a drill press. Quickly recovering his composure, he said that no, of course you couldn't, actually. You had a heavy steel square that just fitted around the drill. It was under enormous pressure, and as the drill proper bored a round hole the corners within the collar chipped out, making a square hole. That matter cleared up, we parted friends.

The Navy contributes more to the Peninsula than Armed Forces Day. If nothing else, the personnel add an air to the streets of the villages, with their immaculate uniforms and their cars carrying German or English or Alaskan license plates. But it's more than that. In times of emergency the Navy ambulance is at the disposal of the civilian population. During the summer of 1957 the life of a man in Corea suffering a bad heart attack was saved by the Navy ambulance, which is equipped with an oxygen tank. He never would have arrived at the hospital in Ellsworth alive if it hadn't been for that. The Navy children attend the public schools. Since many of them have lived on bases all over the world, they often have enlightening bits of information to offer to geography classes, and interesting souvenirs to exhibit. Some of the local girls marry men from the base; and my oil man, who was born in Brooklyn, fell so in love with this coast that when he and the Navy severed connections he returned, married, bought a house in Birch Harbor, started a family, and is a good and enthusiastic citizen.

Quite a bit of literature has been founded on the degeneracy, due to generations of inbreeding, of isolated and bypassed parts of New England. This does not obtain on the Peninsula. Starting with the English Crowley who was washed up on Outer Bar, there has been a constant introduction of new blood. The forebears of the Andersons of Corea arrived a generation ago on a Norwegian fishing vessel, for example, and Katie Young, as I have said, was born in Hungary. Vincent Young met and married his wife, Noel, while he was with the Armed Forces in Belgium; and there are many other instances. And, of course, we always have the Navy at Schoodic.

There is also a small group of outsiders who have come from other places to make the Peninsula their permanent home. Some of these are men and women who have reached retirement age, as the modern world judges, and are spending their declining years here. On the Peninsula the age of retirement is regarded differently. You retire when you are under ground, and not before. Therefore most of these people have found, happily, that here at least they are still regarded as active citizens with many useful years before them. One, a psychologist, serves as advisor and guidance director not only in the local schools but in schools of adjacent communities. Another, a Navy chief, operates an electrician's shop; while still another has set up in his back yard a powerful telescope trained on the heavens. Whenever the light is on over his garage door he is At Home to anyone who wishes to view the stars and have them explained.

Not all these newcomers are over sixty-five. Some younger people have come, just because they like it; and—not being lobstermen —have devised ways of making a living in order that they may stay. Syd and Sandra Browne are artists who also own and operate an art gallery in Winter Harbor. Chenowyth Hall is an excellent sculptress who assists Miriam Colewell, a writer, in the Prospect Harbor store and post office. Bernice Richmond owns, writes, edits, publishes and prints the little *Peninsula Gazette,* the weekly newspaper without which no Peninsulan could get along. It fulfills the true function of the small-town weekly by leaving world events to the Bangor and Boston papers and concentrating on purely local news—parties, weddings, illnesses, and who is reroofing his fish house. Since inbreeding is not only a physical matter, but a matter of ingrown ideas and attitudes as well, this small group so thinly sprinkled about the Peninsula contributes just as truly to the health of the body politic as does the introduction of new blood.

One summer a few years ago there was great excitement on the Peninsula. A movie director named Jean Oser, sponsored by Twentieth Century-Fox, arrived in Corea to make a documentary film about lobstering. Coreans aren't used to this sort of thing and were inclined to take a rather dim view. They weren't going to dress up like fools and put on some sort of idiotic act for any such silly project. They had traps to haul and work to do, and they had no time for nonsense. Let the man take his foolishness elsewhere

Jean Oser surprised them. He and his cameramen didn't expect any picturesque costumes and acts of derring-do. All they wanted was an accurate record of life in a community devoted to lobstering. They went out with the fleet at dawn, perched dangerously and uncomfortably on the sheer crags of Sheep Island for shots down into boats, and wandered unobtrusively about the village for sequences of everyday life ashore. They behaved, in short, like men with a job to do and the ability to do it—a manner and attitude that the people of Corea recognized and respected. Very soon the whole population was taking the idea in stride, going about business as usual, which was exactly what Jean Oser wanted.

I saw the movie on TV two years ago. It was called *Lobster Town*, and has, I understand, been shown in forty-one countries and translated into twenty-one languages. The Army shows it in Germany, Japan and Korea nowadays as an example of one way of life in America. It's an excellent job, honest and unadorned. It's also very beautiful. The lobstermen don't need costumes. Their everyday wear is picturesque—the hipboots, peaked caps and oilskins—whether they know it or not; and their weathered faces are extremely photogenic. As for background, it would be impossible for a cameraman to go wrong with all those longlegged wharfs and staunch little boats against the islands and the ledges and the great, curling combers rolling in. He could shut his eyes while at work and still have a good picture.

When I told Marcia Spurling that I had seen the movie she asked at once, "Did you see my cow?" Then she started to laugh. "I still had a cow then, the only one in the village, and Mr. Oser wanted to put her in his picture. He thought it would be nice to have me feeding her a bunch of daisies. Now you know as well as I do, Louise, that cows won't eat daisy blossoms if they can help it, but I was willing to try. We spent one whole forenoon out in the pasture trying to get that cow to cooperate. All she'd do was sniff at them and turn her back to the camera. Finally she got disgusted, I guess. She turned her back again, up went her tail, and—well, what she did wasn't very ladylike. I thought the cameraman would die laughing, but Mr. Oser didn't think it was very funny."

Jean Oser travels all over the world making documentaries, but between trips he and his wife come back to the little cottage that they built on the scrap of land he bought after making *Lobster Town*. The Peninsula got under his skin during that brief period of filming, just as it has got under mine.

On the Peninsula you never can tell in the morning what the day will bring forth. Once an enormous sea turtle wandered into one of the weirs and became tangled in the nets. The owner of the weir towed it into harbor and confined it in Don Anderson's lobster pound. The whole village dropped everything to go look at the turtle. It must have weighed well over a thousand pounds. I have a picture of two quite large boys sitting cross-legged on its back with plenty of room to spare.— Oh, sure, I went to look at the turtle, too. Unless you can enjoy that simple sort of diversion the Peninsula is no place for you.

In 1957 there was an unexpected event that might almost be termed an Act of God. It happened when the fortunes of the village were at very low ebb. For various reasons the price of lobsters all along the coast had dropped to the point where it simply did not pay to haul. Therefore what was called locally a lobster war went into effect. The lobstermen from Kittery to Eastport refused to go out unless they could be assured thirty-five cents a pound from the buyers. Being put on the beach in the summer, when the demand for lobsters is usually greatest and the labor of hauling least difficult, is a real tragedy to a hamlet that depends almost entirely on this source of income; but the men of Corea felt obliged to cooperate for the common good. They puttered at odd jobs ashore or sat unhappily around the store, at loose ends for occupation.

All summer long we'd seen passing along the horizon small tugs towing huge barges of pulpwood from Down East to some port to the west. They passed well out by 'Titm'nan Light and were no concern of ours, except that we were glad it was the islands near Jonesport and Machias that were being stripped of their blackgrowth, rather than our own. Right in the middle of the lobster war, however, the pulp became very much our business. A tremendous "old" sea rolled up out of nowhere, and one of the barges lost her load directly off the Peninsula. The four-foot logs strewed the ocean as far as one could see and came tumbling onto the shore with every breaker. The entire shoreline was walled with cords of pulpwood, and more came in on every tide.

Nobody had to be told that pulpwood is expensive to cut and ship, or that this was a plain case of salvage, with its accompanying remuneration. The only question was how much the lumbering company would be willing to pay to get its wood back. It turned out that they would pay handsomely by the cord, and every man in the village left the Liars' Bench and set to work. There must have been fifty cords on Cranberry Point alone, but every stick was picked up and sold back to the company. The pulp salvage was truly a Godsend to the village—or one of those occasional relentings to which the sea is subject, perhaps in recompense for demanding so much of those who depend on her. Not that salvaging pulp is easy work; but at least the sea gave an opportunity to those who were willing to take it at the cost of lame backs and sore muscles.

But it doesn't take an auction or a movie filming or a salvage operation to keep the Peninsulans occupied or entertained. Everything, no matter how trivial, is important and interesting. Take the affair of Dinah's being marooned on Inner Bar Island. She went over there with a visiting friend, walking across the long bar which is exposed at low tide and which is the best place to find sand dollars. She'd made the excursion many times before and knew that she had to watch the tide; but she and her friend became absorbed in exploring the back side of the island, and when they arrived back at the bar it was under eleven feet of water. They stood there helplessly until Vincent Young, the husband of Noel, came past in his lobsterboat on his way into harbor from tending his traps. Highly amused, he picked them up and put them ashore.

When Dinah told me about it, I, knowing that she had had no money on her person, said, "Well, I guess I'd better see about paying him. Did you mention the matter to him?"

She said that she had, but he'd told her to forget it, that the big laugh he got was pay enough. And in a way I guess it was, because now, several years later, people still refer to the incident and still laugh about it.

However, at the time I felt that I owed Vincent something, so I went to the store for a conference with Herb. I started to tell him the circumstances, but he cut me short. "Yup, I heard about it already," he said, and laughed.

"Now," I said, "I want to give Vincent some token of my appreciation. Does he drink?"

"Nope," said Herb.

"Does he smoke?"

"Nope," said Herb.

"Well," I asked, becoming a little desperate, "does he like candy?"

Herb said yes, Vincent had a great old sweet tooth. So I bought the best box of chocolates that the store afforded and left it with Herb to give to Vincent, with my heartfelt thanks, the next time he came in. And that, I thought, took care of that.

I couldn't have been more mistaken. A few days later I encountered Vincent, who had acquired some fresh mackerel out of a herring weir. He asked me if I wanted some, and I said yes, because mackerel nowadays are hard to come by. I assumed he was selling them, but he said no, this was in return for the candy. I suppose I could have bought another box in return for the mackerel, but there's a lot in knowing when you're licked. I could see from where I stood that this game could go on forever unless someone hollered Uncle; so I thanked him very much, took the mackerel home, cooked them and ate them. They were good.

This brings up one of the things that I find remarkable and endearing about the people of the Peninsula. They really possess very little and have a hard time making ends meet, but with that little they manage to create an impression of riches and bounty. If you go into a house where a woman is baking brambles, she is certain to press upon you a bagful, saying, "Here, take these home for your lunch. Don't know how good they are, but they're fresh, anyhow." They're always delicious. Or the cultivator of a small vegetable plot will insist on your accepting a huge head of lettuce or a basketful of tender beet greens. A man who has spent the morning laboriously digging clams will tip out of his bucket onto the floor of your car enough to make a good chowder and dismiss your thanks with, "Oh, 'tain't nothin'." Women give you flowers from their gardens, telling you that unless they're picked they'll stop blooming; or if you admire the candle holders some of them make by cementing tiny shells to the tops of the doughnut-shaped corks used to float nets, they'll present you with a pair. When you point out that those things sell for seventy-five cents at a gift shop up on US 1, they'll say, "More fools, then, the folks who buy them." There's no limit to the generosity of the Peninsulans.

Summer with its mild flurry of activity is only the minor portion of the year and soon over. The wild roses and sea lungwort fade and die, and goldenrod and asters take their place along the narrow roads and stony beaches. The blueberries ripen and then the cranberries, and the tops of the rowan trees—called roundwood here— bow heavily with orange fruit. In the swamps single maples blaze —torches which kindle the countryside until all the world flames scarlet and gold. By day the sea is a cold, hard blue, and at night the long streamers of the Borealis leap and crackle in the polar sky. The swallows assemble and depart, and great flocks of fall robins wing in from Canada to settle on the rowans and strip them of their berries before continuing south. Wedges of geese go over in the rarefied heights of the clear and luminous atmosphere, and the wind takes on a chilly edge. The *Bluenose*, to the general gratification, goes onto her winter schedule of two, instead of seven, trips a week. The summer visitors pack up and go home, leaving behind them a Peninsula that for a brief space seems strangely unpeopled. It feels

like a large room after a big party is over and the guests have departed, when the members of the family look about them at the
emptiness and disorder, and then sit down gratefully to relax and
talk it over in peace and quiet.

It's not too unlike that, either. After a short period of adjust-
ment to a regime of fewer contacts, less excitement and no unusual
demands, the Peninsulans, as does a family on the day after the party,
return to routine.

Fall is the loveliest time of all the year. The days are balmy and
bright, the nights crisp, and the world too beautiful to believe.
Now, instead of staying in the house doing washings for pay, the
women stay outdoors doing all manner of things for their own fun
or satisfaction. They walk along the shore picking up Irish moss
or shells, or rake cranberries down on the Point, or pot up in
readiness for winter the houseplants that have been summering in
gardens. And they go on all the expeditions for which they have
not had time during the summer, driving to Ellsworth or Bangor or
especially to Bar Harbor, where the fancy branches of New York
stores are holding wonderful clearance sales to save themselves the
trouble of shipping left-over stock back to the city before putting
up the shutters for the winter.

Many of these autumnal expeditions are local. People go to the
little cemeteries to dig up and take home for winter keeping the
geraniums with which they decorated the graves on Memorial Day.
Or they visit the various family reunion grounds, to make sure that
the lunch shelters are snug against the imminent foul weather. This
is a great area for family reunions, since every family has so many
branches and ramifications. Around the Fourth of July the *Gazette*
is filled with accounts of these get-togethers, where the attendance
sometimes runs into the hundreds. Most families maintain a reunion
ground, usually on the site of their original common progenitor's
dwelling. The buildings have long since vanished into dust, leaving
only a cellar hole surrounded by grown-up fields and worn-out
orchards—pleasant, half-wild places which are, on reunion day,
thronged with those who can trace their being back to this spot.
Then the air is filled with voices and bustle as lunches are unpacked

and men and women who have never before met try to determine their exact relationship to each other. But in the fall there is only a bright stillness, threaded with the murmur of bees about wild asters and the sighing of the breeze in the tall, neglected grass. Then you can sit quietly in the sun on an overthrown stone wall and think about the long-dead who carved this vanishing clearing out of the wilderness.

My own favorite autumn expedition is Up the Guzzle. Up the Guzzle represents to me at any time a sort of retreat. Once in a great while the space and brilliance and majesty of my surroundings on the Point overwhelm me, and my own smallness and insignificance strike me with an almost stunning impact. "What is man, that Thou art mindful of him?" becomes a real and personal question to which I cannot find a satisfactory answer. Then I know it's time to go Up the Guzzle.

It's not far. You leave the Peninsula by the West Bay road, cross US 1, and turn into a narrow road that follows a small stream back from the sea. You're still in Gouldsboro, but you might well be in another world than that of surf and moor and open space. The road winds past the old silver mines and the dam at the outlet of West Bay Pond into a little hollow in the low hills. Here there are fields of hay enclosed by stone walls, and maple groves, and the placid, sun-glinting surface of tideless fresh water. In the plashy marges of the pond grow pickerel weed and water lilies, plants you had forgotten existed in your weeks along the scoured and battered coast, and dragonflies dart and hover over them. Everything is green and very quiet, and, more than that, everything is small and close enough so that you rediscover a confidence that man has a place in a world which is at least partly manageable, and that God is mindful of him for mysterious reasons of His own. The Guzzle is a great comfort to me in my hours of doubt.

It's more than that in the fall of the year. Then the maple groves turn scarlet, and the flaming hills are reflected faithfully in the still waters of the pond. You seem to be entering a shallow bowl into which all the color in the world has been spilled. The air itself, hazy and motionless, glows with a faint rose. I cannot tell you how beautiful it is, nor how solacing to senses exhausted by the constant assault upon them of the violent and restless beauty of the Point.

On fall evenings a favorite diversion is to drive over to Schoodic to see the *Bluenose* come in to Bar Harbor, across Frenchman Bay. Schoodic Point, between Winter Harbor and Birch Harbor, is a part of Acadia National Park, the main body of which is over on Mt. Desert Island. It's a dramatically beautiful place, fringed with enormous crags and ledges against which spectacular surf rolls in from the open Atlantic, and crowned by the eminence of Schoodic Head, from the top of which you can, on clear days, see way over into the Bay of Fundy. Excellent roads wind about the shore, picnic areas have been equipped with fireplaces, and at the extreme end a terraced parking area has been laid out on the ledges so skillfully that nature does not appear to have been tampered with at all. If you have a guest during the summer, one of the obligatory gestures as host is a visit to Schoodic Point; but otherwise, during the summer, the native population doesn't go there much. There are too many tourists in Bermuda shorts cluttering up the place, fishing, eating lunches, feeding the gulls and taking pictures.

But it's different after Labor Day. Everybody has gone home and Schoodic is once more the Peninsulans' own. On warm afternoons you can take your dog and your book over there and climb over the rocks or sit in the sun, reading, for hours without seeing a soul. Even the Park ranger, who in summer would tell you sternly that your dog must be leashed or confined to the car, ignores you beyond a cheerful, "Nice day." Twice a week, after the supper dishes are done and the sun has set, a few cars from all over the Peninsula make their way to the end of Schoodic Point to watch the *Bluenose* berth. It's not like summer evenings, when the parking lot is jammed with out-of-state cars and the sound of the surf is drowned by radios turned high to rock-and-roll stations. It's very quiet, so that you can hear the breathing of the sea. Everyone parks at a considerate distance from everyone else and just sits and looks at the twilit view. Then the *Bluenose* appears over the horizon behind 'Titm'nan Light. Her decks and portholes are ablaze, and she rolls across the ocean like a great, low-floating fire balloon, becoming larger and larger as she nears port. If the wind is right the sound of her engines throbs faintly across the water. Nobody around here likes the *Bluenose* much, but everyone agrees that she's quite a sight to see, swanking into harbor.

As the season progresses the land sinks deeper and deeper into what is almost a hibernation. If it were not for the smoke plumes wavering and flattening from the chimneys, the villages would seem to be truly abandoned. The streets are empty except for the prowling wind, and silent but for the hoot and clangor of whistle and bell buoys and the sound of the offshore rote, borne in fitfully on the gusts. The men are at sea and the women confined to their houses by the biting cold and penetrating dampness. The empty lot across the road from Herb's store, a tip-tilted patch of rock and weeds with a large tree in the middle, is deserted. All summer long the big boys pitched horseshoes there before an admiring audience of girls, and the smaller children took turns swinging out over the road in an old tire suspended from the tree. Now the children are gone all day long to the consolidated schools back inland, and the tire swings eerily in the wind, as though impelled by a ghost child. Only at mail time do bundled figures scurry against the wind to the post office, bringing animation briefly to the winter-bound hamlets.

But life goes on beneath the dormant surface. I have never lived in a place where there was so much neighboring, as it is called, as there is on the Peninsula in winter. Women drop in on each other at all hours of the day, to "set and have a good visit," as they say. Every event of the area—Junior Jordan's plans for a new boat, Nancy Farnsworth's loss of her dearly loved cat, a man's new car or a woman's new coat—all undergo a thorough verbal exploration. When current events have been exhausted the talk goes back to other times and happenings, either within the memory of living man or known only by the hearsay of parents or grandparents. The Peninsula is one of the few places left in the modern world where story-telling still exists as a means of entertainment and as an art. It's a survival from colonial days when there were few books and no radios or TV's, and from before that: from Homer and the caveman. It's a natural medium in such a community, and to me inexhaustibly fascinating. I've heard some wonderful tales while sitting in Peninsula kitchens, but I'm not going to repeat them. They'd lose their flavor and point in cold print. They have to be told in a slow Maine voice, using the impossible-to-reproduce coastal elisions and inflections and understatements, and they have to be heard against a background of sleet on windowpanes and foghorns moaning dismally.

In winter the Peninsula is a barren and sinister place, scourged by gales, battered by tremendous seas, lost in epic fogs, or gripped by a steely cold; but once in a while there is an unbelievable day. Suddenly the sky is clear and soft, the sea quiet, and the air gentle and balmy. The frozen ground may ring like iron under foot, but the sun is warm and sweet overhead. Then, leaving the housework undone, the women go outdoors, strolling about with open coats and bare heads. They walk across the causeway onto Crowley Island, or down the road onto the Point, or the three miles over the heath to call on friends in Prospect Harbor. The day is like a holiday, like a reprieve from winter.

Walking on these rare days is fun. The earth is frozen, so that you can go places which in summer are inaccessible, stepping confidently over the surfaces of bogs and marshes. The grasses are beaten flat and the leaves are off the bushes, so that areas previously veiled in mystery are candidly revealed. You learn a lot of things you didn't know before about the land; and of course, there is always the highly satisfactory feeling that you have somehow managed to outwit the climate. On the coast of northern New England, in winter, you're supposed to be hugging the stove. Instead, you're sauntering along without mittens or scarf, blandly taking the air. Although you are perfectly well aware that this fine day is not of your personal manufacture, nevertheless you feel unwarrantably smart and smug.

And still I haven't told you what it's like on the Peninsula today. I haven't told you about the Old Folks Party that the Gouldsboro Society of Service, or S.O.S., gives every May for those over seventy-five. It's usually a turkey dinner at the Prospect Harbor Community Hall. A grand march opens the festivities, music is furnished by local talent, and awards are made to the oldest man and woman present. All the rest of the guests take home May baskets, candy, flowers and cigars. It's a nice affair. I haven't told you about the baptisms. The creed of the Baptists requires complete immersion upon joining the church, but none of the little local churches possesses a baptistry in which the water can be suitably tempered. Therefore a mass baptism takes place in July in Jones Pond, when the outdoor water is as warm as it is ever going to get. Even so, it's pretty chilly, a true test of the strength and sincerity of one's belief.

I haven't told you about going to the drive-in at Trenton, over toward Bar Harbor. Where I come from, people go to drive-ins in their old clothes, although they may be driving beautiful new cars. That's one of the advantages of the drive-in—that you don't have to dress up. Before the picture starts, the children amuse themselves on swings and jungle-gyms provided by the management for the purpose, while their elders talk or listen to canned music. At Trenton, everything is upside down. People come in pickup trucks or ancient jalopies, but they wear their best dresses and their good blue suits. The entertainment provided to keep the audience quiet until it's dark enough for the show to begin consists of a series of pits in which the men pitch horseshoes. The women and children provide their own entertainment, visiting around with each other or playing games of tag. Sometimes, if there is a particularly close match in the pits, the picture waits until it is over. The movie there is only incidental to an evening of general sociability, an excuse for getting together with your acquaintances.

But chiefly I haven't told you what it means to live in a community where everyone has a place, even you yourself. If someone mentions a Cowperthwaite, you immediately think, "Birch Harbor." You know the Coleses and the Rays belong in Prospect Harbor and the Tracys and the Guptills in Gouldsboro, just as the Youngs and the Crowleys belong in Corea. And when you go into a store anywhere on the Peninsula the attendant asks, "How are things down on Cranberry Point, Mrs. Rich, and what do you hear from the Albrights?" You, too, have your own place where you are known to belong.

When you return to the Peninsula after an absence you know

that everything will be as it has been. The sea and the ledges and the heaths will not have changed, and the winding roads will not have been rerouted to accommodate a heavy flow of traffic that does not exist. You will be able to find everyone where you found him last year and will find him next year and every year until he dies. In a world where there are hordes of migrants and armies of the displaced, where thousands of those in better circumstances think nothing of moving across a continent to a better job, and where families change houses and apartments and even towns almost as readily as they change their coats, this is somehow wonderfully reassuring. Everywhere today things shift and alter too rapidly, both physically and idealistically. It's good to know one place where there is permanence.

7. As a Man Speaketh

ONE DAY AS I WAS SITTING IN MARCIA SPUR-
ling's kitchen exchanging the time of day with her while she did
her ironing, she suddenly looked over my head out the window and
exclaimed, "Here comes Mattie Manson tacking up the hill under a
full spread of canvas. Let's pray her by! I ran afoul of her in the
store yesterday, and that'll do me for a while."

Without turning my head, I was able to form a complete mental
picture of the progress of Mattie Manson, which is not her real
name. She is a large and self-important woman, a professional
bearer of the latest tidings, good or preferably ill. Her purposeful
advance on any objective very closely resembles the massive descent
of a six-masted schooner with all sails set. Since I, too, on occasion
had run afoul of her—or had encountered her and been pinned to the
spot by her gimlet eye and nonstop oratory—I wholeheartedly co-
operated in the business of praying her by, or of hoping sincerely
that she would not turn in at Marcia's house, but continue along the
road.

It was not until our prayers had been answered that I had time
to consider Marcia's remarks and to realize that I had just been
treated to an example of the Peninsula language at its best and
purest. In no other place that I know would the situation have been
outlined in just those words, or more exactly. The people of the
Maine coast have a speech of their own, and it's a speech that I love

and find inexhaustibly fascinating. I hesitate to use the word *picturesque* in connection with it, because *picturesque* and *quaint* are two words of which the Peninsulans take a dim view when applied to them or theirs. They are summer-people words, pregnant with patronage. But if *picturesque* may be allowed its true meaning of vivid, graphic and evocative of pictures in the mind's eye, then I shall apply it to the language of the Peninsula.

When I drive from Massachusetts to Gouldsboro, at a point a little north of Waldoboro I leave US 1 in favor of Route 90. This is a narrow and winding road which passes through some very pretty farming country and two or three crossroads villages, finally to rejoin US 1 near Camden on Penobscot Bay. The primary purpose of taking it is to avoid the traffic around Thomaston and Rockland and to save mileage and time, but there is a secondary purpose. Situated on one of the crossroads is a little country store, and I always stop there, if only to buy a candy bar that I don't particularly want. You see, it is there that I can be sure of hearing, usually for the first time since my last visit on the way home from Corea, the unmistakable accents of a Maine voice speaking its own special brand of English. Many of the business enterprises along the coast west of the Penobscot have been taken over by outlanders, since that is an area of tourist concentration, so that the youth who pumps your gas may have come from New Jersey, or the waitress who serves your hamburger may have grown up in Georgia. Their speechways are interesting, but they aren't Down East. Down East begins for me when people start talking Down East; and the first place I can depend on for that is the crossroads store.

I stopped there first by accident. My daughter was thirsty and had to have a Coke. As we climbed the steps I could see two men sitting on the ubiquitous Liars' Bench, and before I opened the screen door, I could hear their voices—the soft, deliberate voices, singing inflections and clipped syllables of the region, which are impossible to reproduce on paper. The subject under discussion was evidently the condition of the local roads, and one man seemed to be far from satisfied with the amount of work that had been done on the stretch of highway near his house. He apparently felt that others had fared better than he, that discrimination against him was in force. "I tell ye," he was saying emphatically, "makes a difference in this town whose ox is gored." (This phrase is by no means unknown to literature, of course, but it survives here orally with a Maine twang.)

I gave him the widest smile at my command, somewhat to his surprise, I guess. I surprised myself a little, as far as that goes; but I felt good to be back in the land where the metaphors spring from the soil as surely as the meadow rue and the oxeye daisies do. And never since has that store disappointed me.

At the time of my most recent call, the gray-haired woman in charge was watering a long box full of carnation seedlings which had been placed in the sunny show window. I myself once tried to raise carnations from seed with indifferent success, and hers didn't look much better than mine had, so before you could say Vigoro we were exchanging notes on carnation culture. She shook her head over her rather pale and spindling crop. "I dunno," she said. "They look like the last run of shad, pretty pickéd an' peazlin'. I'm in hopes, though, once I set them out an' they get their feet braced, they'll amount to somethin'."

Back where I come from, a sophisticated gardener might have said, "After transplanting, when they've become acclimated and their root systems established—" But I knew precisely what she meant. The purpose of language is to communicate ideas, and her idea was perfectly clear to me. Furthermore, her method of expressing it was to me much more graphic than any purist's choice of words. That's what I like about Down East talk. It doesn't concern itself much with grammar, syntax and vocabulary, but simply with getting the meaning across as succinctly as possible. To this end it leans on well-tried expressions which are firmly rooted in the old regional occupations and the way of life.

This language of the Maine coast is of rather complicated origin. It rests on a base of Elizabethan English, the English spoken by the early settlers. When a man asks, "What be ye going to do?" he is not speaking ungrammatically, but only as Shakespeare, Mother Goose, and his own great-great-grandfather spoke. Richly overlay-

ing this fundamental structure is a bright mosaic of expressions derived from all the means of livelihood by which Down East
Yankees have managed to keep body and soul together for over
two centuries—the shoptalk of the sea, the farm, the woods and the
tavern—absorbed into everyday conversation. Then there is a thin
gloss of modern usage learned in school, picked up from the radio,
or brought home by boys returning from the various armed services
—a gloss which rubs off very easily to reveal the solid stuff underneath, but part of which may be sufficiently durable eventually to
make a permanent place for itself in the language. Added to all this
is the coastal conviction that a man has a right to do a little improvising. If he can't find a phrase by which to express himself exactly, he makes one up. The result is sometimes incomprehensible
to anyone except another Yankee, but it's usually worth listening to.

Since fishing and seafaring were the earliest occupations along
the New England coast and are the commonest occupations today
on the Peninsula, conversation is naturally thickly sprinkled with
sea terms. Some of them are of such ancient origin that they are
in common use almost everywhere, and people like me who don't
know port from starboard—or didn't until recently—not only understand them but employ them constantly and unconcernedly. All
of us, probably, have at some time said that a person knows the
ropes, indicating that he is equal to coping with a given situation or
set of involved conditions. In places far inland, an individual who
enters a room awkwardly, noisily and heavily is said to have come
barging in. A barge does not handle easily, so its entrance into a
harbor or slip may be disruptive. People who have never been
aboard a sailing vessel in their lives have been known, when they
reached the limit of their resources or patience, to declare, "This
is the bitter end." Actually the bitter end is the last few feet of
cable on a windlass bitt. When you've paid out all except that you
really are reduced to a desperate circumstance, since you have
nothing in reserve for an emergency.

These expressions and some others are used all over the nation—
in the valley of the Mississippi, on the flat plains of Kansas, and high
in the mountains of Oregon, but they are nevertheless Down-East

forms of speech. The coastal Yankees on their various exoduses took a great many things with them in their covered wagons and their carpetbags, but the truly imperishable heirlooms they carried in their heads and on the tips of their tongues to pass down to generations of descendants.

Very seldom do Peninsula people arrive at the true bitter end. Usually, no matter what ill fortune besets them, they still possess a reservoir of courage, initiative and humor on which to draw. For generations they have coped with assorted troubles until it is as natural as breathing to them. However, once in a while a man will run into a stretch of really tough luck. Let us say that in the autumn gales he loses his boat. Shortly after that his wife dies, and two weeks later his house burns flat. In fighting the fire he falls down and breaks a leg, lies on the cold ground for an hour, and as a consequence develops double pneumonia. The seafarers have a description for his situation at this point, inherited from the days when a clipper to China might run into a sudden typhoon which carried away every thread of her canvas. "Poor Jack," they will say. "I cal'late he's about stripped to bare poles." The accustomed language of the sea comes more easily to their lips than the unimaginative vocabulary of the land.

Another expression used to indicate that a man is in dire straits is "He's on his beam ends." A ship that is stricken suddenly by hurricane winds sometimes careens so far that the deck beams are almost vertical and she is, in effect, riding on the ends of her beams. This is a far from safe and happy situation for a vessel, or a man.

In the old sailing days ships were rather frequently kept at sea long after expectation because of bad weather. When that happened, provisions ran low and the cook was hard put to it to feed the crew. He literally had to scrape the bottom of the flour barrel to get enough to make bread for the men. So when a family is in financial difficulties, with barely enough money to meet their expenses, the head of the family may say, "I'm going to have to scrape the bottom of the barrel to buy school clothes for the kids."

Windlasses are common pieces of equipment on ships and along waterfronts. They are used to raise anchors and lobster pots, to lift heavy pieces of cargo, and for a variety of other purposes, so the command, "Wind her in" is very familiar. It, too, has moved ashore, so that a mother may say to a child who is dallying with his food, "Eat your breakfast"; but she may equally well say, "Now wind that cereal into you." For some reason this use amuses me very much; but not as much as a use I once heard for the word caulking. Caulking is, of course, the oakum or other material forced into the cracks between the planking of a ship to prevent leakage. On this occasion an old bachelor lobsterman uncle of a new baby had been given the child to hold. Suddenly he jumped up, surveyed a damp area on his best pants, and exclaimed, "Hey, she needs caulking!"

Lobstermen put out to sea in the very early morning and are usually not back in harbor until after noon, so they customarily take with them a lunch which includes hot tea or coffee. This is called a mug-up, I suppose because they up with their mugs when they drink the beverage. However, the term has expanded to include any informal meal, so that a woman may say, "Stop in for a mug-up some afternoon," meaning "Drop in for tea." Even if no liquid refreshment is involved the word is used. Once I was going on a day-long trip to a sparsely settled stretch of the coast, and I was warned by Herb, "There ain't no roadside stands along there, so you'd better take a mug-up." He meant simply a picnic lunch.

Because they get up before dawn and work so hard all day, by nightfall lobstermen are ready to retire. Early to bed and early to rise is their schedule, only they state it differently. "We pry up the sun in the mornin'," they say, "and go to bed as soon's it's dark under the table." I like that. To me it's evocative of a whole way of life in which little boats are abroad on the wide ocean before the sun climbs over the eastern horizon, and men are yawning and stretching in the kitchens of their homes while the western sky is still pale gold. It's *true* language, spontaneous and unstudied.

When a ship is caught by a sudden change of wind, so that the sails are pressed back against the mast instead of billowing forward as they should, it is said to be taken aback. Temporarily, at least, it is thrown into confusion, and its proper functioning is disorganized. Thus a sea-wise person who has been surprised by a startling piece of news or suddenly disconcerted by an unexpected development will say, "I sure am some old taken aback!" And on the Peninsula they do not speak of successfully snubbing an objectionable person or of putting him in his place. Instead they say that they spilled the wind from his sails. They dismiss a slovenly housekeeper as slack, or of about as much use in performing her duties as a slack rope is in hoisting a sail. Of one who is puffed up with pride they say—referring indirectly to the duties of a ship's cooper, who made the hogsheads and barrels— "He'll bust if we don't hoop him." If rain threatens, or if you're going out in a boat on a choppy sea, they don't say, "You'd better wear a raincoat." People don't own raincoats here; they wear oilskins: jackets, pants, hats and aprons. So they say, "You'd best oil up."

In communities that have been exposed to the jargon of popularized psychiatry there are those who are catalogued by their peers as being emotionally unstable. That's not what they are called on the Peninsula. There they are described as not having much ballast. George Crowley was once talking to me about a ballast-lacking youth of Corea, and he carried the comparison to its logical conclusion. "He's riding too high," George said. "Sooner or later he's bound to go on the rocks." A ship without sufficient ballast naturally rides too high in the water and, a prey to wind and wave, it may be wrecked on the reefs.

I like too the Peninsula way of giving directions, although I took a little while to get the hang of it. Early in my residence I asked how to find an old cemetery I'd heard about. "Go along the road," I was told, "keeping a snug watch out for a dead apple tree. When you come to it, steer a course nor'east-by-east for about a furlong across the hayth, and you'll raise her." That left me knowing just about as much as I had before I asked. The same was true when I inquired about the depth of Simeon Young's old well, from which I draw my water. " 'Bout a fathom and a half," I was informed. Now that I have the points of the compass from most parts of the Peninsula roughly in mind, however, and the units of measure employed transposed into yards and feet, I can usually find—or raise—what I'm looking for.

As for the snug watch: in times of impending storm the ship is prepared for danger by taking in sail, lashing down loose gear, and closing hatches; or, in nautical language, it is snugged down or made snug. This is a time when those on duty are supposed to be extra alert; and the combination of precaution and attention is called a snug watch. It is a natural linguistic step for a seaman to speak of snugging his house for the winter: preparing for bad weather by banking the foundations and putting on the storm windows, or making everything snug. *Fast,* too, is an amphibious word. "Make it fast," nautically speaking, means "Tie or fasten it securely." Ashore, where others might say "She has been confined to her bed since September" or "She is bedridden," on the coast they say, "Oh, she's been bedfast all winter."

Seafaring was not the only means of livelihood in the early days. Farming was an almost equally important occupation, and although very little farming is now done on the Peninsula, many of the old agricultural expressions survive. A woman may say of another who is encouraging two suitors about equally, "She's keeping an anchor to windward"; but she is just as apt to say, "She's not one to put all her eggs in one basket." A man who is on his beam ends may alternatively be said to have a hard row to hoe, an expression often used in cities, but nevertheless having its origin in horticulture. George Crowley's nephew, Twink Crowley, who operates the lobster car, was telling me once about a man whom he had to fire because he was lazy and no-good. Twink has followed the sea ever since he was big enough to handle a pair of light oars. However, he said disgustedly, "He warn't worth firewood nor fencin'"; he was, in other words, like an old stick, which is too rotten and punky to burn and too crooked to be used as a fence post.

In rural England there is a form of barrier used between fields consisting of a fence or hedge placed in a shallow ditch. This is called a ha-ha, and as far as I am aware the name has been obsolete in New England since early colonial times. One day as I was waiting for the mail in the store my daughter Dinah joined a group of her young friends on the steps. As adolescent girls are prone to be, they were very shortly overcome by a mass seizure of contagious giggles, probably over nothing. An old lobsterman paused to regard them with some concern, and finally proffered his diagnosis of the situation. "Looks like you girls've found a tee-hee's nest in the ha-ha hedge," he said. Where could he have found that except in his glossarial heritage from agricultural days?

A great many proverbs in common use and familiar not only in this country but in others derive from farming. Those who have engaged in cultivation of the soil, no matter when or where, have observed the same phenomena and, with the economy of words characteristic of farmers everywhere, have framed them into approximately the same easily understood aphorisms. "The willing horse pulls the load" can be found in many languages, as can some equivalent of "All cats are black at night," "Birds of a feather flock together," and "All his geese are swans." These are clearly comprehended when applied to human behavior, and all of them are used on the Peninsula, as elsewhere. On the Peninsula, however, there are some variations on old themes, and some departures that are new, to me, at least.

For example, instead of saying "Birds of a feather . . ." Peninsulans may say, "Lie down with dogs, get up with fleas." Their version of "All signs fail in dry weather" is "When it looks like rain and don't, 'twun't." To indicate that a person who keeps his own council may be working deviously to attain his own ends, they say not "Still waters run deep" but "The still pig gets the swill"; and to put you on guard against becoming too confidential with a notorious and indiscreet talebearer they warn, "The bitch that fetches will carry." If a man has more creditors than he can satisfy, he pays the most insistent, not because "First come, first served," but because "The wheel that squeaks the loudest gets the grease." Of a stingy man it is said "He's still got his huckleberry money." (He's still hanging on to the pennies his mother paid him when he was four years old for picking huckleberries.) Some of these expressions are not very elegant or delicate, I realize. Farmers as a class know the facts of life and face them with composure, an attitude that is sometimes reflected in their speech. Whatever else you may think of these little maxims, though, you must admit that they are comprehensible and to the point.

One day I went into Marcia Spurling's house and found her in a

state of intense irritation. Several years before she had been harshly criticized by a relative for something she had done, and now she had just discovered that the relative was guilty of similar conduct and was justifying herself uphill and down-dale. In the circumstances I should probably have made some reference to the shoe's being on the other foot, but that's too shopworn a metaphor for the Peninsula. Marcia announced, scowling, "Makes a difference, don't it, just whose cat's tail's caught in the door!"

Some expressions come from so simple a thing as just keeping house. Once I wrote Marcia a long letter explaining why I had to put off a proposed visit to her. I had a number of engagements ranging from a dentist appointment to a meeting of the PTA, and I would come, I said, as soon as I had fulfilled all my obligations. She replied on a two-penny postcard. "If you're ever going to make it here," she wrote, "looks like you'll just have to sneak out the back door without washing the dishes." And that's about what I finally did. "Cupboard love," the kind of affection bestowed in hope of gain, derives from housekeeping, too.

Butter, a household commodity, figures largely in country talk. We all know about buttering somebody up. On the Peninsula, one who is trying to excuse himself for some error of omission or commission by making profuse apologies and explanations is told "All that palaver won't butter no parsnips." And of a husband who is suspected of having romantic interests outside his home it may be said "He needs to have his paws buttered." This goes back to an old remedy still applied to cats who, when the family moves from one house to another, refuse to accept the new quarters but persist in returning to the old. The cat's paws are spread with butter and he is shut up in the cellar for three days. This is supposed to cure him of his roving tendencies.

"I'll manage, by the Grace of God and a longhandled spoon," people say. I have lived most of my life in the country, and much of the cooking I have done has been on a wood-burning range. When the top of the stove becomes red hot you have to use a very longhandled spoon indeed to stir the contents of kettles unless you want to roast the flesh of your hands. Not long ago I was talking with a Peninsula woman who was concerned about some business dealings her husband had entered into with a man who was noted for his sharp practices and lack of scruples. "He's too slick for Ed," she said. "Ed expects everyone to be as honest as he is himself, but when you sup with the Devil you've got to use a longhandled spoon."

I like the way the Peninsula women talk about their household chores. They have some very taut and economical phrases. They speak of baking off their bread and turning out their bedrooms and redding-up their houses. When weather conditions make it uncertain exactly when their men will return from the sea, they plan keep-warms for supper. Baked beans and fish chowder are good keep-warms, while an omelet or a soufflé would not be. They speak of glory-holes and hurrah's nests, those closets or sheds that anyone who has kept house knows all about. This accumulated litter is called cultch or sculch. They say of a neighbor that it takes her a month of Sundays to get her work done because she is slower than Death's warping bar. I assume that the reference comes down from the days when every woman spun yarn from the wool of her own sheep and wove it into fabric. It has a much more poetic ring than the cold molasses usually invoked for comparison.

In the woods of northwestern Maine where I spent fifteen years before I came to the Peninsula, the colloquialisms stemmed from the chief occupation of the country, which was lumbering. A lumberjack would say, for example, that he had the downriver cant and cal'lated to spring-out in the Stewartstown jail. Most of the lumber camps were in the hills along streams which ran down to the towns below, so the victim of the downriver cant was one who was completely fed up and bored with the drudgery and routine of work in the woods and entertained a strong inclination (or cant) to go to town (or downstream) and get drunk. As a result he would live out the spring (spring-out) in jail. To this day I sometimes say that I have the downriver cant simply to explain that I'm going to a poor movie to break the monotony. Another name for the same state of mind is cabin fever.

If I ever thought that the lumbering vocabulary was confined to the woods I was disabused of that notion when I started living on Cranberry Point. The people of the Peninsula do almost no lumbering now, but they have inherited the language of the trade from way back. They are very likely to say that they live three hawserlengths up the road; but if you tell them that you left your car a couple of twitches down the hill they know what you mean. A twitch is as far as an average horse can drag a long log without resting. They use haywire, not in the modern sense of crazy, but in the old sense of makeshift. One thing that is plentiful around lumber camps is the heavy wire that binds the hay bales, and it is used extensively to make emergency repairs on practically everything from a man's belt to a broken-down tractor. Therefore anything haphazardly patched together is a haywire affair, whether it be a water pump, a home-trimmed Easter hat, or a casserole consisting of the cleanings of the refrigerator. I once even heard an unsuccessful marriage called a haywire rig.

During log drives men are stationed along the rivers at narrow points to prevent the logs from jamming. This duty is called *tending out*. On the Peninsula there have been no log drives since I don't know when, but *tending out* is still legitimate linguistic coin, although the use has changed. If someone says "Oh, he's been tending out on her for two years" he means nowadays that the subject of the discussion has been giving the damsel of his choice his undivided attention, or courting her, for that period.

Or he may be said to be sleevin' her 'round. One who fancies himself as a ladies' man is called a great old sleever. He offers his sleeve to anything in skirts. This doesn't derive from any occupation, but is a sample of the Yankee gift for close observation and brief, accurate description. *Sly* used as a verb comes under the same heading. "I'll have to sly out before the meeting's over," a woman will say, meaning that she'll leave early and quietly. Another word that is just plain Down East is *towse* or *catowse*. It means fuss or scene. "He made an awful towse about it" is a common statement all along the coast and among the islands.

In some of the older coastal villages, many of which were established in the days of the molasses-slave-and-rum trade, the first public building to be erected was the tavern. This was not true of Gouldsboro, but two expressions of tavern origin exist there today, nevertheless. One is familiar in most parts of the country, where people say of an individual who has obviously met with physical violence, "He's all bunged up." In early tavern days the liquor was stored in casks which were closed by driving wooden stoppers, or bungs, into the small holes through which they were filled. When the cask was thus sealed it was said to be bunged up. If a customer became obstreperous and refused to leave when invited to do so, the bouncer seized the first thing available, which was usually the bung starter, to aid in enforcing his discipline.

The other tavern word is one that I have never heard used in this particular way except Down East: the word *tapster* employed jeeringly to taunt the last member of the household to arise in the morning. In that country everyone who can lift his head from the pillow and get his feet under himself is expected to rise with the sun, and no nonsense about it. Lying abed in the morning for no good and sufficient reason is frowned upon, and being called the tapster is an adverse comment on a man's or woman's nature and habits. It means the heeltap or worthless dregs left in a glass after drinking.

If we're going to start calling names, the Peninsula has some good ones. There is the big gawm, who wanders clumsily through life breaking dishes, knocking over small tables, and in general doing everything ineptly. If you barge around heedlessly you are said to be gawmin' along, or you may be described as kind of gawmy. There is the chowderhead, an impossible slob who shouldn't be confused with the chucklehead, who may not be quite bright but is nevertheless harmless and even likable. The muttonhead is just plain stupid. A spiritless and colorless nonenity is a yard of cold pumpwater, while one who is full of conceit and overweening self-esteem is said to treasure herself. It's no compliment to say a man is plausible. It means that you wouldn't trust him as far as you could throw him. A woman with middle-aged spread is called a Jonesport model after a type of boat characterized by its broad stern. A gunkhole is, as nearly as I can make out, the coastal equivalent of the one-horse town of the interior: a small, backward hamlet situated on some lost little cove among the long capes and scattered islands. There are some other graphic epithets in circulation, but I can't tell you about them, because they are unprintable.

The place names of the Peninsula charm me. There is nothing affected or pretentious about them, no grafting of flowery labels onto the stripped and skeletal structure of the barren land. The names mean something here. A slight eminence is not called Buena Vista Heights, as it might be in a region where housing developments flourish. It is called Porcupine Hill because a great many porcupines have been killed there over the years. Cranberry Point is thickly covered with cranberry vines, while Sand Cove, or The Sands, boasts the only sandy beach in the district. Pond Road passes between Jones and Forbes Ponds. Old Maid's Landing was owned by a spinster long ago, and an anchorage near a rock in Gouldsboro Bay is called Eel Rock because eels run there. A certain swamp is called Pretty Marsh (pronounced Mash) simply because it is a pretty marsh; and the Dyke Marsh is threaded by the remains of dykes built a century and a half ago to reclaim it from the sea for use as a hay field. The Watering Cove at Prospect Harbor is where ships used to anchor to take on supplies of drinking water. On the heath (hayth) at Corea is a small pond in which lilies grow, formed by the building of a beaver dam across a brook. This is Beaverlily Pond, and the brook is Beaverlily Brook. The Potato Field is an area of wild and overgrown land where potatoes were once raised, and Grindstone Neck is composed of the kind of rock suitable for grindstones, although some say that a vessel carrying a cargo of grindstones was once wrecked there.

The islands have simple and descriptive names, too. Ironbound Island looks ironbound and rather forbidding, and Bald Rock is bald. Eastern and Western Islands are at the eastern and western ends of the archipelago known as the Sally Islands, and between them lie Sheep Island, where sheep used to be pastured during the summer months, and Inner and Outer Bar Islands, which are nothing more than oversized bars, one inside the other. Turtle Island looks like a turtle, and herons used to nest on Heron Island. Thrumcap resembles one of the little caps, like toboggan caps, that weavers used to make out of the thrums, or tag ends of the warp; while Yellow Island is largely composed of yellow rock.

A chart of the waters off the Peninsula bears some nice names— names like Bonny Chess and Abijah and Stone Horse Ledges and Roaring Bull, a bare rock over which the sea roars when the wind and tide are right, and Halibut Hole, the passage between Ironbound and Jordon Islands, where halibut sometimes school. Jo Leighton Ground is an inexplicably shoal area more than two miles out from Petit Manan Island, named by Champlain, where the depth of water is only fifteen feet. I suppose Jo Leighton, whoever he was, went aground there at some time.

I understand about Schoodic Point, which is part of the Acadia National Park. Schoodic is Indian for "burned over land," and the point must once have been burned over, although now it has some of the biggest trees on the Peninsula. I can more or less figure out Aunt Nabby Noah's Cellar Hole, a common point of reference in Corea. There isn't any cellar hole there now, and no one knows

exactly who Aunt Nabby Noah was, but she must at one time have
lived and had a cellar in the weedy field that is her only monument. Some names, however, are harder to account for, although I
am sure, knowing the country, that they must have reason behind
them.

Let's take Drunken Pole Hayth as an example. It's a stretch of
heath like any other, covered with low bushes and pitted with
quicksands. Was there once a pole there, leaning at a drunken angle? Or did a native of Poland fall into one of the bogs after im-
bibing too freely? I don't know. I don't know about Chicken Mill,
either. It's a little pond behind a small dam where there was once
a sawmill. Several varieties of water lilies have been planted there
by the present owner, there's a little grove of pine trees, and all in
all it's a nice place for a picnic. But I haven't been able to find out
where the chickens come into the picture. There aren't any there
now, and I'm not sure that there ever were any.

Then there is what is designated as Up the Guzzle, mentioned
previously. It's not at all the sort of place you picture when you
first hear the rather unpleasant-sounding name. I suppose *guzzle*,
which to me means to drink greedily, must be a regional variation of
gulch or gully, but if so it's new to me.

I like the Christian names common on the Peninsula, too. They
aren't popular names, such as Shirley and Kim, bestowed during
the flush of a brief vogue. They aren't even modern. They are
names which have seen generations of Yankees safely through life
and are therefore considered good enough and proud enough for
anybody. Some of them, like Corydon, Virgil, Homer and Horace,
are classical. Some—Gideon, Ishmael, Ira, Elijah, Nathan and Eli-
phalet—are biblical. Quite a few men answer to Ivory or Harvard,
and quite a few women to Persia, India or Ceylon. These last were
inherited from their great-grandmothers, who were born in the days
when the sails and lovely sheers of the American clipper ships were
familiar on every horizon and in every port in the world. Then a
captain often took his whole family with him on a two-year jaunt
to the other side of the globe; and sometimes when a child was born
on one of these voyages it was named for the place of its birth.
These names have been handed down in seafaring families as

proudly as have been the camphorwood chests, Paisley shawls and dinner dishes of Canton china brought home from the ends of the earth.

Then there is a whole division of names which fall into a classification of their own. These—Cedelia and Lovisa, Emmadene and Ogretta, Allura and Alfaretta—were bestowed simply because they were musical and exotic. The same deeprooted need for beauty and color that drives the Peninsula women to work so hard in their brief-blooming flower gardens dictated their choice. The land is so bleak and the sea so cold and cruel, the climate is so ruthless and the life so hard and demanding that the hearts of the Peninsulans reach out hungrily to the pretty and gay wherever it may be found. They have little enough frivolity otherwise.

A love of language inherited from a long line of word-bemused ancestors would in any case have made the speech of the Peninsula a subject of great interest to me; but there is another reason why I consider it worth dwelling upon. Talk here is more than a matter of picturesque phrases and interesting origins. I doubt if anyone who has not lived in a sparsely settled country can understand and appreciate the importance that can accrue to the spoken word. Even those to whom words are the tools by which they earn a living— lawyers, preachers, actors, lecturers, politicians or salesmen—can have no conception of their power and endurance in a place like the Peninsula.

More than twenty years ago the Reverend Mr. Williams of the Maine Sea Coast Mission made a pastoral call on a lobsterman of Corea, Phil Workman. At the end of the call he said, "Well, I guess I must be going."

As any good host would, Phil expostulated, "Oh, don't hurry."

"I don't intend to hurry," Mr. Williams said. "That's why I'm leaving now."

Even longer ago than that, the then presiding minister, a gloomy man who bore his responsibilities heavily, met Marcia's uncle, a lobsterman not noted for his piety, in the store. "Mr. Spurling," he said in a voice fraught with doom, "are you prepared to meet your Maker?"

"Golly," exclaimed Marcia's uncle, "is He headin' this way?"

These exchanges are being repeated verbatim today. They are mildly amusing, it's true; but other long conversations holding no spark of humor or even of any particular interest or importance can be recounted with absolute accuracy decades after they took place.

The store is being added to continually. Just a few Sundays ago there occurred an exchange of remarks that I have already heard repeated six times with no variations. A friend of mine had rented one of Lee Stewart's housekeeping cabins for a month and had improved the Sabbath by attending church. When he got back, Lee was changing the sheets and towels in the cabin. "Did you pray for me?" she asked.

"Certainly I did, Mrs. Stewart," he told her, probably falsely. "I prayed for you and your family and for everybody in these cabins." He then became carried away by the sound of his own voice. "And I prayed for all the good folks of Corea and for sailors at sea everywhere and for—"

Lee stopped him there. "Don't thin the soup *too* much," she advised tartly, and left with her linen. I know very well that ten years from now, and twenty, people will still be repeating what Mrs. Stewart said about Mr. Fager's prayers.

Words live forever in a tiny hamlet. They are almost concrete things, ageless and potent. I know two women who didn't speak to each other for seven years, although they met daily, because of an ill-considered comment one made to the other. The unforgotten and unforgiven words stood between them as solidly as a wall. In more thickly populated places people don't have memories like that. There the air is so full of words that half of them aren't listened to and the other half go in one ear and out the other, like a breeze through the open windows of a house, briefly noted and then dismissed into oblivion. Other things claim the attention in a more complicated civilization.

On the Peninsula the people live in a climate of silence for much of each day. A man alone in his lobster boat on the face of the sea hears no sound of human utterance for long hours; nor does his wife (the children being in school or at play) as she works about her kitchen or garden. Under those conditions any sentence, no

matter how trivial, is engraved on the mind as indelibly as the lines of acid on an etching plate. It is not only remembered, but it is weighed and considered until every possible implication has been extracted.

There is a story, supposed to be funny, about two men who were walking along a road together. They passed a third, a mutual friend, who said "Hello." After about five minutes of deep concentration, one of the original two said to the other thoughtfully, "Now what do you suppose he meant by that?"

Remarks that to me sound almost stupidly innocent are interpreted, and correctly, to contain intended insults, sly warnings, or hidden congratulations. It is perfectly possible on the Peninsula for a man to say *hello* in an ambiguous or deeply significant manner. This being the case, words are weighed before they are spoken, in the sure knowledge that they will be subjected to thorough scrutiny. The result is inevitably the laconicism typical of the Down-Easter, who believes that what you don't say can't be held against you.

I have purposely refrained from trying to reproduce the sound of the Peninsula language as it is spoken. In the first place, the only way this could be done successfully is by tape recording; and in the second place, I myself am always intensely irritated by written attempts at any dialect. They slow the reader and distract his attention from the content; and, even at best, they fall short of their mark. A collection of apostrophes and misspellings is a gratuitous nuisance when you are trying to extract a meaning from a printed page, and I'd like to avoid committing this nuisance.

In my opinion, an index to the character of any people lies in its speech. A soft and indolent people have a vague and sloppy way of speaking, while the hardworking, clearheaded and self-sufficient use an exact, graphic and economical language. Such is the speech of the Down-Easter, who is just the way he talks: direct, thrifty, and yet imaginative. As long as he pursues his present way of life he will continue, I believe, to express himself as he does now and as his forebears did. If and when his means of livelihood changes, probably his language will undergo a change, too—not at once and completely, but gradually and in varying degrees. It has happened in other places where the sea has been given up for the easier and more profitable business of catering to the summer influx. Sometimes exposure to the invaders' talk has altered and enlarged vocabularies and corrected accents until it is hard to tell whether you are talking with a native in his shore clothes or a tourist in vacation costume. Sometimes the Yankee, who is no fool, has perceived that his "quaint" sea-flavored way of talking is a professional asset and good for trade; so he has cultivated an exaggerated old-tar saltiness that rings as false as brass and has developed a habit of synthetic bucolic philosophizing which would make his grandfathers spin in their graves for very shame if they could hear him.

Whichever happens on the Peninsula will be too bad. The language there is as much a part of the country as the twisted firs and surf-washed ledges. When it is no longer heard, something that was real and valuable will have vanished from the land.

8. People Have to Eat

ALMOST EVERY GEOGRAPHICAL DIVISION OF
the world has a regional cookery of its own, an inevitable result of
its climate, its topography, the nature of the materials to be found at
hand, and the type of occupation commonly pursued. This volume
of lore surrounding indigenous foods and their preparation is as
much a part of the culture of any people as are their arts and arti-
facts, their beliefs and systems of education, and their manners and
mores. Not only is it a matter of local pride, but it also affects
directly the physical condition and even the mentality and morale
of the population. "Tell me what you eat," remember, "and I will
tell you what you are."

There was a day when culinary boundaries were clearly defined.
That day has passed. It is now possible, through the offices of various agencies, to eat chow mein in the hills of Vermont or Boston
baked beans on the pampas of the Argentine. All you have to do is
open a can and heat the contents. Now you can buy frozen pizza
pies or Cape Cod scallops no matter where you live; and live lobsters, flown there in tanks of sea water, are by no means uncommon
in the upper Mississippi valley. Eventually, I suppose, there will be
no regional cooking at all. Everyone, everywhere, will be eating
the same things—and very dull it will be, too. It was better when
you couldn't buy a crisp cucumber in January. When you finally
got it, along about July, you really appreciated it.

The Peninsula has fallen victim to this general standardization of foods less than any other area I know. It is possible to buy at the chain stores of Ellsworth or at Charley Small's supermarket on US 1 all the various and fancy viands available elsewhere, but people here don't go in much for strange and outlandish dishes. This is partly because nobody has money to gamble on doubtful experiments, especially when the land and sea will supply a good meal free, and partly because Peninsulans are sot in their ways. They're used to their own foods and like them and see no reason for changing their eating habits. The summer people and the radio homemaking programs have introduced a few new ideas to Peninsula cooks, but by and large the cookery retains its original and distinctive character.

Here are found all the dishes recognized generally as typically New England: the baked beans and boiled dinners, the codfish balls and Indian puddings and applesauce cakes brought here by the first settlers from Massachusetts. In addition there is a special category of foods resulting from the special situation of the Peninsula. Understandably a large part, but not all, is sea food. Peninsula cookery is distinguished by simplicity, inexpensive treatment, and "heartiness," as it is called. By this is meant the virtue of assuaging a man's hunger, of filling him with food that will stick to his ribs for more than five minutes, of putting heart into him for his work. It's easy to do this if you have plenty of butter, rich cream, prime cuts of beef and other costly ingredients. Anybody can be a good cook under those circumstances. It's different when you have to deal with ordinary inexpensive foodstuffs, substituting time and care for the things money would buy. That's where the really good cooks are separated from the dubs, and that's where the Peninsula women shine.

It will come as a surprise to nobody that the lobster, elsewhere a luxury and An Occasion, is commonly served in every household hereabouts. It's what you have when you can't think of anything else for supper, the local version of hamburger or frankfurters. In fact, most of the population would prefer hamburger or hot dogs. Lobsters are an old story, all in the day's work. Unless they are at the peak of perfection people here won't eat them at all, but will sell them to those who don't know any better.

Perfection in a lobster involves several factors, best understood, perhaps, through an examination of its life and habits. This is a subject still under study, as there are large gaps in the information possessed by scientists. The matter is of more than academic interest, since so many people depend on lobstering for a living. Therefore the State of Maine supports a large experimental and research project for the gathering of more data by which control of propagation and an increase in the lobster population may ultimately be accomplished. Lobsters are very strange creatures indeed, both in appearance and in their activities, and I find them interesting as well as succulent. So I'll tell you what I know about them.

The body of the lobster consists of two parts, the cephalothorax, or coalesced head and thorax, and the abdomen, commonly called the tail. The tail has six armored joints or somites joined by bands of tough membrane, so that it is flexible, like plate armor. There are eight little appendages called swimmerets on the under side, and it broadens at the end into a five-sectioned fan. Females carry their eggs on the under side of the tail, packed around the swimmerets. From each side of the thorax grow four walking legs by which the lobster manages to crawl along the bottom of the sea seeking food, or water of a more comfortable temperature. In front of these legs are the most conspicuous single feature of the lobster's anatomy: the two enormous claws or pincers with which it holds and tears food, and fights. Between them, growing from the head, are six antennae —two long and four short—and two stalked eyes. These are instruments of sensitivity by which the lobster finds food and detects enemies. The rest of the body is presumably insensitive, since it is completely covered by the tough shell, actually an outside skeleton, vitally essential for protection.

As soon as the eggs are inseminated they are detached from the body of the female and rise to the surface of the sea, where they float around for about ten days. During this period they hatch, go through a larval stage, and develop into microscopic lobsters They are a part of the ocean plankton up to this point and as such suffer a ninety per cent mortality, some of them being washed ashore and many of them being eaten by fish and other sea life. The survivors finally sink to the floor of the sea and with luck grow up to be lobsters of legal size—a process which takes from four to six years.

In most living things growth is a fairly steady process. With occasional spurts and slowdowns, children or puppies proceed evenly from infancy to adulthood. This is not true of lobsters. They can grow only at the cost of shedding their complete confining shells. Then in the short space of time before a new shell is formed they go through a period of frenzied growth. Very young lobsters may molt as many as twenty times a year, but the mature lobster changes shells only once annually, usually in the summer.

Before the shell is cast some internal changes take place. Most of the calcium in the old shell is absorbed into the bloodstream and deposited in a pair of sacs in the walls of the stomach. At the same time the flesh of the lobster takes in great amounts of water, swelling up and becoming spongy. This makes it almost useless as far as edibility is concerned. The meat is soft and flavorless and nobody who knows lobsters will touch it with a ten-foot pole, although it is occasionally palmed off on the uninitiated. Then the decalcified shell is cast, and the soft, swollen pink body begins to manufacture another to fit it, getting its calcium salts from the deposits in the stomach and from the sea water. When the new green shell is hard, the meat returns to its normal firm texture and is again suitable for eating.

I have gone into this in some detail because it is one of the factors in choosing a lobster for the pot. Nobody on the Peninsula would dream of bothering to cook a shedder. The other factor is freshness or liveliness. Some sea-food restaurants feature a lobster tank from which you may choose your own live lobster. The Peninsulans view this practice with amused disdain. Captive lobsters stay alive all right, but they "g'ant up" (lose weight) fast in a tank and become listless. On the Peninsula it isn't enough that a lobster be alive. It must be alive and fighting. Its claws must clash loudly and its tail must thrash wildly, alternately curling over the head and wedging tightly against the thorax. A languid lobster is discarded with contempt, to be sold for export. Even after it is cooked, if the tail seems a little limp and won't spring back against the body with a snap it is put aside for the cat. As I said, Peninsulans are fussy about lobsters, and they've taught me to be fussy, too.

When I want lobsters I go over to Twink Crowley's lobster car on the island and, standing on the wharf, shout down my needs to him where he is standing on the car. I want them to run around a pound and a half apiece, I tell him, and he opens the hatch of the compartment containing lobsters of that size and with a landing net fishes out a few. He holds them up, and I either accept them or tell him I want them with bigger claws. The claw meat is the best and tenderest. Or else he tells me that I don't either want that one, it's a shedder. One claw of each lobster has been immobilized by the insertion of a small wooden or plastic wedge so that it can't pinch the handler, but as a concession to me Twink wedges the other claw. I once picked up a single-wedge lobster from the wrong angle and thought I was going to lose a finger before I could pry it free. So now I'm a little leery.

The easiest way to cook lobsters is to boil them, and it's best to boil them in sea water if possible. You need a large container. I use a clean, covered garbage pail, bought for the purpose. When the sea water is briskly rolling you drop the lobsters into it and let them boil for about twenty minutes. By this time they have turned bright red. Remove them, drain them, place them on their backs, split them down the entire length with a heavy knife, and crack the claws with a hammer—unless you are on a picnic, when you use stones instead. Remove the meat, dip it in melted butter, and eat it. On a picnic the butter is served in large clam shells that you gather during the boiling period. Eating lobster is a messy business, so it's a good idea to provide yourself and your guests with small ten-cent store turkish towels in place of napkins if you're in the house. On picnics you can wash your hands in the sea as often as necessary, so you don't bother with the towels. A by-product of a boiled lobster is the tomalley, or liver, which is found in the thorax. This is a greenish substance rather like paté de foie gras, and some people regard it with aversion. I like it. Spread on crackers and eaten before the lobster proper is tackled, it makes a wonderful appetizer.

In Corea nobody ever cooks just enough lobsters for the current meal. As long as you have your pail boiling anyhow you might as well dump in a few extra, because cooked lobster meat is a handy thing to have in your refrigerator against an emergency. You pick it out and store it in a glass jar for the making of salads or Newburgs, which you concoct according to your favorite recipe. If it's necessary to stretch the Newburg or salad, local cooks add a cup or so of boiled or steamed halibut, and no one ever knows the difference.

Good lobster stew is a little more tricky. You boil about two pounds of lobster and remove the meat at once, saving the tomalley, the coral and the thick white substance (which is really lobster blood) found in the shell. These you simmer in half a cup of butter for seven or eight minutes, using the heaviest kettle you own—an old iron one if possible, although heavy aluminum will serve. Add the lobster meat, cut in fairly large pieces, and cook all together for about ten minutes. Push the kettle back on the stove and allow to cool slightly. Then, *very slowly*, and stirring *constantly*, add a quart of whole milk. Unless you merely trickle the milk in and unless you stir faithfully the stew will curdle. The mixture now blossoms into a rich salmon color, laced with golden butter, and the really hard part approaches. You remove the kettle from the stove and put the stew aside to age. It should stand covered for at least six hours, but if you can bear waiting until the next day to eat it, so much the better, as every hour that passes blends and improves the flavor. Masters of the dish set up two days as the ideal aging time, but I have never had the moral stamina to postpone consumption that long.

I have never broiled or baked lobsters because the first step in either case is the splitting of the live lobster down the entire length of the body with a sharp knife. I simply cannot do this. I'm afraid it will hurt the poor creature. As I don't hesitate to plunge live lobsters into boiling water, and as I'll eat any number of broiled or baked lobsters of someone else's concoction, I know and admit that my attitude is illogical, cowardly and untenable, but I can't help it. However, I can tell you how the dishes are prepared, having watched more intrepid cooks than I at work.

After splitting the lobsters, you clean them by removing the stomachs, intestinal veins and tomalley. For broiling four lobsters, you prepare a stuffing made of one and a half cups of cracker crumbs, salt, two tablespoonfuls of Worcestershire sauce and four tablespoonfuls of melted butter. This you spread generously in the body cavity. Place the lobsters on a buttered broiler, stuffing side up, and broil for eight minutes. Turn them over and broil for eight minutes on the other side. Serve with lots of melted butter.

The stuffing for four baked lobsters is made by rolling sixteen common crackers into fine crumbs and adding salt and pepper. Mix with a quarter of a cup of melted butter, a quarter cup of whole milk, and enough cooking sherry to make it of a good malleable consistency. Stir in about two pounds of fresh crabmeat and stuff the lobsters as full as you possibly can, pouring melted butter over the whole and sprinkling generously with grated cheese and paprika. Bake in a very hot oven for nineteen minutes and serve at once. This is a very rich, filling and delicious dish, but it's also quite a lot of work.

May I remark in passing that lobster meat *per se* has a very low caloric value? It's all that melted butter that does the deadly work.

The other crustacean commonly eaten on the Peninsula is the crab. These crabs are about as large as the palm of a man's hand and are caught among the rocks of the shore or are taken out of lobster traps. They're boiled, and the meat is picked out. This is a terrible job. It once took me all day to pick out a pailful of crabs. Fortunately many women are more nimble-fingered than I, and pick out crabmeat for sale by the pound. Now I get mine from Noel Young over on Crowley Island, and I must say that in my opinion she earns every cent of the far from exorbitant price she charges.

This fresh crabmeat is of extremely delicate texture and flavor— the best I have ever eaten anywhere. It's used in salads, Newburgs, stews and sandwiches, just as lobster is. Sometimes it is combined with lobster meat to provide variety; and sometimes it is combined with bread crumbs, an egg, and a little chopped onion, green pepper and celery as a stuffing for green peppers or even poultry. Or the same mixture may be placed in scallop shells or ramekins, sprinkled with buttered crumbs, paprika and grated cheese, and browned in the oven or under the broiler. If you do this you'd better allow at least half a dozen shells per person. It's wonderful. I like it, too, creamed with mushrooms and served on toast points, or baked into a sort of soufflé. In the latter instance you beat two eggs lightly into a cup of milk, add salt, a quarter of a teaspoonful of baking powder and a tablespoonful of flour sifted together, a little Worcestershire sauce and a generous cup of crabmeat. Top with buttered crumbs and bake in a greased casserole set in a pan of water for about fifty minutes, or until it is firm.

There are a great many kinds of fish caught in the waters surrounding the Peninsula—some in the weirs, some in the lobster traps, some by dragging, and a few on hand lines. Not very many natives bother with the hand lines, though. They can get all the fish they need by the other methods, as by-products of their real business. The only person I know who regularly fishes with a line is George Crowley, and he does so only to supply his very persnickety white cat, Fuzzy, the darling of his heart, who won't eat anything but fresh pollock, sometimes called bluefish—and by fresh, she means *fresh*, right out of the sea.

So George stands patiently on Twink's lobster car, pulling in pollock, which infest the water thereabouts. They're attracted by the abundance of feed there where the lobstermen pitch overboard from their boats all the left-over bait and gurry when they come into harbor. George really doesn't like fishing, so once in a while I give him a break by taking over his drop line. It's no sport, because the pollock are so greedy or stupid or both that they will grab even a bare hook as soon as it touches the water. In spite of this, the car is frequently so crowded with city-slicker fishermen that the boats have difficulty in docking, and Twink has had to put up a sign forbidding fishing when the lobstermen are delivering their hauls. These pollock are small, bony fish which are edible, but few natives eat them. Better fare is too easily available.

The most common fish are halibut, haddock, cod, herring, hake and flounder. There are still some mackerel (although they, like porgies, are becoming scarcer each year) and some cusk, considered locally one of the best fish. In the spring smelts and alewives run up the streams to spawn and are dipped out with nets, and in the spring also comes the lumpfish to spawn on the rocks. This is a very odd fish about fourteen inches long, jelly-like on the outside and pink on the inside. You slice, drain and fry it. It has a very distinctive flavor, but it's a little too oily for my taste. Around Christmas time tomcods or frostfish are caught for a brief period. They resemble herring. Almost any of these fish—but particularly the cod—are used to make strip-fish, which is simply fish filleted, salted, and dried in the sun. Sun-drying fish is the oldest industry of the Maine coast. It was being pursued decades before the Pilgrims landed on Plymouth Rock. Ships from European countries made three or four trips a year to these shores, dried their enormous catches on pole racks in the sun, and went home with their holds crammed with strip-fish, which was sold at a handsome profit. Quite a few New England fortunes were found on strip-fish.

Nowadays most salt codfish that you buy in stores is processed in modern factories, but on the Peninsula it is still dried in the sun by the ancient method. If you see someone walking along with his jaws moving rhythmically, he's probably chewing neither gum nor tobacco, but a hunk of well-dried raw strip-fish. I do it myself.

There are two versions of the salt codfish dinner on the Peninsula. Both require salt cod or other strip-fish which has been freshened for two or three hours in cold water, salt pork, potatoes, onions and beets; and in both the potatoes and salt fish are boiled together, with the fish, cut into serving pieces, resting on top of the peeled potatoes. In both, the salt pork is fried very crisp and put into the oven to keep warm. In the simpler version, the beets have been cooked the day before and put into vinegar to pickle, and the onions are sliced raw and covered with vinegar or not as you choose. That's all there is to it. The codfish and potatoes are drained and served just as they are, with the diner adding salt, pepper and butter to taste; and the pork scraps and vegetables are eaten on the side. It tastes much better than it sounds.

In the dressier version, the beets and onions are cooked separately and served hot. A white sauce is made, using some of the fat from the tried-out pork instead of butter to combine with the flour for thickening. This gives the sauce a special, delicious flavor. Diced, hard-boiled eggs are added to this sauce, which is poured over the fish. The beets, onions, potatoes and pork scraps are arranged around the fish on a hot platter, and the whole thing looks very colorful and festive. It's a simple and inexpensive meal, and very good indeed. If the fish has been cut into small cubes and added directly to the white sauce it becomes creamed codfish and is equally good.

Strip-fish is also used to make fish balls. Boil six or seven medium potatoes together with about two cups of cut-up codfish, drain, and mash. Whip in two lightly beaten eggs and a little butter and pepper. Don't add salt. It's salt enough already. In other places, fish balls are usually really balls, rolled in cracker crumbs and fried in deep fat. On the Peninsula, they are more apt to be flat cakes with no crumb coating, fried in a spider. The fat used is salt pork fat, about a quarter of an inch deep, and the pork scraps are served with the fish balls, along with chili sauce, piccalilli, or mustard pickle.

I'm not going into broiling, baking, boiling, steaming or frying fresh fish, because methods on the Peninsula differ not at all from methods elsewhere. Anybody who knows one end of a stove from the other should be able to manage with no help from me. There is always Fannie Farmer, after all. Just be sure that the fish is really fresh before you start operating. The way you tell is by putting it in a pan of cold water. If it sinks like a stone it's fresh.

I would like, however, to mention scrod. The authentic scrod is a small codfish, under two pounds, filleted; and on the Peninsula you can be sure that's what you're getting when you ask for it. Small cod are frequently taken from the lobster traps here, or from the dragging nets, but they are not common on the general market. When you order scrod in a restaurant you'll probably get a large cod cut into small pieces or even a fillet of some altogether different fish. This is too bad, if not actually dishonest, because real scrod is so superior that there's no use even in talking about it. It's best broiled, but it has to be broiled carefully and correctly. Brush it lightly with butter, salt and pepper it, and broil it one minute on each side. Then butter, salt and pepper it again, and this time broil it a little further from the flame, five minutes on one side and three on the other. Serve immediately with just a little lemon juice.

If the Peninsulans have nothing else, they have the best lobsters, crabs and scrod in the world, and plenty of them. I no longer even consider eating any form of them in any other place. Instead I devour my year's quota while in Corea and then forget them until my next visit.

I'd like also to say one thing about herring. No matter whether you bake, fry, broil, pickle or smoke them, they are still bony. Peninsulans conclude a meal of herring with the remark, "We won't be able to get our shirts off for a week." They're referring to the needle-like bones that will shortly be working their way through the consumer's skin—or so they pretend—until he has as much chance of removing his shirt as a porcupine would have.

My brother-in-law, who was brought up in the Middle West, used to wax eloquent on the subject of the New England predilection for chowders. "A criminal waste of good food," he'd say. "You people are chowder-crazy. If I wanted to throw away a pair of old worn-out galoshes I'll bet someone would stop me. 'It would make an awful good chowder,' someone would say." This is an exaggeration; but the fact remains that Down-Easters do eat a lot of chowders.

There are several reasons for this. The first is that along the coast the ingredients for a chowder are to be had almost for the taking. The second is that chowder is a good keep-warm. If the man of the house is delayed at sea for hours, the waiting does not ruin the dish. On the contrary, it improves it, allowing the flavors to blend. In the third place, a chowder is easy to eat. New Englanders as a whole have poor teeth, due to deficiencies of salts and minerals in the soil. My husband was once forced to go to a dentist in Texas, a stranger to him. After one glance into his mouth, the dentist said, "Hmm. New England. Typical soft teeth." This is not as true now as it once was, because dentistry has improved and besides, New Englanders now eat vegetables shipped in from areas where the soil is richer in the necessary elements; but it still obtains among middle-aged and older people and in the more remote areas. So easy eating is a factor to be considered. And last, Down-Easters *like* chowders, which alone is reason enough for serving them.

Let us have it clearly understood at once that no New England chowder ever comes within shouting distance of tomatoes or any other vegetable except potatoes and onions. If you want to make a vegetable soup with a fish base, all right, only don't call it a chowder. That is heresy.

The best fish for a proper chowder is haddock, and cod is the next best, although almost any fish may be used. You need a three-pound haddock, which you simmer until the flesh will come easily from the bones. While this is going on, fry a quarter of a pound of diced salt pork in the kettle in which you are planning to make the chowder. Remove the pork scraps and save. Put into the kettle about three cups of raw diced potatoes and three medium-sized raw onions, sliced thin. Cover with the water in which the fish was boiled and cook until the potatoes are tender but not mushy. Add the fish, from which all skin and bones have been removed, keeping the pieces as large as possible, and the crisp pork scraps. Season with salt, pepper and butter, and add a quart of scalded whole milk, the richer the better. If you have cream to spare, it improves the dish, or a can of evaporated milk may be used. Allow to stand and blend for an hour if possible. In spite of my brother-in-law, the chowder now smells and looks marvelous, with the butter and brown pork scraps dotting its creamy surface. Into soup plates put two or three common crackers, split, and ladle the chowder over them. The meal tastes as good as it looks.

An easier way to make a chowder is to alternate in a greased casserole or covered baking dish layers of fresh fish, sliced raw onions and sliced raw potatoes, salting, peppering and dotting with butter each layer. Cover the whole with rich milk to one inch deep over the last layer and bake for an hour in a moderate oven. Serve in soup plates wtih common crackers. This version will pass, but it's not as good as the other, traditional chowder. The chief advantage is fewer pots and pans to wash and less time and fussing in preparation.

All the preceding seafoods can be purchased from men who make it their business to catch them. I find it even more satisfying to prepare and eat a meal the components of which I have gathered myself. I enjoy accepting what the land so freely offers—not only the actual work involved, nor the comfortable knowledge that I am saving money, but also the whole frame and setting of the venture: the things I saw and heard and felt and thought while wresting my living from nature. You'll forgive the rather pretentious expression, I hope. I could speak of digging clams or picking berries, I know, but classifying these activities as *wresting* et cetera puts them into the realm of adventure, where indeed they belong. While in this day and place one is not actually engaged in an epic struggle for survival when he picks a quart of berries, there are other forms of adventure.

The most interesting area of all to explore in the search for food is the world between the tide lines. This would appear to be very unpromising territory. At the lower limits are the wrack-covered rocks. At the top is a disputed strip which owes allegiance both to the land and to the sea, where bindweed and rugosa and sea lavender spring from between the cobblestones and ships' timbers that have washed up during exceptionally violent storms. Between are the bare ledges and small pockets of beach over which twice daily the cold tides wash. There would seem to be very little of an edible nature here

Even if there were nothing, I would still like to walk the shore. Here in this narrow and peculiar world between the tides you are very much aware of standing on the extreme edge of a great continent. Behind you stretches the land, rising in mountain ranges, cradling gigantic river systems, supporting cities and towns and hamlets. On and on it goes, covered sometimes with tall forests, sometimes with prairie sod, until it reaches the night-shrouded Pacific. Before you lie all the peace and mystery of the sea, sunny and

empty to the curve of the earth. Here you are in a buffer zone, belonging neither to land nor to sea, but occupied alternately by citizens of both. On the flood the fish swim wide-eyed over it and crabs scuttle across its floor; and at the ebb the gulls who have been congregated in waiting swoop down to feed on its bounty. And so do I.

One of the things it offers is clams. Surrounding the islands and on the seaward side of the Peninsula is what is called *bold water*. By this is meant water that comes directly in from the open ocean to the steep ledges, water that is deep enough to admit boats, always providing that the surf is not too heavy. Here there are no mud flats exposed at low tide, and the effect is one of clean-cut edges, of decisiveness and strength. It's beautiful, but it's no place for clams. They live in sand or mud flats, and to find these you have to go over onto the Gouldsboro Bay side of the Peninsula. This involves quite a bit of walking. Leaving the road at a point near the Corea cemetery, you strike down across a heath toward the Bay, which you can see glimmering below you. There is supposed to be a path following the course of an overgrown lumbering road of the days of long ago, but time has almost obliterated it. Hampered by bucket and clam rake, pausing now and then to take your bearings or to investigate a pitcher plant or observe a bird, you make your way as best you can to the shore.

It's best to arrive at the clam flats on the lowest tide possible— not an ordinary low tide, but the exceptional low run that occurs monthly at the full of the moon. Somehow this seems always to take place very early in the morning. The last time I went clamming was with Marcia and her brother Merrill Spurling from Prospect Harbor, and George Crowley. On the day before, after a careful study of the tide chart which the *Peninsula Gazette* issues as a courtesy, George informed me that I would have to be at the rendezvous (Marcia's house) not one minute later than 4:45 A.M. So I was, having eaten my breakfast in a hurry and having left my cigarettes on the dining-room table. Herb's store was closed at that hour, so I couldn't get any more, and I burst into Marcia's kitchen demanding a cigarette before I even said "Good morning."

Neither George nor Marcia smokes, and Merrill looked at me resignedly. "Haven't you got any either?" he asked. "I came off with a flat pack, and didn't go back for more because I was sure you'd have plenty. Well,"—he inspected his pack—"I've got three. You can have *one*, but you've got to make it last."

"You're a gentleman," I told him sincerely.

We made our difficult way across the heath and came out on the Bay near Mill Pond, an almost landlocked inlet of the sea across the narrow entrance of which there was once, a hundred years ago, a dam. The granite abutments are still to be seen, with the icy water flowing swift and deep between them. This is the site of a long-vanished tidal mill at which the timber taken from the vicinity was sawn into lumber. It was an early precursor of the Passama-quoddy Project, where the tides were to have been harnessed by dams to provide power. Standing there on the ruined remains in the sunrise, it was easy to see how it worked, with the water falling over the dam alternately into and out of the pond as the tide turned, to rotate the dripping mill wheel. But all that was a long time ago.

"Right out there," Marcia remembered, pointing, "my father set a trap for me, the year I was eight. He only caught one lobster in it all season long, but that one was a real buster. Pa took it out to the lobster-buying sloop, with me right on his heels like a little tag-along boat, and the captain weighed it. Came to ninety-five cents, but he gave me a dollar. I can tell you, I was some old proud."

"Tide's almost slack," George said. "Can't stay here all day." He picked up his bucket and led the way along the shore toward Mill Cove, a half-hidden little estuary in which now, with the tide so low, the rotted, barnacle-crusted and kelp-draped ribs of an old ship were visible. It had been there always, Marcia told me; some said it was the wreck of an English boat driven there by Sam Bel-lamy, the pirate who had had a stronghold at Machias in the early 1700's, while others claimed that it was a Yankee vessel, chased in by British patrols during the Revolution; but nobody really knew. It didn't make any difference now, anyhow.

We continued our way along the shore, past the broken stakes of a long disused lobster pound, past a beautiful little spruce-covered point, until we came to some grassy mounds. It was a queer place, like a tenantless landscape of the moon. The sea, which lately had washed where we were standing, had retreated to the furthest limit it would achieve in the next twenty-eight days, and all the area ex-posed was pocked with half-tide ledges—flat mesa-like formations of rock separated by threads of shallow water. Their shadows lay long and surrealistic in the clear morning light. Beyond were the clam flats. Marcia and I sat down on the mounds to rest, but George and Merrill set off for the flats, leaping the little streams, disappearing behind ledges and reappearing in unexpected places, strangely diminished by distance. Finally they vanished altogether, and Marcia and I sat quietly, chewing spears of wild wheat and enjoying the warmth of the climbing sun.

Then Marcia picked up a short length of driftwood and began scratching in the earth. "Maybe we can find an arrowhead," she said. "We used to find a lot of them here when I was a kid, before the grass and briars grew so thick. These mounds are really shell heaps, though you wouldn't guess it now. They say the Indians used to come here on clambakes, and I suppose they'd be bound to lose things. I found a perfect white one, once. Real pretty, it was. A man who was visiting around here took it over to the Abbe Musuem on Mt. Desert. Far as I know, it's there yet, with a card with my name on it, saying I loaned it."

Inspired by this tale, I too found a stick, cleared an area of sod, and began digging. It was easy now to see that this was indeed a shell heap, although the shells themselves had crumbled almost to white powder and most of the mound consisted of the rich leaf mold and loam that had sifted down between them over the centuries. We uncovered the charred remains of an ancient cooking fire, but the only Indian relic we found was an unfinished flint arrowhead which had evidently been discarded because of a flaw in the workmanship. It didn't matter to us, though, that it was worthless. It was enough to conjure up a picture of the Indians who had sat around their fire on this very spot, hundreds of years ago, shucking out their clams and tossing the shells onto the heap behind them, eating their fill, and then busying themselves with the small accustomed chores of every day—minding the babies, probably, mending their clothes with bone needles and sinew, and, to pass the time while talking, chipping out new arrowheads.

The sun was now well up, and we could see the lobsterboats tending their traps out beyond the flats, and a big sardiner from Prospect Harbor making its way toward the weir further up the Bay. The little rivulets between the ledges began to swell almost imperceptibly at first and then with increasing volume, and Marcia stood up. "Tide's turned," she said. "If they don't start back pretty soon—

you know, it's easy to get caught on these half-tide ledges. More'n one's had a narrow escape— Oh, here they come." Then she laughed. "This is my idea of going clamming. Let someone else do all the work."

I agreed with her. Digging clams here is real labor, like chiseling nuggets out of solid rock.

George and Merrill leaped the last channel, trudged up to us with their pails of clams, and sank down onto the ground. Merrill reached into his shirt pocket, took out his flat cigarette pack, removed the last cigarette, and carefully cut it in two equal parts. "Here," he said, handing me one, "I know your tongue's hanging out for this." I was speechless before this display of chivalry.

"No sense lugging all these shells back up over the hayth," George remarked, practically. So we shucked out most of the clams into one of the buckets, saving a few for steaming, eating a few raw, and tossing the shells onto the Indian heap with a fine sense of making our contribution to the accumulation of the ages.

When we got back to the village we were surprised to find that it was only half-past eight, not yet the shank of the morning. We felt as though we'd been long gone on a distant journey through time and space. That's what I meant when I said that wresting a living from nature on the Peninsula can be a form of adventure.

The simplest way to eat clams is, of course, raw; and the next simplest is steamed. Scrub the clams thoroughly with a stiff brush to remove sand and grit. Throw away any dead ones—and they're probably dead if their necks hang out and don't retract when you touch them. Have ready boiling on the stove about half an inch of water in a kettle of suitable size. Put the clams in, cover tightly, and allow to steam until the shells open, or about twelve minutes.

The eating is a messy business best undertaken in the privacy of one's own home. Each person is provided with a soup plate full of clams, a shallow dish of melted butter, a cup of the hot liquid from the kettle—really a clear clam broth—and a small bath towel. In the middle of the table should be a large pan for the empty shells. Remove the clam from the shell, rinse it in the broth, dip it in butter and eat it. Some people don't eat the stomachs, some don't eat the tough black necks, and nobody eats the cellophane-like membrane that encases the necks. From time to time take a drink of the hot broth. When I serve steamed clams I also provide rolls and sometimes a green tossed salad. That's enough. I also save all the leftover liquid, after allowing the inevitable sand to settle to the bottom, and keep it in the refrigerator. This I drink either hot or cold because I like it, but many consider this a perverted taste.

New England clam chowder is made as fish chowder is, with potatoes, onions, salt pork, whole milk and maybe cream, and *no* tomatoes. It's made by the same method, too. The pork is diced and fried crisp, and the potatoes, onion and a little water are added. When these are soft, add the clams, from which the inedible parts have been removed, and cook for not more than three minutes. Longer cooking makes them tough. Move the kettle to low heat, pour in the milk slowly to prevent curdling, salt, pepper and butter to taste. Clam chowder, like other chowders, should age a few hours to be at its best.

Clams may be fried in batter. The fried clam is as common at coastal wayside diners as the hamburger is elsewhere. The batter is made by beating the yolks of two eggs hard and adding half a cup of milk, a teaspoonful of olive oil, a tablespoonful of lemon juice, and a cup of sifted flour. Fold in the stiffly beaten egg whites and about a pint of cleaned clams, and let stand in the refrigerator for at least two hours. Fry in deep hot fat. Adding the lemon juice and olive oil is a local refinement aimed at preventing the clams from soaking fat and becoming indigestible. As far as my experience can indicate, it succeeds. Clams done this way are much better than the commercial variety, in which I suspect the use of baking powder to swell the batter. I base my suspicion on the fact that those you buy often consist of a lot of batter (relatively cheap) and very little clam (quite costly), and I apologize to any vendors who don't employ this dodge.

Or clams may be deviled by chopping them fine, simmering them for five minutes in their own juice, adding minced onion, green pepper and celery leaves to taste, along with a touch of prepared mustard and enough cracker crumbs to make a fairly firm paste. This mixture is baked in a moderate oven in clamshells or ramekins for about twenty minutes and served with lemon juice.

It's very good, but to me its chief virtue is that in an emergency it allows the stretching of a few clams into a lot and is a far more elegant company dish than the admittedly sloppy steamed clams.

The local mussels (*Mytilus edulis* or blue mussel) were probably eaten by the Indians and early settlers, but then they fell into a period of disfavor for no particular reason that I know. Now—and I think perhaps the summer people with their more sophisticated tastes may be responsible for this—they are coming back into popularity. Recently the cannery in South Gouldsboro has been processing them occasionally, so that they may be bought at almost any supermarket. Since they are rather fussy to prepare, this is the easiest way; but, if you live on the Peninsula, buying canned mussels when there are bushels of them at your door is considered extravagant. I myself consider it cheating. Half the point of serving mussels is that you gathered them yourself.

You have to keep a snug watch on the mussel colonies in your walks around the shoreline if you want to be sure of finding them when you need them. Because there was a large bed near Shark Cove last year doesn't mean that it will be there this year. One season I could get all I wanted over on the back of Cranberry Point, but now there aren't any there and I have to go clear over onto the other side of the harbor and out onto the sand bar that connects Crowley and Inner Bar Islands at low tide. Formerly there were none there, but only a great plenitude of sand dollars, a variety of sea urchin which are interesting but inedible.

Nevertheless, there seems to be a general mania for picking up sand dollars and taking them home. Almost everybody in Corea has a fine collection of them on the window sills, with the overflow piled in a heap by the doorstep. I do myself, but I'm sure I don't know why. I don't know either, why I persist in filling my dungaree pockets with every pretty shell and pebble I find whenever I walk along the tide line. There is no virtue in mere numbers, and one perfect little alabaster-like whelk shell with its delicate whorls can teach you as much about both whelks and beauty as a thousand can.

Trying to justify my compulsive action, for a long time I told myself that I needed them for doorstops, which I made by filling the half-gallon jugs in which I buy orange juice with assorted shells, small sand dollars, skates' eggs, banded pebbles and other curiosa These are rather attractive and interesting objects, and they actually will hold a door open. Peninsulans sometimes put three or four clean beach pebbles into milk they are scalding to prevent its catching on the pan, and some of my better pebbles I allocate to this department. But there is a limit to the number of doorstops one needs, to the number of friends who will accept one as a gift, and to the pebbles required in milk-scalding. Still I pick up shells and pebbles, and the heap outside the cabin door grows daily. Some archeologist of the race that succeeds ours will find them, maybe, and will draw some totally erroneous conclusions.

When there were mussels on Cranberry Point backside, I one day discovered something of no importance whatsoever, but I loved it just the same. Mussels must be gathered at low tide. On this day, time got away from me and the tide turned before I knew it. If I was going to get to the mussel bed before it was submerged I'd have to find a quicker route than my usual long way round the perimeter of the Point. So I struck bravely off across what appeared to be a field of tall grass between the sea and a tangled copse of stunted spruces and tamaracks.

This was a mistake. What looked like smooth terrain was nothing of the sort. Here where the gales of winter strike with undiminished force, the surf sometimes thunders up onto the land for an unbelievable distance, bringing with it stones of all sizes from boulders down to coarse sand. The heavy boulders are dropped first, so that the exposed parts of the Point are walled by a breastwork of sea-smooth rocks, sometimes head-high. When an "old" sea attacks the base the whole structure shifts slightly, giving out a faint musical chiming as stone knocks against stone. It's eerie. Back of this breastwork is a strip of varying width paved entirely with smaller rocks, loosely strewn, up through which grow weeds and shrubs and grass. This was the area in which I now found myself.

It was an impossible place. The grass that had looked so harmless at a distance turned out to be waist-high sedge, each tough blade of which was a saw-toothed bayonet, and every time I took a step a rounded cobblestone rolled under my tread. It was a good place to fall down and break an ankle, but that's all it was good for. After picking myself up half a dozen times and licking the wounds inflicted by the vicious sedges, I decided that enough was enough and started looking around for a way out of the mess. The further I went inland, I reasoned, the smaller would become the stones and the firmer the footing, so I started working my way back from the sea.

My theory was correct, and within fifty feet, halfway to the woods, I was able to proceed with confidence over a surface of packed gravel which marked the extreme of the deposits made by the storm tides. Low turfy grass grew out of it, and small flowers, and a healthy crop of daisies in full bloom. It wasn't until I had gone for some distance that I realized that the daisies stuck strictly to the four-foot sash of gravel. There were none to the seaward and none to the landward, but only here on the dividing line; and I found that I didn't have to pick my way at all, but only to follow the gold and white daisy trail winding so airily and brightly across the bleak terrain. Forgetting all about the mussels, I let it lead me clear around the Point. It was wonderful. Lots of people have a red carpet laid down for them, but very few a mile-long runner of daisies, dancing and tossing and beckoning in a fresh and salty breeze.

The next day I went back and got the mussels, which I baked according to a very old recipe. Take six or seven dozen mussels, scrub them and let them soak for several hours in fresh cold water. Any that float to the top, throw away. Steam them until they open, or for about fifteen minutes, in a pint of sea water to which you may add a clove of garlic if you wish. Remove from the fire, drain, then pick the meat from the shells, using scissors to trim off the little beards that are found under the black tongues. Place in layers in a casserole, seasoning each layer with a little chopped onion and parsley, salt and paprika. Lay five or six slices of bacon on top, sprinkle with grated cheese, and bake in a hot oven for fifteen minutes or until the bacon is crisp. This is really delicious.

You can do lots of things with mussels. You can steam them and serve them on the half shell, or roll them in batter and fry them, or scallop them, or stew them in white wine, or chop them up raw, add onion, Worcestershire sauce and celery salt and serve them on crackers as an appetizer.

Then there are what are called locally "wrinkles," fairly large snail-like gastropods with coarse brown shells. They're found attached to rocks at low tide. Here they are boiled and the flesh is picked out with a long pin and pickled in vinegar. The flavor is good, but they are almost as tough as an old rubber boot. Probably a chowder could be made of them, but I haven't got around to that experiment yet.

The strip between the tide extremes offers other forms of food than shellfish. After an "old" sea has been running, quantities of dulse may be found on the outer beaches. This is a fine, ferny seaweed, white or pink or pale tan, that grows in lacy bunches. It's pretty. Many specialty stores sell a dried and packaged form under the name of Irish Moss Blancmange, but on the Peninsula we have no truck with such effete nonsense. We don't make blancmange. We make seaweed pudding, which is the same thing.

First you gather a couple of handfuls of dulse and wash out all the sand, salt and shells—quite a job in itself. Let it stand in cold water until it has expanded, drain it, and add it to a quart of milk in a double boiler. Cook until the milk coats a spoon, remove from the fire and strain, rubbing the weed lightly through the sieve. Add a teaspoonful of vanilla and chill in greased molds until it is firm. Serve with cream and sugar. Don't try to cook the sugar into it, as it is very apt to whey.

Drinking hot dulse lemonade is a standard treatment locally for coughs and colds. You put the juice of a lemon and a tablespoonful of sugar into a tall glass and fill the glass with hot water in which a handful of dulse has been boiled. Drink the brew as hot as you can stand it. I never had occasion to try this remedy, but others swear by it.

Higher up on the tide strip, growing out of impossible crevices in the ledges, there is goose grass, which can be used as a green. This grows in thick bunches from a central taproot. The pale green leaves are rather fleshy and arrowy in shape, like the tongues of geese—if you've ever had occasion to examine a goose's tongue— and you cook them as you would any other green, picking them in the late spring and early summer and boiling them. Most people here include a small piece of salt pork in the cooking, but that isn't necessary. They taste a little salt and more than a little peppery, and I like them very much. They must be good for what ails you, being full of iodine and other components of sea water, like the mineral-trace salt that health fiends advocate. In colonial times, when people had gone all winter long without green vegetables, they ate bushels of goose grass, come spring, drinking the liquid in which the greens had been boiled as a sort of spring tonic. They didn't know about vitamins then, but evidently a natural craving dictated this procedure. They probably ate them raw, too. I know I find myself absentmindedly chewing on a goose-grass spear as I walk along the shore, and without doubt beachcombers before me have done the same. As the season progresses, though, you have to give up this practice. The leaves become more and more peppery until they almost burn the tongue. They're still good in a tossed green salad, however, adding a tangy zest.

Along the upper limits of the tide strip, where the sea washes only during storms, are the big rugosa bushes and the small wild roses. The hips or ripe fruit of these are added to jellies during the boiling to stiffen them, as commercial pectin is added elsewhere; or they are ground up—either cooked or raw—with other fruits to make relishes, conserves or marmalades. In the early times such expedients were necessary in a place where food was scarce and hard-won, and these uses have survived to the present day, when scratching a living is still a problem.

Like the rich pastures of the sea and the surf-scoured amphibious between-tide territory, the land proper, barren and unproductive as it may appear, provides the Peninsulans with a variety of indigenous foods. The first to be available in the spring are the greens: dandelions, dock and fiddleheads. Almost everybody is familiar with dandelion greens. Nowadays they may be bought in cellophane bags at most chain stores, but that isn't the same as digging them yourself. Digging dandelions is something to do outdoors when it's too early to spade the garden and you can't stand being housebound another minute. You provide yourself with a basket and, an old knife and, dressed in old clothes, go looking for dandelions.

They grow in abandoned meadows or on the open moor, and it's best to dig them before they blossom. Afterward they become increasingly tough and bitter. The taproot should be cut below the surface of the ground, so that the whole plant hangs together. Holding it by the root, you can shake out the dead grass that is inevitably lodged among the leaves. This saves cleaning time later. To reduce bitterness, you can soak the dandelions overnight in cold water with a teaspoonful of salt and the juice of half a lemon added. Then drain them, simmer for an hour with a ham bone or a piece of salt pork, and eat with or without vinegar.

Dock greens are good, too. These are the young, tender leaves of what will grow up to be the common coarse burdocks found along all New England country roadsides. Their season is short. They grow fast and soon become too tough and hairy to eat. You boil them as you would any other green.

Fiddleheads—so called because they look like the head of a violin—are the tightly curled stems of various ferns before they unfurl. There are three kinds: the ostrich fern, which grows in clumps in swampy places and is covered with a brown scale that must be removed; the cinnamon fern, which is covered with a yellowish fuzz that must be soaked and rubbed off; and the common bracken, a more delicate single stalk covered with a silvery bloom that also must be rubbed off before cooking. Having cleaned them, you cook them as you would asparagus or broccoli, allowing twenty minutes for the ostrich type, thirty for the bracken, and thirty or forty for the cinnamon. Serve with melted butter; or they're good cold, with French dressing, as a salad.

I like fiddleheads. They have a faintly earthy flavor, evocative of marshes basking in the thin spring sunlight and slowly coming to life. When you wrest your living from nature it is almost impossible to keep the end food product free from the context in your mind. A mess of dandelion greens, for example, is not merely something to eat but an emotional adventure involving the first robin of the year, a short talk with another digger, the sound of the bell buoy drifting over the moor, and long thoughts of other women who dug dandelions in this same place a century ago.

After the greens come the berries, one replacing another from mid-June to early October, so that you are never left without berries to pick. First, in June, come the tiny ambrosial wild strawberries, brought to early ripening by the heat of the sun reflected by and stored in the basic rock of the Peninsula, so that the whole seagirt tongue of land is virtually a natural hotbed. In July there are raspberries and blackberries, growing on rank canes in open places. August brings great misty-blue clusters of blueberries, so thick on the low, dwarfed bushes that the earth seems to reflect the blue of the sky and the sea. In no time at all you can pick a whole milk-pan full. The foxes pick them, too, and the gulls and curlews, looking strangely domestic as they peck about what passes for the cabin dooryard. Sometimes during blueberry season the whole Point seems to be covered with drifted snow as the great white flocks of gulls settle upon it to eat berries; and when you drive slowly along the rough track of the road, the earth ahead of you dissolves into a cloud of strong, beating wings as the startled hordes take flight. It's like proceeding through a crowd of archangels, an otherworldly experience.

In August, too, wild gooseberries ripen over on Inner and Outer Bar Islands, and later in the month the tiny highland cranberries are ready for picking. These are the same as the lingenberries of Sweden, and are greatly prized on the Peninsula. They grow on the higher, dry land, their miniature vines mingling with goldthread, violets, pussyfoot and cinquefoil to form a rich and various carpet. They are hard to pick, being so small and low, which may be the reason they are held in such high esteem; although they really do have a flavor and color superior to the bog and heath cranberries, which come later, after the first September frost. The heathberries are speckled brown and white and are not very plentiful, but there are bushels of bogberries on Cranberry Point. That's where it gets its name.

In late August there are also what are called colloquially baked apples. These are really heath mulberries and are new in my experience. They're found on the big heath back of the cemetery and on Drunken Pole Heath, but those more traveled than I tell me that they also grow on the lower slopes of Mt. Katahdin, on Petit Manan Point, and in Alaska. They are the size and shape of a blackberry, but they are golden in color and grow one to a six-inch stem rising erectly between twin leaves like tulip leaves. They taste like condensed milk—the thick, sweet kind—when eaten raw, or they may be made into jam by boiling with an equal amount of sugar, pound for pound, and sealed in glass.

In September the sides of all the narrow roads are lined with fruit free for the picking. There are chokecherries, used to add color and pectin to apple jelly; and sugar pears—small, plum-like fruit which makes wonderful jelly by itself; and rowan, or round-wood berries, which attract great flocks of south-bound migrating birds. They also make a very good conserve, and I will quote you verbatim the directions for making it as I received them.

"First pick yourself a good lot of berries and blanch them for a few minutes. Then add what you think is the right amount of sugar—half and half, maybe—and bring the kettle to a boil. After a while, slice in a nice apple or pear or both, with the peels but not the core, and keep on cooking until you think it's probably about the right consistency. Pour it off into jars and seal it with paraffin. That's all there is to it."

Since these directions require a culinary intuition that I do not possess, I have never made roundwood-berry conserve. I've eaten it, however, and it is delicious, both tart and sweet, with an unusual, exotic flavor, like no other fruit I know. Some day I'll learn to make it.

The other berries are easier to deal with. All, except the cranberries, may be eaten raw, with or without sugar and cream. Sometimes I think this is the best way to eat them, with their natural flavor undisguised. I always eat wild strawberries raw because I never manage to pick enough to make a pie or shortcake. They are so tiny and fragile. Once I did amass almost a pint and, as an experiment, made a small jar of sun-cooked strawberry jam, the way the early settlers did. The berries are cleaned, spread in a pan, lightly sugared and placed outdoors in the sun with a net over them to discourage bugs. The hot sun cooks them slowly until the juice is a thick syrup and the berries are almost translucent. This takes several days, but the jam is wonderful, with a flavor exactly like that of fresh berries.

However, the whole process is a great strain on the nervous system. At night, or the minute you see a fog bank on the horizon, or if you hear thunder in the distance, you have to rush to carry your jam under cover. This isn't so bad if you are at home anyhow, but it's definitely inconvenient when you happen to be miles away. I suppose colonial women stayed home where they belonged, though, and I know they were much more efficient in all departments than I. They probably turned out quarts of strawberry jam as easy as rolling off a log.

The next most obvious way to treat berries is to make them into pies, adding sugar to your own taste—I like berry pies rather tart, so I skimp the sugar and sprinkle lightly with flour before topping with crust to prevent juice leakage. I add a little lemon juice to gooseberry and blueberry pies, and a pinch of salt, as otherwise they may be a trifle flat.

One day, on my way to the supermarket, I stopped to call on Ida Buckley on the Pond Road. Ida is Town Clerk, Town Treasurer, Tax Collector, a justice of the peace and a notary public, among other things. Therefore a call upon her is liable to interruptions. You frequently have to amuse yourself while she issues a dog, marriage or hunting license, notarizes a paper, registers a deed, accepts tax money, or even performs a wedding ceremony. It was during one of these interludes that I, sitting in her kitchen, picked up her I-don't-know-how-many-great Aunt Cora Guptill's cookbook. Ida was a Guptill before she married, a descendant of one of the original settlers who spelled the name Gubtail; and this cookbook had been in the family for generations.

It was a very old copybook, the pages foxed brown with age and decorated with faded spatters of batter. The recipes were written in perfectly lovely, carefully shaded, copperplate script. I turned the leaves respectfully, thinking how much could be learned about a way of living, even about dreams and beliefs and longings, from so homely a thing as an old cookbook.

There was, for example, a recipe for mock cherry pie. It could have been evolved only by one who came from a far place where cherry trees grew to a land too newly settled to have brought orchards into bearing, by one who remembered with nostalgia the cherry pies of her homeland. Employing the ingredients at hand, she did her best to duplicate for her own children an experience of her childhood.

"Cut one cup of cranberries in halves without crushing," she wrote in her beautiful hand. "Add ⅔rds of a cup of seeded raisins cut in quarters, and ¾ths of a cup of sugar mixed with one tablespoon of flour. Put crust in pan, crimping edge, add mixture, and make a lattice top. Dot with butter. Bake." It's a lot of work to halve cranberries and to seed and quarter raisins. There were no seedless raisins in those days. I hope the pie tasted as good to her as she thought it would.

The same woman also made "blueberry tilt." She used saleratus and soda, but when I made it I translated into baking powder. You make a batter of 2 cups of flour, 2 teaspoonfuls of baking powder, one egg, one cup of milk, ⅔ cup of sugar, and salt. Add a cup of blueberries, floured to prevent their sinking to the bottom of the mixture. Bake for half an hour in a moderate oven and serve hot with foamy sauce, cream, or stewed blueberries. Or, in my case, with vanilla ice cream.

She made strawberry dumplings, too; and so would I if I could ever collect enough strawberries. Since I can't, I use blueberries with good results. Following her general plan, I stew two cups of blueberries with a cup of sugar and a cup of water. When they are briskly boiling I drop in dumplings made of soft biscuit dough to which a cup of blueberries has been added. I cover the pan tightly and allow it to simmer and steam for twenty minutes. Serve in a cereal dish, drowning the dumplings in the blueberry sauce and cream—or vanilla ice cream.

It was from Aunt Cora Guptill's cookbook that I learned about putting dried marigold petals in steamed suet puddings for flavor, and about clover honey. You gather equal amounts of red clover blossoms, white clover blossoms, and wild rose petals. These you boil in half the amount of water by volume and an equal amount of sugar by weight, until the liquid will spin a three-inch thread when dribbled from a spoon. Strain and allow to cool. The result is a thick, pale gold syrup that really does taste like honey.

Besides pies, "tilts" and dumplings, you can make blueberry cakes, muffins and pancakes simply by adding the floured berries to your favorite basic recipe. They're good for a change. I especially like blueberry pancakes with butter and brown sugar instead of maple syrup. I use them as a dessert during blueberry season. If there's any batter left over from dinner dessert it keeps nicely in the refrigerator, and I have blueberry pancakes for breakfast the next morning if I want them.

There is game, too, on the Peninsula. Almost every man and boy gets his deer in the fall, and rabbits for the pot. There are coons and bears and porcupines, but the first two are seldom eaten and the last never, although porcupines are said to be edible. Then there are pheasants and partridges in the woods and on the heaths, and canvasbacks—called simply sea birds—and black ducks and what are known as whistlers along the shore and out on the reefs and islands. Stews are made from the birds and rabbits, and the deer are cut up into chops, steaks and roasts, the odd scraps and necks being made into mincemeat. But I won't go into all this, because those who hunt have their own methods of game cookery, and those who don't hunt have no need for any advice.

On the Peninsula there is a rule governing the making of vegetable soup. You start with a marrow- or shinebone, which you simmer until the meat is almost tender enough. Then you add cut-up raw vegetables, but the rule is that you must use only those which grow underground: carrots, potatoes, turnips, onions, parsnips and the like. No string beans or tomatoes, you notice; and you don't thicken the brew with flour. You just let it boil down to the proper consistency.

Then there is succotash chowder, about which an old cookbook carries the parenthetical note, "Good for a cold day." You try out a half cupful of cubed salt pork and fry two small onions, sliced, in the fat. Add one cup of whole-kernel corn, one cup of cooked Jacob's cattle beans, three pints of milk, and pepper to taste. Jacob's cattle beans are peculiar to this area. They're about the size of yellow-eyed beans, but they're white and irregularly spotted and striped with a rosy brown. They're named after the "ringstraked, spotted and striped" cattle that Jacob bred from Laban's flock, according to the book of Genesis.

Carrots were apparently a very useful vegetable to bygone generations of cooks on the Peninsula. Aunt Lutee Martha Guptill, who inherited Aunt Cora Guptill's cookbook and added recipes of her own, gives directions for making a carrot pie. Boil and mash three carrots and add them to one cup of milk and two beaten eggs, spiced with cinnamon, nutmeg, allspice and ginger. This is baked in a single crust and looks and tastes very much like pumpkin pie. And in a day when citrus fruit was scarce and hard come-by, one orange and one lemon were stretched into a lot of marmalade by adding to them two cups of sugar and two cups of cooked carrots. This was boiled until the juice would jell and was sealed in glasses; and I don't suppose anyone knew the difference.

But the recipe I like best is the one for carrot cough syrup. It's very easy to make. To a cupful of boiled-down carrot water you add half a pound of loaf sugar and cook until it is syrupy. What I like about it, though, is the footnote appended, which states categorically and with no foolish false modesty, "This is the cheapest, best and safest cough medicine now or ever in use."

Then there's Haymakers' switchel, which was carried in stone jugs to the Dyke Marsh during haying season. To a quart of cold water was added a cup of brown sugar, a half-cup of molasses, a tablespoonful of ginger and a cup of vinegar. This really is a refreshing beverage, much more so than the case of cola that the hayers would probably take with them if there was any haying on the marshes today.

There's vinegar candy, too, made by boiling together until brittle when tried in cold water two cups of sugar, half a cup of vinegar and butter the size of a pullet's egg. This is poured onto a buttered platter to cool, pulled until it is snowy, and cut with scissors into manageable pieces. This was a very popular confection in the early days for two reasons. First, the ingredients were a part of the standard basic stock of every pioneer larder; and second, a candy pull could be used as a device to keep the kids occupied and happy on a stormy afternoon, or even made into a social event by inviting in the neighbors. People were easily entertained in those days.

There are many more foods prepared and eaten on the Peninsula today than those I have told about, of course, and each month when the women's magazines come out with their new ideas more are being tried. Just the other day Marcia served me a cracker spread which she'd picked up from Arthur Godfrey. It's made of sour cream and dehydrated onion soup, and you've probably served it yourself. But I have confined myself to dishes made from native produce and from ingredients—like oranges and spices—brought in on the sloops in the old sailing days, and cooked in the old ways. Salt pork, you will have observed, is used in a great many recipes. That isn't because Peninsulans have an uncontrollable craving for salt pork, I'm sure, but because it, along with potatoes, onions, and salt fish, was one of the few necessary and plentiful staples of olden days.

But it isn't only the recipes that have been handed down. A woman I know, Julia Stewart, makes the best doughnuts I ever ate anywhere. So good are they that she has found herself in the doughnut business and daily makes dozens and dozens for sale. Part of her success she attributes to the fact that she fries them in her great-great-grandmother's old black iron doughnut kettle, which always did turn out superior doughnuts.

On the same day that Marcia served me the Godfrey spread she was busy making yellow-hammers, which are saleratus (or baking powder) biscuits with a tablespoonful of molasses added to give them a golden color. The pastry board she was using was an enormous affair with a retaining rim on three sides to prevent flour spillage. On the fourth side was a smooth-edged notch at least four inches deep, the purpose of which was not apparent to me. So I asked.

"Oh, that wasn't meant to be there," she said. "This was my mother's board. Her brother made it for her as a wedding present, and she used it as long as she lived. She started right in the day she was married. She didn't have any wedding trip. She and my father moved into their house at West Bay right after the ceremony, and the first thing she did, almost before she took her coat off, was stir up a batch of hot biscuits for supper, the first meal of their married life. I can hear her tell of it yet. Nobody thought to give her a rolling pin, so she had to roll out the dough with a bottle. This front edge of the board was straight then, but she used to rap it on the edge of the flour barrel to shake the loose flour off when she was done baking. I remember when it was only a small gouge, but it grew over the years. They did a lot of baking in those days."

They must have. The board is made of heavy stock and the notch is deep. It made me tired even to think of the scores of barrels of flour that must have crossed the surface of that board, and the thousands of times Marcia's mother must have rapped it on the barrel rims.

"I suppose," Marcia went on, "I could get me a smaller, lighter board. I don't do the baking she did, and this is heavy and inconvenient. But I don't know. I just can't seem to make up my mind to give it up. Whenever I use it I get to thinking of my mother and the times we had—both good and bad—when my brother and I were children. Things I thought I'd forgotten come back to me. So I guess I'll just keep right on using it. It'll last out my time all right, and after that it won't make any difference what becomes of it, because there won't be anybody left to remember how it was in those days."

That's how Peninsulans are, not only about cooking but about all other aspects of living as well. Old things are not given up lightly here, nor old methods or ideas or attitudes. In keeping them, the Peninsulans keep their sense of security and continuity and serenity, blessings which elsewhere in the world are becoming increasingly rare.

9. In the Midst of Life

WHEN I FIRST STARTED SPENDING SUMMERS on Cranberry Point I was struck by the frequent use of illness, tragedy and death as conversational material. It seemed to me that these subjects exerted a morbid fascination on Peninsulan minds and hearts. Where I came from, one murmured the conventional phrases upon being told of a death in the family of a friend, following his topical lead and never asking probing questions, on the theory that dwelling on the particulars might be painful for the bereaved. On the Peninsula it was different. People seemed to me to take an almost ghoulish pleasure in recounting or hearing every detail not only of the deathbed scene and funeral, but of the events leading up to them as well, from the first trivial symptom of disease to the last gasping breath. I thought it was an unhealthy preoccupation, depressing and morbid.

Now I have been here longer, and I understand better. Far from being abnormal, this is a perfectly natural attitude that has been retained from the past, along with other manners and mores, because the circumstances surrounding these occasions have changed very little in the past century. In most places today the sick are taken to hospitals as soon as the situation borders on the serious and are kept there until they either recover or die. There modern medicine reduces suffering to a humane minimum; but if suffering is unavoidable the hospital staff, whose business it is to do so, acts as a buffer between the patient and those who love him. The family is spared sitting helplessly through the scarifying periods of agony implicit in many diseases and through the endless night watches. It is relieved of the wearing and often unpleasant chores attendant upon care of the desperately ill. The family no less than the patient benefits from hospitalization.

If death occurs, the buffer is still in effect. No longer do people lay out their own dead in their own homes. Instead, a team of professionals smoothly and sympathetically takes over the responsibility, so that often the bereaved never see the face of the departed until the lines of suffering have been skillfully erased. No longer do children tiptoe wide-eyed about their homes and adults speak low in constant awareness of the coffin in the best parlor. The modern funeral home now houses the dead until the day of the funeral, which may take place there or in the church of the deceased's affiliation. The emphasis now is on the comfort and convenience of the living rather than on the performing of last sad services to the dead. I do not mean to sound censorious. Actually I think this is a very sound state of affairs, but it is unlike the state that prevailed even fifty years ago.

Today, also, the mentally deficient and the harmlessly insane are more often than not committed to institutions operated specifically for their protection and well-being; and very often, too, the elderly move or are moved into rest homes designed especially to provide for the needs of those of their age group. Less and less are the young, sound and vigorous subjected to reminders in the persons of those who are old or ill in mind or body that man is frail and liable to flaw, and that where there is life there is also, by corollary, aging and death.

Things were not thus in the past, and they are not thus on the Peninsula today. The last century was characterized by, among other things, a fashion for tears and grieving, for widows' weeds and a whole year of full mourning after the death of a near relative. This included the wearing of unrelieved black by women and of black ties and armbands by men, the use of heavily black-bordered stationery, and the eschewing of all social events whatsoever and all public appearances except church services. During the second year of bereavement the strictures were slightly relaxed. Men shed their mourning bands and women added touches of white to their weeds; or in summer, under exceptional circumstances, all-white costumes were permissible, as was attendance at small informal parties in the homes of close friends. It wasn't until the third year that the mourning period was officially ended and the bereaved could wear bright colors again and take up the normal activities of every day.

Inevitably there were some who had withdrawn so far into a life of seclusion and had become so accustomed to the lachrymose consideration given a mourner that they never did re-enter the hurly-burly of the world. Rather, they spent the remainder of their days on the fringes, like pale wraiths whose bodies continued to occupy the terrestrial plane, but whose thoughts and spirits were elsewhere. These were greatly admired as being good grievers and were spoken of with awe and respect. Today, in most places, they would be considered neurotics and would be bundled with all possible haste by concerned friends to the nearest psychiatrist. The pendulum has made the full swing. If in other times death and sorrow were surrounded by too much emotion, today their treatment is too curt and brusque. But not on the Peninsula.

Why? Because on the Peninsula today illness and death are familiar and intimate things, as they were everywhere in the past. There are good hospitals available in Bar Harbor, Ellsworth and Bangor, and they are being used with increasing frequency; but still many children are born and many adults waste away and die in their own homes, attended by members of their families. The old are cared for by their sons and daughters as they were in bygone days, and the insane and mentally deficient are tended and kept out of trouble by their relatives and neighbors. This is due partly to lack of money to provide other care for them, it's true, but not entirely or even largely. After all, there are various social agencies that will render aid if approached. No, the chief reason why Peninsulans assume the often very heavy burden of the care of their old and ill is that they retain the old-fashioned virtues: a strong sense of duty and a deep feeling of responsibility for their own. I know that the word *duty* has fallen into disrepute and that enlightened persons do not allow themselves to be hampered by any such consideration. They explain plausibly that it is really nothing but a guilt complex, easy to cure if taken in time. They have a right to their opinion, of course.

On the Peninsula, however, *duty* is a word often used and a concept constantly put into practice. Women watch their children toss in delirium or, heartsick but steady-handed, bathe their fever-wasted bodies. They nurse—sometimes for years—a mother or husband through incurable disease until death comes. A man is regarded as none the less a man for tending faithfully a fatally ill wife: cooking, mending, keeping her clean, changing her bedding and hanging out lines full of spotless sheets. Whole families down to the youngest child live always in awareness of the mental aberrations of a mother or brother or grandfather, are continually watchful for the first indication—a restlessness, a vacant stare, a meaningless laughter—of the approach of a "spell." Entire communities know who is feeble of intellect ànd stand guard over him to protect him from himself and from strangers. It is no wonder that illness, insanity and death provide the coin for conversational exchange. The people live too closely with them for it to be otherwise.

For you cannot inhabit for weeks or months the world of the ill and, when death releases you from this bondage, return at once and unchanged to the world of the sound and vigorous. For eons—or so it seems—you have lain down nights, fully clothed to meet emergencies, and slept as a cat sleeps, lightly and fitfully, hearing every turning of the patient, listening for his voice, conscious of his every breath. Summer may come and go and winter snows fall silently, lie deep, shrink and vanish almost without your noticing, so narrowed is your field of perception to the demands of the sick-room. A sudden brightening of your charge is more miraculous than a shower of gold would be, and a trace of blood in a bodily secretion more terrifying than an earthquake. You learn to speak soothingly and to tread softly, and the words "Everything's all right" comes constantly to your lips, false and unfounded reassurance which gives unreasonable comfort. Then at last it is over and you are spent, physically, mentally and emotionally. You go abroad among men who walk upright, women who laugh with full-throated enjoyment, and children who leap and shout; but you are a stranger among them. You have forgotten their ways.

You are like a person who has lived long in a far, foreign country, speaking a different language, following alien customs. Now that your exile has ended you must learn all over again to live among your own kind. But before you can be repatriated you must tell of your exile, comparing notes with others who have in the past undergone the same experience. Only by putting it into words can it be given significance. Only through the exchange with and the understanding of others can it be softened and transformed into a banishment with a purpose and meaning rather than a witless ordeal. So, slowly, through words do you come back to life.

That is one reason for the Peninsulans' preoccupation with death. There is another. In most of the civilized world today, people regard death as something that will inevitably overtake them, but at a date so far in the future and under circumstances so unforeseeable that there's no present need to think about it. Death never has to overtake men who daily venture far from land on the tumultuous wastes of the North Atlantic. Always it rides side by side with them in their small boats or lurks beneath the angry waters, ready to turn a wrist or stretch out a clasping hand and say, "Now." Under these circumstances, death cannot be regarded as a distant and nebulous threat. It is rather a close-pressing enemy whose shape and lineaments are clear and well known. To speak of death as it came to others is to spy out the enemy's territory, to learn of his sly subterfuges and crafty means. To discuss death is as natural as discussing a shipmate or a neighbor.

These discussions do not confine themselves to the present day, but range back over the decades. George Crowley was telling me one day about the shipping in the harbor of Corea when he was a boy. Boats came in from all over, he said, mooring so close together that it was possible to cross from the mainland to Crowley Island by jumping from deck to deck. Things certainly hummed in those days, he said. The crews were always rarin' to get ashore and whoop it up, and their favorite form of whooping was dancing. If there was a dance in the vicinity they attended in a body, and if there wasn't a dance scheduled they held one anyhow in the home of some cooperative citizen who had a large enough room for the purpose. The kitchen of the house now occupied by Caspar Anderson, which is the oldest house in Corea, a Cape Cod type with a long ell, was a favorite rendezvous. These dances were not the unbridled orgies sometimes associated with shore leaves. After all, many of the sailors were local boys with the welfare of sisters, wives and sweethearts to consider, so they kept matters under excellent control. The affairs were more in the nature of noisy, high-spirited good times.

"Sounds like fun," I commented. "I'd like to go to one myself. It's too bad the shipping has declined so much."

George looked out over the harbor below, where only the lobsterboats of Corea rode at anchor, curtsying in a lazy swell. He knew and I knew that if three strange vessels of outside registry entered the sheltered basin during the summer it would be a cause for marveling. "Oh, I don't know," he said surprisingly. "All them boats from all over warn't an unmixed blessing. We had good times, it's true, and things were a mite more prosperous around here then. But money warn't all they brought into the place."

Then he went on to tell me about the terrible epidemics of smallpox and what was known as black typhoid—which may have been some form of pneumonic plague—that used to sweep the Peninsula in the olden days. They always started shortly after a ship from a foreign port arrived in one of the little harbors, and there was no stopping them until they had run their course. By that time, half the population would be dead. Children, who carried over no immunity from previous epidemics, were especially susceptible. Whole families would be wiped out, the parents losing all of their eight or ten children within a week. This happened not once or twice, but often. How could people bear such a crushing blow? Even if they were shocked into merciful numbness at the time, there would have to come an agonizing return to realization. The only alternative would be flight into the untroubled world of the insane, which some took. How can one blame them, faced with the horror and terror of such an experience following so closely upon the lighthearted dancing and laughter?

To make matters worse, the bereaved were denied even the comfort of a funeral to dignify their disaster. I know that many consider funerals a barbaric and unnecessary pillorying of the bereaved. There is much to be said for this attitude, but it isn't the attitude of the Peninsulans, now or then. Their view—and it has its points, too—is that a funeral is absolutely necessary for several reasons, the least important of which is that it gives those left something to think about and busy themselves with as they arrive at the difficult acceptance of and resignation to their loss. It is a therapeutic outlet for pent emotions.

But more than that, it gives shape and form to events. A man can't just be alive for seventy years—or a child for five—and then the very next day dead for eternity with nothing to mark this greatest transition of all. The funeral provides a definite period to what was. It formally closes a door on the irreclaimable past, making easier an unencumbered approach to the future. And finally, it is still considered by Peninsulans as the last opportunity to give fitting and decent recognition and homage to one who walked among them and shared their lives, one who had his faults and frailties, as we all do, but who had also his own virtues and nobilities. To deprive a man of his funeral would be to take from him personally, even more than from his surviving family, a right.

But the victims of the epidemics were so deprived. So contagious were the diseases in those days of medical ignorance that the dead were buried at night. Sealed in hastily constructed rough-lumber coffins, unaccompanied by any cortege, they were carried secretly to their last resting places on crude farm carts and interred without ceremony.

A very old lady who is now dead herself told me about it. During one dreadful plague-stricken winter of her childhood, her family lived near a bridge on the road to the cemetery. Time and again she was awakened in the dead of night by the slow and muffled drumbeat of horses' hooves striking hollowly on the planking of the bridge. She would lie there quaking in the darkness, her scalp crawling, wondering, "Who is it this time? When school reopens, whose seat will be empty?" She knew there was only one errand to take men abroad on that road at that hour. They could only be going—shamefully, furtively, with none of the trappings that ordinarily would have veiled the unbearable truth—to bury their dead. It is not remarkable that eighty years later she remembered and talked about the horror of those nights, as others remember and talk about similar experiences.

In the olden days everywhere and today on the Peninsula there remains after the funeral one more service that the living can render the dead—a fitting obituary. The modern trend toward streamlining the whole treatment of death has reduced the obituary to a few factual lines comprising the vital statistics of the subject, the cause of death, his accomplishments, if any, and a roster of his survivors. Very seldom do you see now an obituary in the fine, old, leisurely, grandiloquent style, with its stately phrases and rolling periods, and its concern with the character as well as the accomplishments of the deceased. I think it's too bad. The old-style obituaries imparted dignity and solemnity to death.

Read this one: "The sunshine of a fair summer day fell very softly on a flower-strewn lot in the little cemetery of this village Friday afternoon, when loving relatives and a host of friends were gathered to pay their last tribute to all that was mortal of Leonard Moore." There follow the pertinent facts of his life. Then, "To do for a friend in trouble, to make the way easier for a schoolmate, to lend a hand to a man less fortunate than himself, that was his daily life, a life which reflected sunshine and happiness wherever his presence was manifested. The sympathetic words and beautiful prayer by Rev. Mathews awakened a responsive chord in every loyal heart present, and as the eye gazed on the mass of purple and white lilacs heaped above the casket, the profusion of honeysuckle and fragrant blossoms plucked and placed about him by the hands of those who had known him from childhood, one felt that his sleep under the whispering pines must be very peaceful—that the great love of humanity he bore was but a reflection of the Father's love, and that he was Home at last."

Stilted and effusive? I don't think so. Beneath the ornate language accepted at that time as appropriate to the occasion there is obvious sincerity. There is also a sidelight on the custom of the era and place, for where now do mourners gather and bestow their own floral offerings? A historian seeking to reconstruct the life and attitudes of the past could do much worse than study its obituaries.

He could, for example, hazard a pretty definite opinion as to the character traits most widely admired and respected. Over and over such phrases as the following appear in old Peninsula papers: "She possessed a keen sense of justice and was a great worker both in her home and in outside affairs"; "Of her it can truthfully be said, 'She eateth not the bread of idleness' "; and "She was a cheerful worker and a thoughtful neighbor." Other qualities received frequent mention, too: "She was generous to family and neighbors alike," "Her many kindly deeds were known to all, who will ever hold her in grateful remembrance," and "The public will never know of her many kindnesses and generous deeds, for it was her way to hide them." Thus emerges the local ideal of womanhood in a woman not necessarily beautiful, almost certainly not greatly talented, but a woman who wore well under the friction of daily living—kind, generous and hard-working.

The men of the Peninsula lived wider ranging lives than did their womenfolk, and their obituaries are full of brief brushes with a greater history. Captain Samuel Oscar Moore of Prospect Harbor "began a seafaring life at an early age and followed it for most of his life. Quickly rising to a master's berth, he commanded large vessels, mostly in the foreign trade. During the Civil War, he served three years as quartermaster on the US sloop-of-war, *Pawnee*. Among his most valued treasures was a pair of marine glasses presented to him by the late Queen Victoria through ex-President Arthur, then collector of the Port of New York, as a recognition of his services in the rescue of the crew of the British ship *Phaola* which burned at sea in the late '70's."

I never knew before that Arthur was once collector of the Port of New York. And I'm fascinated—but not surprised—at the punctiliousness of Victoria Regina, who, like any properly reared, good,

fussy little matron, sat down at her desk and made a note of the
fact that she really must do something about Captain Moore in return for his gallantry. Hardly a place on the Honors List, and a
medal wouldn't be quite— Maybe something of a practical nature,
he being a Yankee? Ah! Marine glasses! Just the thing. And the
glasses are still on the Peninsula.

Captain George Bunker of Gouldsboro also went to sea young
and "was in command of small vessels when a mere boy. Later he
commanded ships in the European and West Indian trade. The
schooner *Onward* drove on the shore of Cow Bay, C.B., in the
hurricane of Aug. 17, 1873, and the barkentine *Alexander Campbell*
that he commanded for sixteen years went down off Block Island;
but he never lost a man while rescuing many. He was in command
of the three-masted schooner *Alasia B. Crosby* at the time the *Portland*, the *Pantagoet*, the *Addie B. Snow* and the *King Phillip* went
down with all hands; but Captain Bunker brought his ship into
Portland Harbor safely before morning. He was strictly honest,
temperate, conscientious and capable."

I'm glad he finally received credit for bringing his ship through
the Thanksgiving blizzard of '98. Usually the emphasis has been
placed on those who went to the bottom that night, even to the extent of sending down divers to find out what really did happen to
the *Portland*. (She was rammed by the *Addie B. Snow*, a granite
schooner out of Rockland, Maine.) But then, his obituary goes on
to say, "Captain Bunker comes from a line of seafaring men. He
was directly descended on his mother's side from Commodore
Preble, sometimes called the Father of the US Navy, and his ma-
ternal grandfather, Esias Preble, was the first keeper of Mt. Desert
Rock Light." He had every reason to be capable, if heredity means
anything at all.

The old-fashioned obituary served a double purpose. It extolled
the virtues of the dead and at the same time paid homage to the
living. Very often we read a statement like "She was one of eight
sisters, who were unremitting in their devotion to the stricken one
and did all that could be done for her comfort"; or "The devoted
husband, who was constantly with her, and the sister who had been

a faithful and loving attendant during the past few months, also friends and relatives who did everything possible to alleviate her suffering, could not realize that they must part with her—that this sweet young life had already passed beyond them."

This particular young woman died of what was then known as galloping consumption, now tuberculosis—a shockingly frequent cause of death among the young of a half-century ago; and I'm going to include the rest of her obituary because it is an almost perfect illustration of the importance attached to what was called—and still is—"a beautiful passing." It goes on, "Just before the end came she said to her husband with a smile of ineffable joy: 'Do not weep for me; I am ready and so happy.' Her last words were: 'They have come to take me over.' Then she fell asleep to wake in that land where there is no sorrow."

I have had occasion to study a great many columns of obituaries in a search for facts, and I have yet to find one that so nearly approaches the classic as that of Louisa Parsons Eppes, who died in Gouldsboro in 1912. It is such a good example of an almost vanished art form that I'm going to give it in entirety, omitting only the vital statistics.

An old resident, a personality respected by all and beloved by many, was removed from mortal sight in the death of Mrs. D. H. Eppes, which took place Dec. 3. She had been so long a helpless invalid, apart from the social life she so much enjoyed, that she might easily have been in a measure forgotten; but her own interest in life had been retained in so vivid a way; her thought for her friends had continued so warm and strong; her devotion to the young had remained so vital that her hold on the life without her home held fast to a remarkable degree.

[Here follow the facts of her birthplace, marriage, and the number of her children.]

Mrs. Eppes was a devoted wife and mother, and found rare compensation, especially in the latter days, in the corresponding devotion of her children. She was of a very social disposition, keenly interested in all her environment, with a particularly warm place in her heart for children. One of the most touching things in her late illness was the thought for her that little ones whom she had known manifested. During the summer past, one and another of these little friends would come to the home with wild flowers which the childish hands had picked. The voices of children at play were a source of constant pleasure to her, even in her darkest days.

Everything pertaining to the church life found a ready welcome in Mrs. Eppes' hands, and its welfare was ever dear to her.

A fall received in the store was the beginning, followed by a paralytic seizure, affecting principally the muscles of her throat. Speech became almost an impossibility; her communication with friends a matter simply of passive reception; and yet all these weary months not one indication of impatience or rebellion was shown.

Her patience had a touch of the vast forbearance of the Infinite in it. Very pathetic was the well-nigh speechless resignation, accompanied as it so often was, with a look of such intense longing for speech with those she loved, that it seemed more than once as if the strong will would break the bonds imposed and force utterance on the palsied tongue.

To few lives has been given more of loving ministry than has been bestowed upon her in these wearing years. Her children at home, the grand-daughter who had been her special care, have vied with each other in sacrificing love. Day and night their care has been unceasing, and their sorrow must be unmixed with reproach or regret.

There. That's my idea of the model obituary. It tells you everything you could possibly want to know, it gives credit where credit is due, it honors the dead, and its style is impeccably suited to the subject.

Epitaphs are considered even more seriously on the Peninsula than are obituaries, possibly because an epitaph, being chiseled into granite or marble, is more nearly permanent than an obituary, which is printed on less durable paper. In fact, the whole matter of grave-marking is of great individual concern to Peninsulans. Many buy their own headstones and supervise their setting while they themselves are still in the land of the living and able to arrange things to their own satisfaction. Sometimes they sacrifice present creaturely comforts in order to pay in advance for this form of near-immortality. Failing in this foresighted provision, others make very clear to their probable survivors exactly what they want and expect in the way of a tombstone and postmortem care of their graves. The mother of one woman I know, for instance, expressed a wish that grass should never be allowed to grow on her grave. She'd had enough trouble with grass and weeds in her flower beds during her lifetime to last her through eternity. She had been dead for many years, but still her daughter faithfully uproots the encroaching grass at frequent intervals from frost-out until snowfall. She considers it her duty.

I grew up believing that what became of one's mortal remains after death wasn't too important; that, the existence of a life hereafter being problematical, the only certain hope of immortality lay in one's posterity, if any, and in the remembrance by friends and acquaintances of one's works and deeds. Therefore an emphasis put on gravestones, epitaphs and the other trappings of death seemed to me to be exaggerated and unnecessary.

But not long ago I was in the Prospect Harbor cemetery with Marcia Spurling, looking for the grave of a Malvina Brown, when we came across an unmarked mound, overgrown with blackberry briers and timothy grass. The Prospect Harbor cemetery is a wonderfully serene place, a little, sun-dappled bowl of peace, approached over a grassy track across a big hayfield and surrounded by pines. All the graves were orderly and well-kept except one, which lay on the edge of the burying ground, close to the encircling stone wall. It looked forlorn and forsaken.

Marcia stopped short. "Why," she said in shocked tones, "that must be So-and-so's mother! She's been dead going on four years, which is plenty of time to put up a headstone. So-and-so doesn't lack for money, so that's no excuse. She was an only child, and you'd think, wouldn't you, she'd attend to her mother's marker the first thing? When *she* dies, there'll be nobody left to do it, and it won't be long before folks forget completely who's buried here. Nobody wants to be forgotten that soon."

I guess that explains the whole attitude. Nobody does want to be forgotten the minute they're underground.

The reason we were looking for Malvina Brown's grave was because I wanted to see for myself a phenomenon of which I had heard. Malvina died a long time ago at the age of twenty, another victim of galloping consumption. On her deathbed she promised her mother, "If I am happy after I leave this world, I will send you a Sign." Within a few months after her headstone had been erected, the profile of a woman appeared upon it, at first very faintly and then with increasing clarity. It was the Sign.

"It's caused, no doubt," I told Marcia with a regrettable lack of faith, "by some flaw in the granite that came out as it weathered."

"Maybe it is," she said stoutly, "but that doesn't prevent it's being a miracle, does it? I never knew Malvina—she was before my time; but my mother did, and she told me that this is the spit'n image of her, you'd know her in a minute. Don't make any difference what causes a miracle to happen, does it, just so long as it happens?"

And I suppose she's right. Miracles will always happen as long as there are hearts that believe in them. That is the true miracle, that there will always be, unaffected by cold logic, such believing hearts.

Marcia and I lightly brushed what may have been another miracle on that autumn afternoon in the cemetery. There had been a storm a few days before, followed by a spell of bright and chilly weather. The storm had thrown over the slate slab that marked one of the graves, and in my search for Malvina I lifted it far enough to read the name on it. Curled in a tight knot underneath were at least a dozen small snakes. They'd evidently crawled under there to enjoy the warmth of the sun that had been absorbed by and stored in the dark stone. I have no particular aversion to snakes, but I'll admit that I was considerably startled by the unexpected rearing of all those spade-shaped heads in my direction. I squeaked and dropped the stone in a hurry.

When I explained my conduct to Marcia, she looked thoughtful. "Whose grave is it? Did you have time to notice?" she asked. Exercising caution, I lifted the slab again and read her the name. "Hmm," she said. "Well, I can't say I'm surprised. I knew him, and oh, he was a mean man, crooked and sneaky as they come. Any tears shed for him were crocodile tears. If he's got snakes in his grave it's no worse than he deserved."

One of these days I must go back and see if the snakes are still there. It takes a little while to authenticate and establish a miracle.

Marcia has a miracle in her own family. Her mother, whom she nursed for many years of incurable illness, had always had her heart set on a white gravestone. Marcia, knowing that it would comfort her mother to be sure her wishes would be respected, started negotiations for the marker during the last months of the invalid's life. It was possible, she found, to buy a small white stone at the price she could afford; but the man with whom she was dealing made her a business proposition. He had had in stock for a long time a large and handsome headstone that nobody seemed to want. Nobody liked the color, which was greenish. He offered it to her at a substantial reduction in order to get rid of it.

Marcia went home and talked it over with her mother, who decided that the green stone was so much better than any she had hoped for that she would be more than willing, indeed happy, to accept it as a substitute. So the deal was made and in due time the stone was set on the Spurling lot in the West Bay cemetery.

Now here is where the miracle comes in. The West Bay cemetery is on a knoll, and while it is partly sheltered by a grove of pines it is still open to winter gales and the heat of summer sun. Whether this was responsible or whether simple exposure to light and air after centuries of being buried deep in the bowels of some quarry wrought the change, I don't know. Whichever it was, slowly the stone blanched until today it is the pure white of Marcia's mother's dreams. It stands there proud and snowy on the knoll, gleaming against the black of the pines and the scarlet of autumn leaves. And when I said to Marcia, "It's too bad your mother couldn't know," she told me, "But of course she *does* know!" Miracles do happen, and I guess their causes really aren't important, at that.

There's another puzzle in the West Bay cemetery. Over near the brink of the knoll under the pines are two adult headstones flanked by a long line of the small markers used on the graves of babies. This is the last resting place of Edwin Young, his wife Margaret, and their eight or ten infant children. Child mortality being what it was in the olden days, the presence of so many tiny graves on one family's lot is in itself not unusual or surprising. It's the story that lies behind it, a story that is frequently told and implicity believed on the Peninsula, that makes this a special case.

It seems that Margaret Tracy—the same Margaret Tracy who discovered the silver mines—was engaged to one of two Young brothers. Her betrothed was a seafaring man, and before setting out on a long voyage he extracted from Margaret her solemn oath that she would wait for him and be true to him. During his absence, however, his brother Edwin disloyally courted Margaret with such success that she broke her vow and married him. Shortly thereafter, the wronged brother returned home.

He was furious when he learned the state of affairs, so furious that he put a terrible curse on the marriage. Not one child of the union, he swore, would ever survive infancy. And not one did. You can put the blame where you want to—on a polluted well, on some inherited weakness, on an Rh factor, or on recurrent epidemics; but, whatever the cause, the curse was fulfilled. There the children lie in a row under the sod of the West Bay cemetery: Charley, Georgey, Winnie, Effie and Justin; and then Margaret and Edwin must have become discouraged, must have decided that it was useless to name a child who would never grow up to know and answer to his name, because the rest of the stones bear bleakly only the word "Baby" and a date. I don't know what to believe; but whatever I believe, I can't help feeling sad for the Margaret of the silver mines, who told about them at a dance, when I stand in the West Bay cemetery and think of what her life came to.

One day I heard about an abandoned graveyard way Up the Guzzle, so I started asking how to find it. This took place in the store at mail time, so the whole hamlet of Corea was at once aware of my project. Evidently it required some explaining, because I overheard one woman tell another, "Oh, cemeteries are a hobby of hers."

That isn't exactly the way I would have put it myself, but I'll have to admit to a great interest in old cemeteries. They are almost invariably beautiful and steeped in a peace that you can find nowhere else. They're good places in which to sit on the ground and think. No problem seems as difficult or crisis as overwhelming as you had imagined, here among those whose crises and problems have all been solved and forgotten. Soon you have your personal difficulties in proper perspective and can give your attention to reading the epitaphs on the stones around you.

Some of the old ones were addressed directly to the living in an apparent effort to influence their conduct from the grave. Very common was

> Behold and see as you pass by
> As you are now so once was I
> As I am now so you will be
> Prepare for death to follow me.

and

> Weep not for me my pains are o'er
> We soon shall meet to part no more.

One I like especially, possibly because the author was aware of the existence of punctuation marks, commonly ignored in such compositions:

> Look up into the blue
> Where, light hid,
> Lives what doth renew
> Man's chrysalid.
> Say not, she is here;
> Say not, she was here;
> Say, she lives in God,
> Reigning everywhere.

Then there are those addressed to the deceased, like

> You're on the Saviour's bosom laid
> And feel no sorrows there
> You're by a Heavenly Parent fed
> And need no more our care

and this:

> Forgive blest shade the tributary tear
> That mourns thy call from a world like this
> Forgive the wish that would have kept thee here
> And stayed thy progress to the seats of bliss

The one I like the very best of all, though, is that of Captain Thomas Boardman, who died in 1815 at the age of seventy. It's my notion of what an epitaph should be. I found it in a cemetery so old that full-grown spruces grew out of the graves and the head-stones were moss-covered and tilted at crazy angles by the tunneling roots of trees. The carving on Captain Boardman's stone had been so blurred by time and almost a century and a half of coastal weather that I had to make a rubbing in order to decipher it at all. After all the flowery verses I'd been reading on neighboring mark ers, the few unadorned and unequivocal words that took slow form under my crayon on the clean sheet of paper were like a shaft of sunlight in a dark forest. They read simply

> The noblest work of God
> An honest man

Here at last, I thought, was a man I could recognize, his quality unobscured over the long years by a haze of ornate phrases. I shall think about Thomas Boardman long after I have forgotten all the rest.

Sometimes, though, it's the unknown whom you remember and about whom you think. I do a lot of speculating about the seaman who was washed up on Outer Bar and buried above the shore of Crowley Island. Then there are the man and woman who lie in a common grave at the Potato Field. The Potato Field is between Cranberry Point and the cove known as the Sands because it contains the only really good sand beach on the Peninsula. Long ago it was just the potato field, but now that potatoes haven't been planted there for almost fifty years and it is no longer a field but a tangled copse of small spruce trees and alder bushes, it has been graduated to upper-case status and is the Potato Field .

But before that happened, the bodies of a couple unknown in the vicinity were washed up on the shore nearby. As widespread inquiry as was possible in those days failed to reveal their identity or even how they came to be in the locality in the first place. So they were buried in the nearest convenient spot, the Potato Field, where the digging was fairly good, in one grave. Since no one came forward to meet the expenses of interment, but since it was unthinkable to leave the grave unmarked, two beach boulders were rolled up from the shore and placed at their heads and feet. You can still find them if you know where to look for them and if you don't mind thrashing through dense undergrowth, but almost nobody bothers about them any more.

I do, though. I wonder about them a great deal. Who were they and how did they come here? Were they husband and wife on a vacation, or fleeing lovers? Did they arrive in a small boat which they sailed for pleasure from some harbor to the west, and which foundered; or did they come afoot overland on one of the walking trips people used to take and, stopping for a swim at the Sands, find too late that the icy seas hereabouts are full of treacherous currents from which there is no escape?

I've gone so far as to develop a theory that they didn't even know each other, that they weren't even nodding acquaintances. It's possible, even without straining coincidence to the extent of requiring that two bodies from widely separated points drift by chance onto the same twenty feet of beach out of a hundred miles of shoreline. They could have been fellow passengers on a passing ocean liner who had never laid eyes on each other in their lives. On the first evening out, the woman might have been leaning over the rail to watch the low dark line of the Peninsula with its scattering of lights slide past on the western horizon. She leaned too far and went overboard; and the man, taking a last solitary turn about the deck before going to his cabin, saw her and impulsively dived in after her. No one saw the incident, and their absence was not discovered until the next day, when it was too late to do anything about it. Naturally the captain reported their disappearance, but word of it never reached the isolated Peninsula. So there they lie, two who were strangers to each other, their dust mingling forever in the close, dark intimacy of the grave.

I rather like this reconstruction. It has a certain irony that appeals to me. But of course, no one knows the truth.

No one knows the truth about the disappearance of Ella Pinkham, either. It's one of the riddles of the Peninsula, which, in common with the rest of rural Maine, has its share of unsolved mysteries. The machinery for tracking down missing persons was not as efficient anywhere in the olden days as it is now, and in the isolated crossroads of the interior and forgotten gunk-holes of the coast it was practically nonexistent. What agencies there were usually were not activated until considerable time had elapsed after the subject stopped frequenting his accustomed haunts. It was generally assumed that he was off somewhere minding his own business and that he'd show up or send word when he got around to it. Down-Easters were and are inclined to be close-mouthed and slightly eccentric; and just because a man didn't advertise that he was planning to visit a relative in Portland or start a sheep ranch in Nevada didn't mean that he had no such plan. He could have been mulling it over for months, and no one the wiser. Then when he couldn't stand the smell of bait any longer he'd just pick up and go. It was nobody's affair but his own, he'd figure; and that was what everybody else figured, too.

In fact, abandoning the seafaring life in disgust was common enough so that there is a standard remark used to indicate such an intention. It's based on the anecdote of the lobsterman who walked up from the harbor and out of the village with a pair of oars over his shoulder. "I'm taking these damn things inland," he told inquirers, "until I come to a place where nobody knows what they are or what they're used for; and that's where I'm going to spend the rest of my life."

Men are still saying that of a pair of oars or a lobster trap or a riding sail. Most of the time they don't mean it; but the thought is there, and if it were put into action nobody would be much surprised or would institute any widespread search.

This did not apply to the case of Ella Pinkham, whose vanishing caused a great stir. I read about the affair in Marcia's Aunt Sarah Tracy's scrap book, a homemade album in which Aunt Sarah had over a period of many decades pasted newspaper clippings that interested her. The account (around 1910) was detailed:

> No trace of Mrs. Ella Pinkham, who left her home last Tuesday, can be found. Lorenzo Whitten was the last person who saw her, when he called there for her order at ten o'clock Tuesday and found her combing her hair. She talked and laughed and everything seemed in her usual health and good spirits.
>
> At twelve o'clock when Mrs. Atwater went to the house she found a note on the door saying "I am gone." Mrs. Burk, who has been visiting her brother and went to say good-bye to Mrs. Pinkham, also saw the note.

As Mrs. Pinkham is lame and never goes far from home, it looked strange, so Mrs. Atwater wrote her daughter in Bangor to see if she had gone there to spend Thanksgiving, although it would be unusual. Word came back:— "No; search the house."

Jesse Stevens on entering the house found another note saying: "Have gone on my visit. Have a free pass and am going right along; don't look for me back until after Cristmas."

A package was waiting for each of the children with what she wanted them to have of her personal belongings. When they arrived Friday, they found each package contained a letter saying good-bye. She had planned this since last fall and was going for a long rest. One other daughter is married. Her husband, Winfred Pinkham, is with Captain Josiah Bunker and is expected home at any time.

Mrs. Pinkham lived alone when her husband was away and the neighbors believe that she had laid her plans carefully. When she knew that it would take only a fair wind to bring the vessel home from the Cranberry Isles, she evidently put the house in perfect order, cooked for her husband's arrival, put down all the grain she had for the hens, locked the door and disappeared. Nothing is missing from the house but her suit of underwear and a calico wrapper, not even her hat. The weather was cold and in her condition she would not long survive.

Mrs. Pinkham is fifty years old, about five feet eight inches in height, weighs 135 pounds, and has dark brown hair and blue eyes. Any information should be communicated to G. W. Pinkham.

I find this a fascinating account, full of incompatibilities that need explaining, and sketching in lightly the outlines of the whole way of life of a woman whose husband was at sea. It needs only a little imagination to fill them in and bring Mrs. Pinkham to life in her daily round of visiting with neighbors and feeding the hens.

Apparently Aunt Sarah Tracy was a woman who did not like loose ends, and at a much later date she had written beneath the clipping, "Mrs. Pinkham's bones were found fifteen years later under a brush pile near her home." The faded characters are still firm and clear, but they still don't answer the question, "What happened to Ella Pinkham?" That's still a matter of discussion and conjecture, with opinion about equally divided among murder, accident and suicide. Her careful preparations would seem to favor the last; but, say the murder proponents, layin' down under a brush pile is a foolish way to commit suicide, especially when she had the whole ocean to jump into. She could have been forced to write them notes. The more temperate promoters of the accident theory suggest that she really was going on a visit, dressed in new clothes that the neighbors didn't know anything about, was overcome by a fainting spell before she'd hardly got started, and just chanced to fall into the brush pile. But no one will ever know for sure.

A lot of things happen on the Peninsula, the truth of which will never be known. Some of them are old happenings, their immediacy lost, their outlines blurred, surviving only as tales to be told and speculated upon in snug kitchens during long winter evenings when the surf thunders beyond the bar, or on lazy summer afternoons in a sunny cemetery overlooking a smiling sea. But death has agreed to no armistice with the living. It lies always in wait—the eternal enemy, the implacable foe—for the unguarded moment in which to strike, just as surely today as in days gone by.

And just as it did in days gone by, an unaccountable death casts a shadow over the entire community. It is a matter of concern and a subject for conjecture superseding all others. I learned that when Raymond Dunbar, a lobsterman of Corea, was drowned. Even I, who knew him only slightly, found myself saddened, found myself thinking, "How shocking and dreadful!" and asking the inevitable question, "How could it have happened?"

For the tragedy occurred on a brilliant July morning, when the sun shone and the sea was almost calm, a perfect hauling day. Raymond was only sixty-three, which is young as Peninsulans reckon. He had followed the sea for fifty years. "He was a pretty man with a boat; an awful pretty man with a boat," they said of him, and he knew the reefs and channels of the area as he knew his own front yard. Nevertheless, when his invisible shipmate of half a century turned to him and said "Come," all his knowledge and skill counted as nothing. His thirty-five foot *Lillian Mae* was seen entering the passage between Western and Outer Bar Islands, proceeding competently into harbor, by men still hauling their traps further out; and only a few moments later Junior Jordan and Vincent Young, returning to port by the same channel, came upon her capsized.

Then it started—all the harrowing business following a drowning offshore. The *Lillian Mae* was towed into harbor and examined for a clue to the accident, but there was none. Her life jackets were intact and her motor in good running order. The failure had not been hers. Long before that conclusion was reached, the waters of Outer Bar Passage and the sky above it were alive with boats and planes gathering for the search. The Coast Guard sent a picket boat and a motor lifeboat from Southwest Harbor and an amphibian plane from Salem, Massachusetts; and the Stinsons, who own the canning factory in Prospect Harbor, sent the big sardiners and their two seiner planes; and of course the lobsterboats of Corea were already covering the area, cruising slowly back and forth, alert for any sign.

Ashore, the women, the children and the old men stood in little groups, their ordinary occupations abandoned and forgotten, talking low and turning their eyes continually to the sea. When two or three boats converged at one point and idled there, all talk ceased. It was as if the whole village held its breath, to release it in one great sigh as the boats parted and the quest continued. "Not yet," women murmured. "They haven't found him yet." And near the surface of every woman's mind was the unspoken awareness, "It could as easily have been my husband or brother," just as every man in the coursing boats knew surely, "It could have been me."

All day long the search went on, until the late, lingering northern dusk crept over the sea and only the high-flying planes caught the light of the vanished sun, but no sign of Raymond Dunbar was found. Bits of floating gear from his boat were picked up, and small personal possessions, mute reminders that only a few hours before he had been alive and going about his accustomed work; but the man himself was gone. Finally the boats returned to harbor, the planes soared away to the south and west, and the officials in charge terminated the search with the terse verdict, "Lost; presumed drowned."

Talk in the store and the kitchens of the village was subdued that night, subject to long periods of silence as each man pursued his own somber thoughts. Almost twenty-five years before, Bernard Briggs and Walter Young had been lost in a December storm when their boat was disabled off Petit Manan Point; and it was recalled with a sense of awe that they and Raymond Dunbar were all members of the same family. Other drownings in other places were discussed; and recent encounters with Raymond were gone over and over, his every word now holding added poignancy and meaning in the light of events. But always the talk came back to the question, "How did it happen?" Had Raymond been taken ill—so ill that he was unable to guide his boat through the narrow passage? Had he run upon a submerged or floating object of unknown origin? Or had he been standing on the engine housing—as all lobstermen do frequently, the better to see their course—when an unexpected swell toppled him overboard and left the *Lillian Mae* to founder on the ledges? No one will ever know.

In places like the Peninsula, where men are not uncommonly lost at sea, it is the custom to hold a memorial service for the victim in place of a funeral. It serves the multiple purpose of a funeral, ending a chapter, bridging a gap, and providing an opportunity for the decent paying of respect to the dead. Such a service was held for Raymond Dunbar, ten days after he was lost, in the church at Corea.

I have never been to a service that I found more moving and impressive, not because of its pomp and ceremony—these qualities were conspicuously lacking—but because of its simplicity and sincerity. There were great bunches of flowers picked from village gardens placed about the severe interior of the little church, and the long windows stood open to the sunny July afternoon. The sound of the sea breaking gently on the ledges drifted in, and the mewing cry of sea gulls, and the sighing of the wind over the heath. They provided a beautiful and fitting requiem for one who had ordered all his days within the sound of their voices. The whole village attended—all the lobstermen with whom he had shared the lonely life implicit to their occupation, and their wives, who were friends of his wife, Amanda. Herb was there, unfamiliar in a white shirt, and Holly Myrick, whom I had never seen except in dungarees, wearing a suit and tie.

There were none of the grimaces of easy grief upon the rugged faces. Rather, the weathered features seemed carved, as granite might be, in strong lines of classic sorrow. They sat quietly, these true Down-Easters, mourning the loss of one of their own in their own Spartan manner. There was none of the subdued and cheerful chatter that usually precedes church services on the Peninsula. Only when Raymond's family—Amanda and their children and grand-children—took their places did a small sound, more like a sigh than a murmur, sweep the assemblage. It was an expression of sympathy;

but, more than that, it was a tribute to their bearing of composed and dignified grief. On the Peninsula, sorrow is a quiet business, and so all the more heartbreaking to witness.

Two ministers officiated. Young Mr. Margeson from Steuben, the regular pastor of the church, conducted the formal opening of the service; but, since he was at the time almost a stranger to the community, he had not known the lost man well. So when it was time to speak of the dead, Mrs. Henrichsen rose and faced the gathering. She had been pastor of the seven churches strung along the Peninsula from Sullivan to Prospect Harbor for several years and knew her people intimately. Slowly, calmly, she began to speak.

It was as though she were talking to a group of friends—as indeed she was—rather than addressing a congregation. She told of small incidents of Raymond's daily life, of his honesty and thoughtfulness of others. Then she went on to the circumstances of his death. "They tell us he is lost," she said, "but Raymond isn't lost. Lost to us for a time, perhaps, but not lost to God. Listen!" And she read from the Psalms, "If I take the wings of the morning and dwell in the uttermost parts of the sea; even there shall Thy hand lead me, and Thy right hand shall hold me." On the wings of the morning, she said, Raymond—as most of the men present did daily—had gone out to sea; and surely, *surely* he was now held in the right hand of God! He was not lost. Rather, he was safe for eternity.

She did not speak for very long, but her words, strong and sure against the surging of the sea, carried great conviction. It was impossible to doubt in the face of such unquestionable faith. It was a wonderful service, full of hope and inspiration, and it brought comfort not only to the bereaved, but to those who must face squarely the possibility of a fate similar to Raymond's, and to all the rest of us as well, who must inevitably be lost for a space to those whom we love.

Ten days after that, Raymond's body was found near Outer Bar Island by one of the sixteen-year-old Young twins, Vin, who was out tending his traps. He lies now in the little cemetery on the hill above Corea overlooking the sea that he knew and loved so well and that was his undoing. It is a good place for a seaman to lie. The wind-blown gulls and the sounds of the whistle buoys and bell buoys and of the sea drift over it all day and all night long. No seaman could rest peacefully, even in death, away from these things.

Perhaps, in the wider world of today, it is no longer important how and where the dead rest, nor how they came to their graves. Maybe in other places it no longer matters that a sailor should lie within sight and sound of the sea for his last sleep, or a plainsman under prairie sod, or a mountain man within the shadow of the hills; but it does to the Peninsulans. When they turn their backs on this last responsibility to their own, then will the place be changed out of all recognition, and the people no longer what they were.

10. One Woman's Peninsula

STILL I HAVEN'T TOLD YOU WHAT IT'S LIKE
on the Peninsula. I'm not sure that I can. It isn't like anything. It's
a place and a way of life with a flavor and character of its own
which it is difficult to convey in words. Too much of its effect is
subjective, belonging to and existing in the mind and heart of the
individual. Some, I know, would consider having to spend a year
here the equivalent of a stretch in the salt mines of Siberia. Nothing would awaken any response in them: neither the hard beauty of
the land, nor the slow sun-paced routine of the days, nor the simplicity of the life and the people. They'd be bored and miserable.
To others of us each small occurrence, each change in the weather,
each new Down-East turn of phrase is a source of interest and true
delight. It's more than a difference of taste or a predilection. It's
almost a matter of affinity.

I haven't even told you what it's really like to live on Cranberry
Point. I've told you a little about the log cabin, and about the birds
and the plants and the animals, and about walks along the shore.
I've mentioned the isolation and tried to describe the view of the
sea and the sound of the wind over the open heath; but still I haven't
given you an idea of what a woman alone does with her days in
such a place, of what she finds to keep her hands and her mind
employed.

I used to think, when I was very young, that I would like to live on an island. Most people at one time or another fall victim to the peculiar spell that islands have from time immemorial exerted. Even those who have never been on one often find themselves in love with the *idea* of an island, seeing in it a symbol of independence and integration and security. Such was I. I hadn't then learned that no matter where you may be, you are still on an island, with only yourself to call upon in the end, whatever your desperate plight. I hadn't learned that islands work both ways. They can serve as fortresses, successfully holding the enemy at bay; but they can also without warning suffer a sea change into prisons, keeping you from aid and succor. This is equally true of geographical and of spiritual islands. It can be very frightening to be trapped on an island in a storm through which no boat could live, with a possible case of appendicitis on your hands, just as it can be frightening to live among friends and feel yourself completely cut off from communication with them.

Now that I have learned these lessons I appreciate the advantages of the Point. It is remote and almost surrounded by water, having the look and feeling of an island; but always there is the winding, grass-grown track that connects it with the village and the world beyond and with the society of one's own kind. Increasing years have taught me the value of a route of escape, whether it be from physical danger or from my own company.

Before I can give you a true picture of my life on the Point I shall have to go into some detail about the cabin itself. I've told you that it is an L-shaped structure of logs with a big stone chimney, crouched on the ledges by the sea as though it belongs here. There is no porch or veranda to mar its low, sturdy lines. Porches here are superfluous, of no use whatsoever. If the weather is fine you sit in the open on the rocks or on the grass in the shelter of the ell; and if it's not fine it's so bad that you can't sit outdoors anyhow, porch or no porch, but stay close to the fire. The front door therefore opens directly from a patch of bare ledge into the living room, and the kitchen door opens onto the small, unroofed platform where the oil barrels rest on a trestle.

Half the floor-space is given over to the big living room, which has a fireplace at one end and a picture window overlooking the sea at the other. It's a beautiful room, open to the rafters. The walls are of peeled log, caulked with oakum which was sealed in by nailing inch-thick alder switches between the logs. This makes a lovely and decorative finish, deep-toned and glossy, and it requires no care —no washing or rubbing with dry bread crusts such as paint or wallpaper occasionally demands. It's a room after my own heart, always looking its untroubled best with little effort on my part. I'm not really lazy, but I don't like to spend half my life doing housework.

The room is beautiful by day, and it's beautiful at night, too. Sometimes the unearthly white light of the moon streams in at the picture window halfway across the floor, where it surrenders to the leaping red of the open fire. Standing in the middle, you imagine yourself on the boundary between two worlds, the cold inhuman world of outer space and the warmer, dearer world of the here and now. But on stormy nights the darkness presses close beyond the glass, making of it a mirror, so that now you stand between two fires, the real and the reflected, guarded by them from all the perils outside the near walls of the cabin and the further walls of earth's atmosphere. The rain drums importunately on the roof, and the wind off the heath prowls at the door; but inside, where the shadows of the rafters waver with the leaping light of the flames in a lovely, fluid pattern on the ceiling, there is a feeling of security against more than physical storms.

The two bedrooms are in the low ell beyond the kitchen, facing away from the sea and onto the moor; but the kitchen windows look east to the islands and the harbor entrance, so that there is plenty to divert the mind and eye from dishwashing and scullery work.

I don't know what happens to otherwise practical people when they plan the household arrangements of summer cottages and beach shacks. They're evidently seduced by the ancient delusion that coming to grips with fundamentals will purify their souls; or else they think that a minimum of essential equipment is enough for a short vacation. This is all very well for everyone except the house-wife, who must somehow manage to produce adequate meals, working with only a too-small saucepan, a spider and a balky wood stove, the drafts of which she doesn't understand. I know. In various shore dwellings I've stewed and cursed over every type of cooking unit from a double-oven hotel range with a burned-out grate down through a small electric plate to a worn-out and smoky oil stove. I've managed, but it's been more like a shift in a stokehole than a vacation.

I assumed that things had to be like that until I came to Cranberry Point. Here the two modest requirements of any cook, a decent stove and decent refrigeration, have been nobly met. There is no electricity, but electricity isn't necessary to convenience in the kitchen, I find. The stove is an old-fashioned black iron range, built for wood but converted to oil, with a hot water tank at the rear. The oil barrels outside the back door are piped directly to the stove, so that there is no filling of jugs to contend with. All I have to do is pay the oil man when he comes. The oven bakes well, there is always hot water, and the one burner that I keep running all the time is enough for ordinary cooking and enough to drive out the damp-ness that is inevitable near the sea.

The refrigerator operates on bottled gas, and I've given up trying to understand how you can light a flame and shortly have ice cubes at your disposal. It's something about the heat's circulating a coolant through a series of coils. I just accept the fact that it works and that all I have to do is defrost occasionally and keep an eye on the gauge. If it turns red I leave word at the store for the gas man, and he brings another bottle.

You can't imagine, unless you too have been victimized, what a difference in your disposition and whole outlook on life having a practical and convenient kitchen can make.

Now that I've sketchily set the scene, I'll tell you about my average day at the Point. I get up early, at about five o'clock, not because I'm ambitious but because the sun and everyone in the village are up at that time. The sunlight floods in at the windows, and the lobsterboats are puttering competently and cheerfully around in the front yard, so I might as well get up, too. I regret to say that I am neither competent nor cheerful when I arise. It doesn't make any difference whether I get up at five in the morning or at noon; I'm still stupid and cranky. I've learned, however, that I'll feel better as soon as I've had my breakfast, so I let the dog out and start the coffee. Sure enough, the daily miracle occurs, and shortly after drinking it I feel well enough to tackle the chores.

One of the definitions of *chore* is "hard or unpleasant work," but I don't think it's a definition that would occur to Peninsulans, who use the word constantly. "I've got my chores done early," they'll say, or "Let's start right after chores." They don't feel abused at having to lift a finger in honest toil. They assume that naturally one has to pay somehow for the privilege of living, and endorse a philosophy that includes physical labor as inevitable and good rather than one which rejects it as being bad or degrading. I agree with them. The danger of the laborsaving device, it seems to me, is that it too often produces idleness rather than leisure—and there is a big difference. Leisure is something earned by work, a reward to be savored and enjoyed. Idleness is a form of poverty, a lack of employment, and conducive to waste of time and talents.

My morning chores at the cabin fill in very nicely the time until my sleep-sluggish mind starts functioning. First I collect all the kerosene lamps, fill them, trim the wicks, and wash the chimneys. Next I make my bed and give the living room a cursory dry-mopping and dusting—a lick and a promise until the weekly cleaning day. Then I wash out some socks and dishtowels, make out a shopping list if necessary, and bring in enough fireplace wood and kindling to last until the morrow. This whole routine takes about forty-five minutes—or less, if I'm spry—except on cleaning day.

On cleaning day it takes a little longer, but still not too long. All the floors are hardwood with no thresholds between the rooms, so it is necessary only to pitch all the rugs outdoors for shaking and to start sweeping at the furthermost corners of the cabin, working toward the fireplace. There's never much dirt, anyhow. The Point is a clean place with little dust and only some dead grass tracked in on wet feet or sand and gravel emptied from sneakers at the end of a walk to be swept up. There's no clutter. Unlike most summer quarters, the cabin has plenty of closets and storage space in which cultch and oddments can be concealed. I know it's there, but nobody else does; and what the eye doesn't see the heart doesn't grieve over.

Most housekeepers, I know, consider sweeping trash into the fireplace a very sloppy practice, but this fireplace really asks for it. It's enormous and the hearth is sunk below floor level. This was accidental. When the Albrights decided to build here it was too late in the season to secure building materials and start the work. They wanted to be doing *something* constructive, however, so they began on the fireplace, which was going to be made of native beach rock. Lisle and his brother worried the stones up from the shore, and their father, Adam, set them. According to my friends of the village, that fireplace sure looked some old funny that winter, stuck up there like a sore thumb on the bleakness of the Point.

When it came time to build the cabin around the fireplace it was found that there had been a slight error in calculation. Sufficient allowance for the floor joists to clear the ledge below had not been made. So the floor was laid several inches above the hearth, with very happy results. It's easy to sweep trash into the pit and burn it; but, more than that, the higher edge of the floor provides a wonderful place to sit and dry or warm your feet, or to sit and toast marshmallows or hot dogs, or simply to sit and look at the fire. If ever I have occasion to build a fireplace of my own I shall purposely sink it below the floor.

Cleaning day or not, my chores end with attending to the water situation. There are two sources of fresh water on the Point. Near the back door is a big brick and cement cistern into which rain water drains from the roof; in short, a glorified rain barrel. This water is used for washing clothes, floors, windows and oneself; and it's pumped into the kitchen sink with an old-fashioned hand-pump. Drinking and cooking water, however, must be carried in buckets from Simeon Young's old well up back of the cabin near the road; and I save this chore until last, as a sort of treat or reward, because I enjoy it.

The dog enjoys it, too. When he hears my pails rattling he comes wagging back from wherever he's been, smiling all over his face and cavorting clumsily. As a matter of common courtesy, I ask him if he'd care to walk up to the well, and at the word *walk*, he falls all over himself in ecstasy. It isn't much of a walk, really, but he thinks it's a big occasion, and so do I. In all sorts of places when I'm away from the Point—in noisy railroad stations, or hot and crowded rooms, or on the paved streets of cities—I remember the walk to the well.

It never seems to be the same on two days in succession. The path itself remains unchanged, a narrow ribbon pressed inches deep into the earth by years of foot-travel over it, crossing an expanse of bare rock, then a wider stretch of shallow soil bearing ladies' tresses and bearberry vines and starred with goldthread and cinquefoil, and plunging into a meadow of high grass grown up to alders and little spruce trees. It climbs a low outcropping of ledge, winds down the other side, turns sharply to the right, and there's the well. I could walk it in my sleep, but in my sleep I couldn't see all the things that make it a new and different walk each time I take it.

In fair weather the grass along the sides stands straight and proud, and the pods of the rattlebox whisper dryly as I brush them with the pails. From the moment I leave the cabin I can see the one great symmetrical wild rosebush near the ledge, beckoning like a beacon above the lower bushes, and beyond it, clear across the Point and the bay, the white spire of the church in Prospect Harbor, miles away. But on foggy days the sodden rattlebox is silent, the grass plumes bow low under a weight of fog beads, drenching my ankles, and the rosebush is invisible until I am almost upon it, when it suddenly looms large, brightening the fog with the glow of its prodigal blooming. Prospect Harbor is lost in a gray limbo. There is no sound of gulls or boats, and I carry the whole fog-circumscribed world with me along the path, its boundaries advancing as I advance.

Sometimes it rains, and then cold, absolutely clear water collects in the vegetation-filled depressions of the rock. It can't sink in and it can't run off, but lies there, still as glass; and all the little yellow and white and lavender blossoms stare up through it like sea anemones or the flowers of a lost Atlantis. Tiny frogs no larger than a fingernail leap crazily from pool to pool. The daisies and steeplebush in the meadow look sad and bedraggled, and the bindweed hasn't bothered to open its pale, corded trumpets.

No matter what the weather, certain things are always the same at the well. I lift the plank cover, fill the first pail, and give the dog a drink in a pan kept there for the purpose. He may have drunk quarts from the puddles we've splashed through, but still he has to have a drink at the well, and if I don't give it to him in his pan he'll take it out of the pail when my back is turned. Then I lower the second pail more slowly, taking time now to admire yet once again the masonry that lines the shaft.

Simeon Young laid these stones a hundred years ago, fitting them carefully and plumbing them surely from the level of the meadow to the dark water with the eye of light in which my face now appears, the latest of a long succession of faces. He used no cement or binder, and yet the facing of the well is as solid as it was on the day, so long ago, that he finished it. Once I sent a sample of the water to be analyzed by the State, which provides this free service to well owners. So old a well, I thought, might easily have become polluted in the course of a century. Back came the report: This water is pure and entirely fit for drinking and household and other purposes.

I don't know anything better that a man could leave behind him to be remembered by than Simeon Young's legacy of a never-failing well of pure water, discovered through his own intuition, dug by his own strong arms and back, and walled with his own knowing and patient hands. I think of him and thank him every morning as I lean looking into the cool and dusky depths.

Then I carry the dripping buckets back through the fog or the rain, or through a brilliant morning clarity in which the islands bask like a school of surfaced whales with the sea breaking in geysers of spray over their outer ledges—"throwing the old rice," as the lobstermen say. My chores are done, and I feel good.

Now it is about half-past seven and time I started earning a living. Everyone else has been at his livelihood for hours. All the lobsterboats have worked their way out so far that they are just white dots on the horizon or flashes of sunlight on spray-shields. I turn rather reluctantly into the dining room, which is really an alcove off the living room, just large enough for its purpose, the consuming of meals.

Here the windows face south and east, commanding a view of the ocean, the islands and the entrance to the harbor, and they occupy most of the wall space. I use it as a work room. The light is excellent, and the table is of good typewriting height and nice and big for the spreading out of notebooks and papers. When I first came here I found the ideal spot in which to sit, where the light fell on my work and I could see almost 180 degrees of the horizon. I placed the field glasses within easy reach in case a strange bird flew past or a strange boat approached the passage between the islands, rolled up my sleeves, spat on my hands, and typed my name and the page number.

That's as far as I got. You'd be surprised how many things can demand your attention on a sparsely peopled shoreline and an expanse of open sea. If there's nothing else to look at, there are always the fountains of spray on Western Island, the turning of the tide, the congresses of gulls, and the bowing of the sedges in the wind. Usually there are also lobsterboats at work, the Coast Guard cutter or the *Bluenose* further out, and some people walking on the Inner

Bar sandspit, half a mile away, whom you can almost identify, using the field glasses.

So I hid the glasses in a drawer and moved to the other side of the table, where I now sit with only the blank wall to look at and disturbed only by a nagging sense that all sorts of things that I shouldn't be missing are going on behind my back, and if I just glanced over my shoulder—but that would be boondoggling.

The morning wears on. I am vaguely aware that the square of sunlight that fell on the table has moved to the floor, dwindled and vanished. Now the soft sounds of the wind and the sea and the mewing gulls are drowned by a crescendo of roaring motors as the lobsterboats, their throttles full open for the homeward run, converge on the harbor. The dog barks apologetically at the kitchen door. It's after midday, and he's hungry; and so, come to think of it, am I. We'll have lunch, then we'll go to the store for the mail, and after that, we'll see what happens.

By that I mean we'll see whom we encounter. I'm not a particularly gregarious type who requires the constant company of others; but nobody can live solely on natural beauty, divorced completely from the society of his own kind. That wouldn't be living at all, but merely vegetating. It's contact with people that keeps the ego whittled down to size and the mind honed to a working edge. I like people, and particularly do I like the people of the Peninsula. I like their coastal faces, all clean brown planes not easily broken into expressions of any emotion—until you come to the eyes, which look out coolly, intelligently, clearly, confidently, ready to give or to withhold. I like the way they talk: tersely, colorfully and to the point. I like their Down-East walk, a sort of lounging stride that seems unhurried but that gets them where they're going. I like the way they treat me, as though I were a person in my own right and entitled to my own opinions, tastes and eccentricities.

Usually my first human contacts of the day are with Herb and the postmistress, Daisy Young, at the store. Herb, who is that rare thing in Maine, a dedicated Democrat, attempts daily to correct my political thinking. Daisy doesn't try to convert me to anything. She sits in her cubicle, pleasant and friendly, whiling away the time between customers by tying bait bags or doing intricate and beautiful embroidery and crochet. I ask her what's new, and she tells me. Or she says that the Condons left word that they'd like to see me; their daughter has arrived. Or she asks, her eyes twinkling in a straight face, if I got my laundry dry; I certainly had it out early enough.

I'm amazed, since neither Daisy nor anyone else, I had thought, commanded a view of my clothesline. "Now who told you that I washed today?" I demand, surprised as always that, while I'm observant of and interested in the doings of my fellow citizens, they reciprocate my interest. Far from being annoyed, I'm always reassured and warmed by evidence that I'm not living in a void, invisible and disregarded. But she won't tell me, not because it matters, but because she thinks it's good for me to have something to ponder; and I leave, wondering *who* in the world—?, which was just what Daisy intended.

Every day, too, I see Marcia or leave word at her house that I am still among the living and reasonably able-bodied. This is an arrangement we arrived at early in my solitary tenancy of the Point. A person living alone can slip on the wet kitchen linoleum and break a leg, or fall off a ledge and fracture a skull, with no one the wiser for days. Nothing of this sort has happened to me yet; but if ever I'm lying helpless and in mortal agony it will be of considerable comfort and reassurance to me to know that, since I haven't checked in with Marcia that day, she or an emissary of hers will eventually come to my rescue. I consider this precaution only sensible, fussbudgety as it may appear to the more valiant.

Then, with the afternoon before me, I consider what I'll do next, which often boils down to on whom will I pay a call. Peninsulans are constantly dropping in on each other informally, a folkway surviving from earlier days when people through lack of means of transportation were forced to stay at home more, and when much of their social life consisted of "neighboring." I think it's a very pleasant custom. Talk is more likely to be easy and relaxed on this haphazard basis. The hostess feels no obligation, since she didn't know you were coming, to dress up and serve tea; nor does she hesitate to tell you that you'll have to do your visiting in the kitchen, since she's in the middle of putting up the last of the raspberries.

Sometimes I call on Captain John Allen, who is now ninety-three years old and long retired from the sea. In the winter he stays at Sailors' Snug Harbor on Staten Island, but summertimes he returns to his boyhood home of Prospect Harbor, where he lives alone, getting his own meals and doing his own housework. He runs his house as he ran his vessels, apparently, keeping everything shipshape. No sweeping trash into fireplaces for him. You could eat off his floors, as they say here, and bounce a quarter a foot in the air off the taut counterpane of his bed. He's a wonderful old gentleman, with his faculties unimpaired by age. Chenowyth Hall and I once agreed that he's a sweetie-pie, but we decided we'd better not tell him so. He wouldn't appreciate it.

When I was new on the Peninsula I was under the influence of sea stories like *Treasure Island* and *Mutiny on the Bounty*, in which the captain is a psychopathic tyrant given to violence and sadism. I hoped I could get some true, original and lurid tales of murder, mutiny and general mayhem at sea from Captain Allen; and since I'd heard that he was not exactly garrulous I'd prepared some leading and prodding questions to ask him.

I guess most of those books I'd read dealt with the exceptions. Aboard the average Down-Easter, at least, the truth seems to have been very different; and yet the truth is dramatic too, in a quiet way. Leading up gently to the subject of bloodshed, I started by asking Captain Allen how old he'd been when he received his master's certificate, and he told me he was twenty-one.

"Isn't that rather young to be responsible for a ship?" I asked.

He smiled. " 'Bout average. There was some younger than me when they took their papers, but not many much older. If you weren't fit to be a captain at twenty-one you weren't going to be. By that time you'd been at sea nine-ten years and you'd learned about all you were capable of learning. If it wasn't enough you'd better give up and go to farming."

Still in thrall to my romantic illusions I said, "You must have been very proud the first time you wore your captain's uniform."

"Uniform," he said in his soft voice, as though it were a new word that he was trying the sound of. "Captains didn't wear uniforms in those days. None of the officers did. Didn't need them. If the crew couldn't tell you were an officer by your manner and conduct, you didn't last long. Uniforms!" And he looked at me as though I were soft in the head.

"But how did you maintain discipline? By force?"

"Never struck a man in my life. Never had to. Hardly ever had to raise my voice, unless in a storm. Same with the other captains. A captain didn't go bawling around the decks at the top of his lungs, now I tell you. It didn't become him."

I was getting desperate. "Did you ever have a mutiny on your hands?" I asked, and immediately wished I hadn't. Captain Allen is a slight man with a gentle voice and a mild blue eye; and I suppose that he is much slighter, milder and gentler at ninety-three than he was at, say, forty-three. Nevertheless, I found out at once why he didn't need a uniform and why he never had to resort to shouting and the belaying pin to preserve order. His faded eyes grew icy and his quiet voice thinned and hardened till it cut.

"Mutiny!" he spat contemptuously. "You've got some pretty funny ideas, young lady. Of course I never had a mutiny. Mutiny!" Unless you have come in contact with pure authority, unbacked by any physical means of enforcement and rising solely from inner strength, you can have no idea of the power that emanated from old Captain Allen. Without moving an eyelash or a finger, he managed to be completely intimidating. I suddenly understood how, with captains like him on the bridge, Maine sailing ships built up the reputation they enjoyed all over the world before the days of steam.

Hastily I asked, "Were you ever shipwrecked?" and then wondered if this, too, were an insulting question.

But evidently shipwrecks were Acts of God and excusable.

"More than once. Never lost a man, though, not in a wreck. Only man I ever lost was on a clear, calm night in the horse latitudes. Wouldn't have lost him, if he'd made any attempt to help himself. He was a big Negro, and as soon's he went overboard, we launched a boat. Everything was going first-rate, but when they were almost up to him he just seemed to give up, and sank. I never did understand it, unless he wanted to die and took this means." He brooded, still puzzled and concerned after all these years over the only man he'd ever lost.

Now when I go to see Captain Allen it's a call and not an interview. We inquire for each other's health, discuss the weather and the local gossip, touch in passing on the olden days, and part with what I hope is mutual esteem and good will.

Most of my cronies, however, are women. This is the natural lot of middle-aged widows everywhere, I suppose; but on the Peninsula compatibility as much as necessity dictates my choice. I like and respect these women who have not been relegated by the society in which they live to the position of dependents or symbols of masculine success. As in colonial times, they are vital and necessary for more than the raising of families and acting as housewives and hostesses. They're valuable, and they know it, and this knowledge colors their talk, their thinking, and their actions.

Because of the precarious economy of the place they do all manner of work to help out the family budget and take over many of the duties that would ordinarily fall to the man of the house, were he not at sea. They work in the sardine or blueberry canning factories, raise vegetables or bake pastry for sale, take in laundry, serve meals, operate small businesses in their homes, or even drive trucks occasionally; and they mow their own lawns, paint their own houses, do carpentry and other odd jobs about their premises, split kindling, lug water, help their husbands build traps or bail out boats and beach them for repairs—all this in addition to the normal duties of a housewife and mother of several children.

They're not too far removed in time and not at all removed in outlook from the pioneer women who helped raise cabins in the wilderness, shot bears that threatened the priceless livestock, brought in the hard-won crops, made adequate clothing and improvised edible meals out of almost nothing, survived unattended childbirth, laid out the dead, amputated gangrenous limbs, or even, as captives of the Indians, made the long and bitter trek to Canada, escaped their captors by guile or violence, and managed to find their way home. It's a little difficult to reduce women of this caliber to nonentities, and any attempts to do so on the Peninsula have been signally unsuccessful.

Peninsula women have always been competent and independent. The first woman to hold in her own right a lobster-fishing license in Maine—and that probably means in the world—was a Corean. This happened before the turn of the century, before my day, I'm sorry to say, because I would have liked to have known her. She was married very young—at the age of twelve, which wasn't too unusual then on the Peninsula—to a man who came in on a sloop from Nova Scotia and settled in the village. In order to make ends meet for a growing family she went into the lobstering business. She hauled from a dory, a type of heavy, keeled, double-ended boat which, with the peapod, vanished from these parts with the advent of the outboard motor. An outboard requires a square stern, which neither dory nor peapod has.

A dory has to be rowed. It's probably the most seaworthy of the small boats, but its seaworthiness is bought at the price of weight as well as design, and this makes rowing any distance a back-breaking labor. Nevertheless, this woman rowed her dory not just around the harbor and nearer reaches of the shore, but clear across to Petit Manan Point, a long distance over rough and open sea. She didn't do this once, you understand, but regularly; and she was not only rowing, she was also hauling, baiting and resetting a big gang of heavy traps. Since her husband was a lobsterman, too, there was no one at home with whom she could leave the baby; so she took him along with her, lashed in the stern sheets. She was quite a woman, in anybody's language; and the baby, far from being injured by this rather rugged early treatment, grew up to become one of the more successful and respected citizens of the vicinity today.

Whenever I look across the gray and heaving waste between the Gouldsboro Peninsula and 'Titm'nan Point, or whenever I see the young boys with their fast outboards hauling their traps in my front yard, I think of her, tossing around out there in the vast emptiness She must almost always have been cold and wet and tired, and some times she must have been frightened, if not for herself, for her child She's one of my favorite women anywhere, at any time.

Contemporaneous with her was Mary Christmas, which couldn't have been her real name, since she was an Arabian. All the older people of the Peninsula remember her. She came from Arabia in about 1885 and set herself up in business as a pack-peddler, going about the countryside on foot and carrying her wares in a basket. Although she wasn't of Down-East stock, she was temperamentally akin to the women of the region, being competent, shrewd and full of git-up-and-git. Everybody liked to see her coming with her basket of gewgaws because she was jolly and cheerful and because—since she traveled tremendous distances on her own two feet and came in contact with innumerable people—she was always full of news, which she happily dispensed. This was undoubtedly a great business asset. You can't very well monopolize an hour of a business woman's time in gossip and chitchat without buying at least a paper of pins and a length of lace from her.

She is described as being a woman of striking appearance, handsome in a dark and exotic way, who wore odd clothes. Sometimes she dressed in modified Arabian style; but sometimes in foul weather she threw convention to the winds and appeared in *pants*. This, if nothing else did, would have given her a place on the pages of local history. But she did something further to win the respect of the thrifty Yankee population. In the twenty years between her arrival in this country and her death in 1905 she managed through her own efforts, alone and with only her basket of trinkets as working material—that and brains—to leave an estate consisting of a brick business block in Belfast and $8000 in the bank. In those days that was a modest fortune. Mary Christmas deserves at least honorary membership in the sorority of Peninsula women, I think.

So, I think, does a woman whom I shall call Sadie Ellis. The people of the Peninsula have their marital difficulties, just as they do elsewhere; and it is the custom here, as it is in some other places, for a husband, if he thinks the circumstances warrant it, to "publish" his wife. This means that he announces in the public print that he will no longer be responsible for her expenditures. Such a thing happened to Sadie Ellis. There appeared in the paper the following notice:

This is to notify all persons that whereas my wife, Sadie B. Ellis, having left my bed and board without a just cause or provocation, I shall not pay any bills contracted by her or for her support from this date.

THEODORE C. ELLIS

Sadie was not one to take this lying down. The next week she did her own publishing:

I wish to answer Theodore C. Ellises notice. I never left his bed and board; we were both working in Bar Harbor; he left me without any reason whatever as far as I know; never asked me to go with him or told me where he was going. As to his bed, he didn't have any. It was mine, bought and receipted for in my maiden name.

SADIE B. ELLIS

That's what I mean when I say that it is difficult to put Peninsula women in any place except the one to which they feel they are entitled. They take no nonsense from anybody.

My friend Ida Buckley is another good example. Ida is a widow with two grown sons, and she lives alone on the Pond Road, except when one of her sons is at home. As I've mentioned, she's the Town Clerk, the Town Treasurer, the Tax Collector, a notary public and a justice of the peace; and if she wished to become Governor of the State of Maine, I'm very sure she'd do so and, moreover, she'd make an excellent Governor. She manages the multiple affairs of the town within her province efficiently and with dispatch, without turning a hair.

One day we were riding along in her car at a moderate rate, minding our own business and enjoying the scenery, when a State trooper passed us with a loud blaring of his horn. We were both startled, not having observed his approach; but where I would have tamely assumed that the police are always right and he was doubtless on urgent business, Ida swore under her breath, stepped on the gas, and leaned on the horn.

"Hey," I said feebly.

"Hey nothing," Ida retorted. "If I'd done that to him, scaring him half to pieces, he'd have had me in jail. He could have put us in the ditch. He always was a show-off from way back."

"Oh, you know him?"

"Darn right I know him. He was one of my pupils when I taught school, and if he thinks— Hey, you Willie Sykes! Pull over!"

The trooper pulled over and gave us a watery smile which faded in the face of Ida's black scowl. "Now you listen to me," she began. "I've shaken the head off your shoulders more than once in the past, and I can do it again if I have to. What do you mean by blasting that horn in my ear? I've got a good mind—"

The affair ended by the trooper's saying he was sorry, Miz Buckley, he only meant it as a friendly greeting. Nobody tramples on Peninsula women.

It's fun to travel around with Ida. She's good company and she knows all there is to be known about the Peninsula. She's lived here a long time, she knows everybody and his dog, and she's in a position to gather information. She tells me lots of thing I would otherwise never know. It was she who told me one day when we were in Bar Harbor that Gouldsboro owns the beautiful little Porcu pine Islands that lie within a stone's throw of the Bar Harboi waterfront.

"Are you *sure?*" I asked. The Peninsula was just a hazy lines miles away on the other side of Frenchman Bay.

"Yes. In fact, the town line used to run down the middle of the main street of Bar Harbor. Made the town fathers mad, too, to have all that tax money go to us over in Gouldsboro. They whined around until they got the State to intervene and move the line offshore. But we've still got the Porcupines, and if they build a causeway and put a motel on that nearest one, like they're talking of doing, it'll sure help our tax rate." Ida takes her position as Tax Collector seriously.

She takes her other positions seriously, too. She can and will give you a great deal of information about a great number of things; but she can also be extremely close-mouthed. It's a very good thing that she can. Through her various offices she's in possession of enough assorted facts about enough people so that she could rip the social and economic fabric of the Peninsula to shreds, simply by talking. She won't, though. I've tried. When Ida shuts her mouth you're just wasting your blandishments.

Another of my friends is Ida's Aunt Linly Prudence Rosebrook. I think that's a charming name, and Aunt Linly is a charming old lady. She lives next door to Ida on the Pond Road in a house that is among the oldest on the Peninsula, having been built over a century and a half ago. By Plymouth and Jamestown standards that is not so ancient, but here it is. Aunt Linly's house is a Cape Cod type, with a large living room, fireplaces, and lovely old Christian doors throughout. These doors, in case you didn't know, are made in such a manner that the borders of the panels form a crucifix, and they were originally intended to prevent the entrance of witches and devils to the house. They're the most beautiful doors I've ever seen.

According to Aunt Linly, they're witch-and-devil bait nowadays. She is frequently approached by such nether-worldly characters as antique dealers and architects with the proposition that she sell them her doors complete with hand-wrought iron latches and HL hinges and buy herself some nice new ones from Sears Roebuck. This annoys Aunt Linly. In the first place, she hates to be considered a fool, and in the second place, she admires and appreciates her doors as much as the next one does, and she doesn't see why she should have to fight a running battle to keep possession of what is after all her own property.

Fortunately there can be no question of removing the walls of one of the rooms of her house, so she is pleased—if she has time to spare from her housework and gardening—to show them to anyone who is interested. These walls enclose a small downstairs chamber which was used in the early days to check babies and wraps during the dances that were occasionally held in the long living room, at the time the largest gathering place on the Peninsula. All the families assembled for the festivities, bringing their children, and the babes in arms were tucked up in rows in the huge double bed while their parents and older siblings danced in the next room to the music of fiddles. Probably the walls were then as they are now; but at various times during the interim wallpaper was hung, so that Aunt Linly scraped off five layers to reveal, to her surprise and delight, what lay beneath.

The entire surface of all four walls is covered with stencils, all in dull red and green against a background of pale gold. They're beautiful. Around the top is a leafy border, and at about four-foot intervals ribbon and flower streamers divide the wall space into panels. Each panel bears a stylized red pineapple, a basket of flowers, or a willow tree obviously copied from the weeping willow on willow-ware. This leads me to believe that the other motifs were also adapted from various sources—from china patterns, perhaps, or from Fortuny or even calico prints. Quite evidently someone who couldn't afford or couldn't acquire wallpaper went to a great deal of painstaking trouble to adorn these walls, cutting the stencils delicately and meticulously applying them.

But the real puzzle is the medium used. It isn't paint. It's been there for well over a hundred years and is still fresh and clear. It must be either tempera or fresco, made with egg white as a base and colored with the juices of leaves and berries. How did the artist know of these methods? The probable answer is that a seafaring man of the family brought home the idea from abroad. Peninsulans got around the world in those days and had, as they do now, a lively curiosity and thirst to learn. Whatever the case may be, I love to call on Aunt Linly Prudence and to have brought to life again the people who lived so long ago in this old house, protected from evil spirits by their Christian doors and cheered by their gay frescoed walls.

Sometimes I go over to Bunkers Harbor to see Mrs. Gossler. She lives behind a high hedge in a low house close to the road that leads to Schoodic Point. The place looks rather secretive and mysterious as you approach it, hidden as it is behind the hedge; but the minute you step through the narrow gate all that is changed. The land slopes down to the sea, opening a wide and airy vista of sunlight and sparkling water and distant white sails and lighthouses. Nearer at hand, below the seawall, are small, freshly painted boats drawn up on the beach, and, closer still, half smothered in rambler roses, two or three little rustic cabins. And everywhere there are flowers —all kinds and colors of flowers, in beds and borders, in tubs and urns, around a small pool, and climbing over trellises and arbors. Often there are water pails of cut flowers standing in a row on a bench in the shade of the lilac bushes. I hate to sound corny, but it really is just like stepping into a fairyland where everything is brightness and sweetness and order. Even the enormous vegetable garden, over beyond the last of the flowering borders, seems unreal, as though elves worked there diligently to keep it weeded and the beets and carrots and string beans in neat and perfect rows.

Actually all this is testimony to Mrs. Gossler's enterprise and energy. She earns her living—and I do mean earns—by selling the vegetables and flowers that she raises without the help of elves. She does the work herself, and as a consequence her blond hair is bleached even lighter by the sun and her nose is permanently freckled. Her produce has a widespread and well-deserved reputation. She sells only that which is perfect, and she never picks it until you show your face at her door, so that it will surely be fresh.

That isn't all she does. She also rents cabins and boats, which she herself keeps clean and in repair. In addition, because the vegetable and rental businesses are summer occupations, she spends the winters making and dressing dolls to sell during the summer months. Her front parlor is even more like fairyland than her yard, if possible. You open the door from the hall, and there, sitting on the chairs and the tables and the mantelpiece, leaning against the walls and lounging on the floor, are hundreds of dolls—Dutch dolls and Aunt Jemima dolls and Swedish dolls and bobby-socks dolls. You feel yourself growing large and clumsy, like Alice in Looking-glass Land, in this composed and diminutive company. It's a very odd feeling, and while it may sound fanciful I assure you that it's real and rather disconcerting.

Sometimes on Tuesdays I go to see Bernice Richmond, who lives with her brother and two great golden Chinook huskies in a house overlooking the Town Wharf of Winter Harbor. Tuesday is the only day she has free to fritter away on callers. Faced like the rest of us with the necessity of earning a living, she owns, edits, writes, prints and publishes the *Peninsula Gazette*, doing job printing on the side. This is in itself a full-time occupation, from Wednesday through Monday of each week. I know all about it, since my father was also the owner-editor-publisher-printer-and-handy-man of a small-town weekly. But Bernice gives piano lessons and plays at various social functions as well. She's an excellent musician—Tony Perkins was once a pupil of hers—who studied abroad for years and played the organ in the original Broadway production of "Our Town." She lives on the Peninsula simply because she wants to; and if she has to work much harder here than she would elsewhere, that's a price she is willing to pay.

I like to call on Bernice. We drink tea and talk about books and watch the traffic of the Inner Harbor; and the two big dogs, Anvik and Norvik, observe us gravely and exchange superior glances when we say something more than usually silly. She, like Mary Christmas, belongs here by adoption.

One of the most enchanting calls I ever made was with Marcia Spurling on George Crowley's sisters, who live Up the Guzzle in the house by the old silver mines. They didn't know we were coming, because we didn't know it ourselves, and when we walked into the kitchen they were giving each other home permanents. I know this is a common practice of American womanhood, but Mrs. Lindsay is eighty-seven and Mrs. Foss is ninety-one. I could have kissed them. The long hard years—for no woman on the Peninsula leads a pampered life—hadn't robbed them of pride or damaged their self-respect. Nobody—as they said—was going to set *them* up in a field to scare the crows! No, they weren't going anywhere special, and no, they weren't expecting company; but if you once started letting yourself *go*— Well!

Sometimes I don't call on anybody in the afternoon, but just drift around, seeing what there is to see. There's always something new and different here on the Peninsula where everything, even the mood of the people, depends so much on the vagaries of nature. I remember one day especially, one day at the end of a long dry spell. There hadn't been any rain for well over a month, or even any fog, which was most unusual. A heavy fog doesn't take the place of rain, but it does help parched gardens. The moisture collects on the plants and is absorbed, or gathers into heavy drops which are funnelled down leaves and stems to the thirsty roots.

For weeks and weeks the sky had been a brazen blue, the persistent warm west wind had blown any fog out to sea, and even the nighttime fall of dew had ceased. Gardens shriveled, the marshy places on the heaths turned to dust, the earth cracked down to the basic rock, and all over the Peninsula wells went dry. Wherever you went you met trucks hauling milk cans of water from shrunken brooks for cattle and gardens; and those who—like me—still had water in their wells filled bottles and distributed them among friends, since a gallon of drinking water was a gift more welcome than rubies would have been. Laundering was cut down to the bare essential minimum, and bathing was done in the sea or the warmer waters of Jones Pond. It was a time of long faces and short answers and of eyes constantly searching the sky for even the smallest cloud.

Then one morning I woke to the sound of rain on the roof and of water gurgling and splashing into the long-empty cistern. The sea was lost in fog and blowing scud, and a raw-edged wind drove sheets of rain against the seaward windows. From out of the obscurity the bell buoy tolled dolefully and the whistle buoy sounded its mournful hooting. It was a mean, miserable, nasty day, fit for neither man nor beast, a good day to stay by the fire and sulk, you would have said.

But nobody on the Peninsula stayed in the house that day. Everybody was abroad, dressed in oilskins that were stiff from disuse, plowing recklessly through puddles, lifting hands and faces to the wonderful rain. Stranger spoke gaily to stranger, and everybody laughed at nothing. That was what impressed me most—the sound of universal laughter here where people are commonly serious and self-contained. A carnival air prevailed everywhere, and the purchase of a bottle of milk was as gala an occasion as the splitting of a magnum of champagne might be in another time and place.

"Looks like a three-day nor'easter," Herb informed me with relish; and the lobstermen on the Liars' Bench, for once undismayed at being kept ashore, chimed happily, "We sure can use it!"

"Got every pail and pan in the house out catchin' water," one woman announced; and another responded, "Me, too. Plan to wash the minute it clears. I've got dirty clothes piled up *so* high." She indicated a point at shoulder level, and the laughter was all out of proportion to the occasion for it.

That was the day I almost acquired a kitten. I was up at Charley Small's supermarket buying a steak to celebrate the rain. "Want a money-cat?" a small boy inquired of me from under the brim of a big sou'wester; and I asked what in the world a money-cat might be. "Some folks call them fourteen-color cats," he said. "They bring good luck. Here." And he hauled out from the pocket of his slicker a very small multicolored kitten with its eyes barely open.

Do you know, so carried away was I by the general euphoria induced by the breaking of the drought that I almost accepted? And I don't even like cats very much. Just in time I realized that, while he might call it a money-cat, it was still a three-colored kitten, and three-colored kittens are invariably females. This is a law as inexorable as that of the Medes and Persians. One cat—especially a lucky money-cat—I might learn to love, but semiannual litters of kittens—! So I said no-thank-you-very-much and sloshed out into the beautiful rain with my steak.

That day too I lingered long over the difficult choice between two identical loaves of store bread just so I could hear the outcome of an argument about the best way to break up a broody hen. I didn't know either of the participants, I didn't own a hen, broody or otherwise, and I didn't expect ever to have a use for the information I gained. Nevertheless, wild horses couldn't have dragged me away from my eavesdropping. This I can't blame on the rain; I have a trivial mind, easily entertained.

It was finally agreed that the best method is to place the hen in a covered tub with two inches of cold water in the bottom. After a day or two of being foiled by the water in her attempts to set on imaginary eggs, she's glad to give up the whole notion of motherhood. An acceptable alternate method is to imprison the hen in a lobster trap and leave her out in a good driving storm such as the present one. I freely pass these tips on to any who may have use for them.

Wherever I have been roaming, whomever I have been seeing, whatever I have been doing, there comes the time when I must return to the Point. Perhaps I have been over at the Sands watching a tall column of gulls waver and blow above a purse seine of herring anchored there. All afternoon they have circled and soared and dived like plummets into the captured school—a shining, shifting tower against the deep blue sky; but as the light drains away and the tide of the dusk rises over land and sea, one by one they take their departure. And so must I, driving slowly across the heath in the half light. Gouldsboro Bay gleams dull silver to the east, and the smell of the soil rises from the marshes. As I pass through the village, single lights show golden in scattered windows, and then I leave them behind. Ahead lies the narrow track, pale and glimmering in the twilight, and the darkling empty shore, and the unlighted cabin.

This is the saddest time of the day, the time when it would be possible to become unbearably lonely, not solely for oneself but for all mankind and indeed for the whole earth, spinning lost and alone into the coming darkness. The moor is dim and featureless, the sea is empty, and the surf breaks on the cold ledges with an endless, hopeless sobbing. For an instant it is possible to comprehend the meaning of panic—the fear of Pan, the strange unreasoning and unfounded terror that strikes those who wander abroad in primitive places.

Then a rabbit flashes across the road and under the woodpile, and as I switch off the motor the sleepy chatter of the swallows under the eaves fills the silence. The dog jumps out of the car and trots to the cabin door, brushing a low bush in passing. Immediately it springs into trembling light as a hundred fireflies are disturbed, and glimmers like a Christmas tree, gold and green and blue and yellow. Somewhere inland a dog barks, the sound carrying easily in the still, clear air. Over on Crowley Island a car swings its headlights in a slow arc. Far away on the utmost horizon 'Titm'nan Light

springs abruptly into being and shines bright and steady in the gloaming, and in the deep and limitless vault of the heavens the stars appear one by one.

And then I know that I am not alone, that none of us is alone, that the earth itself swings through space in brilliant company. The fireflies, the rabbit under the woodpile, the swallows in the eaves, the women in Peninsula kitchens and their men plodding up from the tiny harbors, the solitary keepers of the light on their sea-washed distant rock and I are all bound together as parts of a colossal plan, the success of which depends equally on the soundness of the greatest and the smallest part.

Perhaps that is what I had to come to the Peninsula to learn: that isolation is not estrangement from life, that across the void that separates man from man and from the wild things it is possible to flash a light, to transmit a voice, to send a glance or a thought; and that one cannot live in true community with others until he has learned to live with himself.

Conclusion

THIS, THEN, IS WHAT IT IS LIKE TO LIVE IN A place that has stood still in time, that exists today in its bypassed and forgotten corner of the world almost as it existed a half-century ago, protected by its harsh coastline, bitter sea, inhospitable land and rigorous climate from invasion and change. It is to come as near as possible to a return to that lost home of racial memory, where life was simple and good, where issues of right and wrong were clear-cut, where all the battles were fought in the open against elemental and tangible enemies. It is to live again the old American dream of a frontier where each man is the equal in all respects of his neighbor, where all men are bound together by common problems and interests, and where no man is limited except by the limitations of his own abilities.

There is a price to pay, however, for this return to an age that seems so golden and uncomplicated. Nothing is free in this world. The most obvious cost is that of physical comfort. The life is really hard, taking its toll on the youth of the men and the women. But more than that, there tends to be in all small and isolated villages all over the world, whether on the coast, among the hills or far inland on the plains, a certain provincialism. The Peninsula is no different in this respect than any other remote district. It would be unfair to pretend that it is.

But it would be equally unfair not to point out that there are rewards and benefits, too. From an intimate knowledge of and identification with the earth and the great natural forces, which are unalterable and unfaltering in their courses, from an immutable pattern of living and an accepted standard of behavior there come a sense of security, an emotional stability, a peace of mind almost impossible to attain in the wider world today, so torn with disturbances outside the understanding and control of the individual. Here the people seem to possess the secret of tranquillity and to live lives of more than surface contentment. That is rare today. Perhaps it is only by going up the old back roads leading to the lost little hamlets of the mountains or the seagirt islands and peninsulas of the world that you can still find it. Perhaps even in such places it has not long to last.

The other day I found Herb alone in the store, leaning gloomily on the candy counter. "What ails you?" I asked.

"Everything," he told me categorically. "Atom bombs. Asian flu. Folks buying fancy gadgets on time. Fat women in shorts. The Russians. The way the whole world's going." He warmed to his subject. "You know what we'd ought to do? We'd ought to put gates across the roads onto the Peninsula and keep strangers out. They got the whole rest of the earth to work ruination on. We'd ought to try to keep one place left the way it used to be."

I said that he had a point there; but both he and I knew that it would never work. Gates might keep strangers out, but they could never serve as barriers against ideas and the change that is a part of life and growth. They could never provide a frontier behind which the old customs and attitudes—the bad as well as the good—could retreat and survive forever. Even if it were possible, it wouldn't be desirable. The world progresses, and those who refuse to progress with it end in hopeless stagnation.

No, we can't go back into the past; but should we leave the past entirely behind us? Should we dismiss the primitive life of long ago as anachronistic and of only academic interest? Was there not something there which we should try to preserve for the future? Did the people not possess things that we can't afford to jettison and forget?

What those things are we must go to places like the Peninsula to learn before it is too late.

Gouldsboro Peninsula - 1972

THE PENINSULA WAS WRITTEN ALMOST FIF-
teen years ago, and in fifteen years—even in as slow-paced an area as
this—change is bound to occur. Time does not stand still, and neither
does anything else. Situations may improve or deteriorate, but one
thing is certain: they do not remain static. This basic fact of life applies here as elsewhere.

Inevitably, some of the old faces are missing. George Crowley, who
took me on my first lobster-hauling trip, is gone; and so is Grattan
Condon, with whom I explored Sheep Island; and Katie Young, who
came to Corea from Hungary by way of Cincinnati and Bar Harbor;
and Daisy Young, the Postmistress; and Herb Young, the storekeeper;
and others who had seemed to me as enduring as the tough little fir
trees rooted in the crevices of the ledges. I miss them all.

I miss Herb's store, too, with the Liars' Bench at one side and the
Post Office to the rear. It was the gathering place, the information center, the pulse of the village. Now there is no store at all in Corea. To
buy a loaf of bread or even a candy bar you must go three miles to
Prospect Harbor.

There is still a Post Office; only now it is in the kitchen ell of Buddy
Crowley's house over toward the head of the harbor. Buddy—whose
real name is Munroe—is the Postmaster. This arrangement will probably last for a while, since Buddy is a comparatively young man; but
it will not last forever. In the interests of economy and efficiency, the

United States Government has adopted a policy of closing the little local Post Offices housed in general stores and private homes when the incumbent Postmaster reaches retirement age. There used to be seven Post Offices on the Peninsula; now there are five. Eventually there will be only one, at Winter Harbor, where the Government has already built a modern brick Post Office building. Everybody not within walking distance of it will be classed as RFD. This seems to me too bad, in a way. The little old Post Offices not only served as social centers and practical conveniences; they also gave each hamlet an identity of its own.

Other institutions have changed. The Latter Day Saints—or Mormon—Church, which was closed for many years, has taken a new lease on life. It has been painted and refurbished, and services are held there every Sunday. It's active now, after years of dormancy.

Don Anderson has moved his marine supply store out of Corea up onto US Route 1, where presumably business is livelier, and his lobster pound is no more. The only pound left is Twink's, and even that has changed hands. It is now operated by a lobstermen's co-operative. This progressive move actually makes little or no difference to the buying public; the change is internal, not external. The place looks and smells and is the same as always, and one can still pick up a few lobsters there or fish for harbor pollock off the float.

The lobster and the sardine are still the backbone of the local economy, but the crop from the sea-pastures is a little more varied now. The clams and scallops have come back, and so have the mackerel. It's easy to understand about the shellfish. The beds were overworked and depleted, so for years nobody wasted time clamming or scalloping. Left to their own devices, the shellfish increased and multiplied prodigally. Now if folks will only use a little restraint. . . . About the mackerel nobody understands. They just went away and now they have returned for mysterious reasons of their own. Now, too, there are the shrimp which have suddenly come to these waters in huge numbers. In winter, the lobstermen rig their boats for shrimping, a profitable venture. Not having all the eggs in one basket—or lobster pot—contributes considerably to the peninsulan peace of mind.

The standard of living among the local residents has improved in the past fifteen years. Almost nobody still depends on a hand pump for water or a wood-burning range for heat. Nearly everyone has an artesian well, indoor plumbing and an oil burner. *And* a television set. Where once a plume of blue woodsmoke rose from each chimney or flattened in a stiff on-shore breeze, now a TV antenna challenges the elements. I miss the old smoke signals, indicating that someone was at home and poking up the fire to cook supper. The village seems a little cold without them. Aside from that, though, it hasn't changed much in appearance. A few people have bought mobile homes and set them up on lots next to their parents' or married daughters' houses, but mostly they still live in the unpretentious little cottages that have been there forever.

The Navy, which fifteen years ago occupied a small base on Schoodic Point, has expanded its operation. The personnel at Schoodic now numbers in the hundreds, and there are two other installations: one on Lighthouse Point in Prospect Harbor, for the purpose of tracking satellites, and the other on the Corea heath, for purposes too hush-hush to mention. To shelter the men and their families, two Navy Housing Projects have been constructed in Winter Harbor. They are very neat, ship-shape and well-cared-for, but they don't look like Down East Maine. Whether this is good or bad depends entirely on your point of view.

Inevitably the land boom has hit the Peninsula. As the choice shore property "up to the westward" has been sold to summer people, the trend has expanded to the east. This area, once impossibly remote and inaccessible, is now easily reached by air or by better cars over greatly improved highways. What was once a two-day drive from Boston is now a mere six-hour spin. Consequently the day of the perfectly gorgeous twenty-acre point of wooded land jutting out to sea that could be had for a song is over. It can be had—but at a price. Real estate companies have bought up enormous tracts of the most desirable terrain, put in roads and power lines, and gone into business. This has happened elsewhere, and now it is happening here.

Actually this invasion, so long dreaded and deplored, has turned out to be an insurance against despoliation. Fortunately the land companies operating in this particular area do so on a rather grand scale. Their lots are large, expensive and well off the traveled highway. Anyone who can afford one is not going to put a tarpaper shack on it; so we are spared the trailer camps and cheek-by-jowl beach shanties that have ruined much of the western coast. Between the land companies' and the Navy's holdings, the Peninsula shore is well protected against shoddy exploitation. Anyone driving over the narrow and crooked roads sees very little change in the landscape.

In fact, the lack of change in a changing world over the past fifteen years is what is surprising here. The lobstermen's co-operative may be new, but it is made up of the same old lobstermen and their sons. They look and act and talk exactly as before. They sit around the stores and Post Offices and hash things over just as they always did. They still pry up the sun in the morning and go to bed when it's dark under the table. "What was good enough for father is good enough for me" remains a working precept on the Peninsula. The people still care for their own ill or indigent, still bury their own dead, still make-do or do without, just as they did a hundred years ago.

In short, the conclusions at which I arrived a decade and a half past are as valid today as they were then. Underneath the superficial changes lie the old attitudes and principles, like granite ledges beneath the shallow soil of a field of blowing daisies.